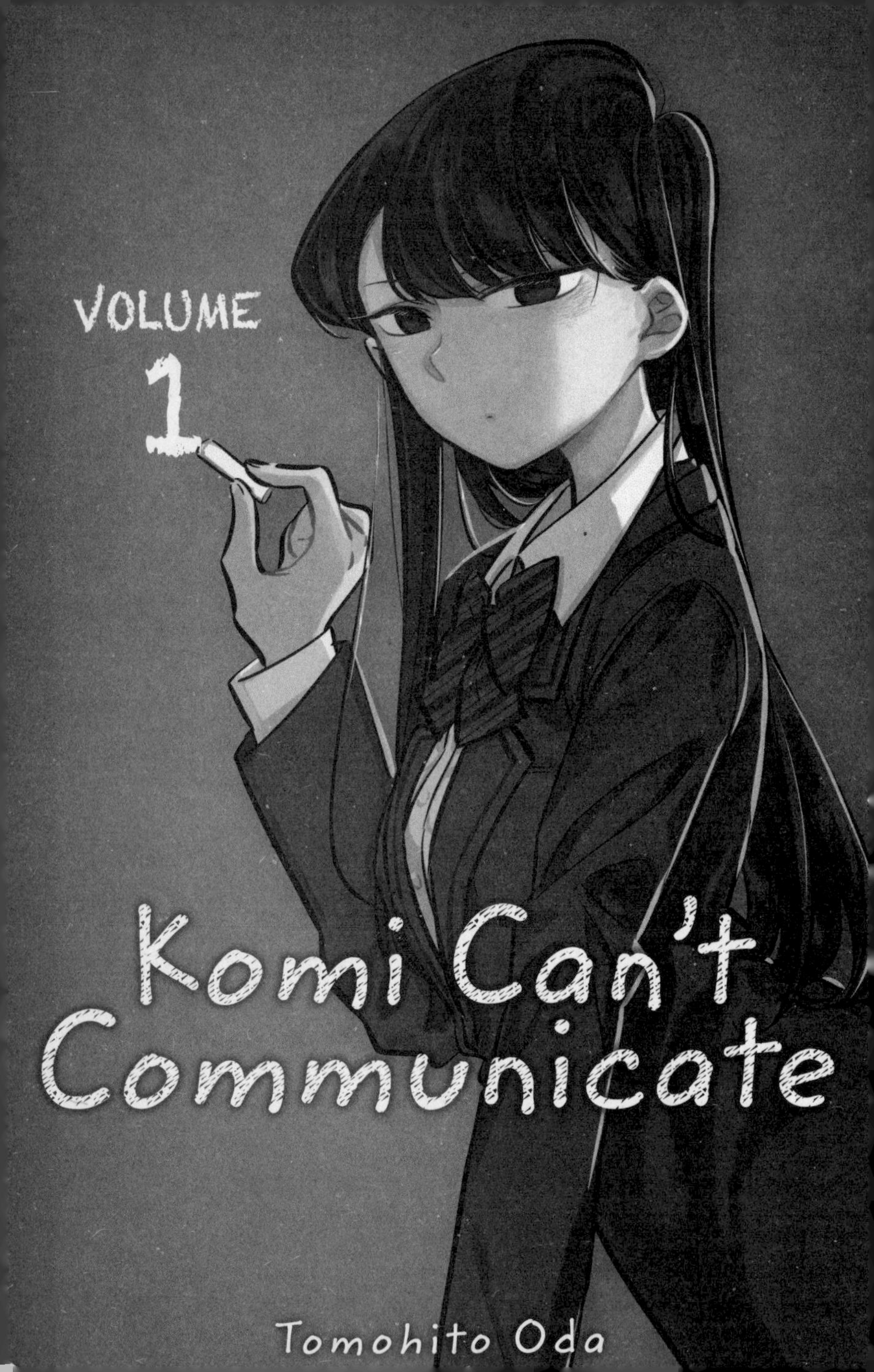
VOLUME
1
Komi Can't Communicate
Tomohito Oda

Contents

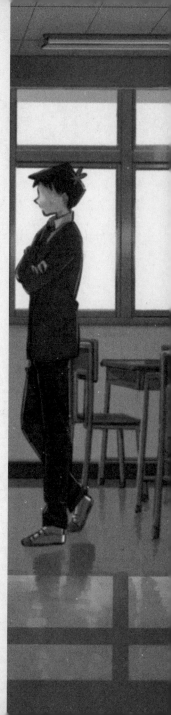

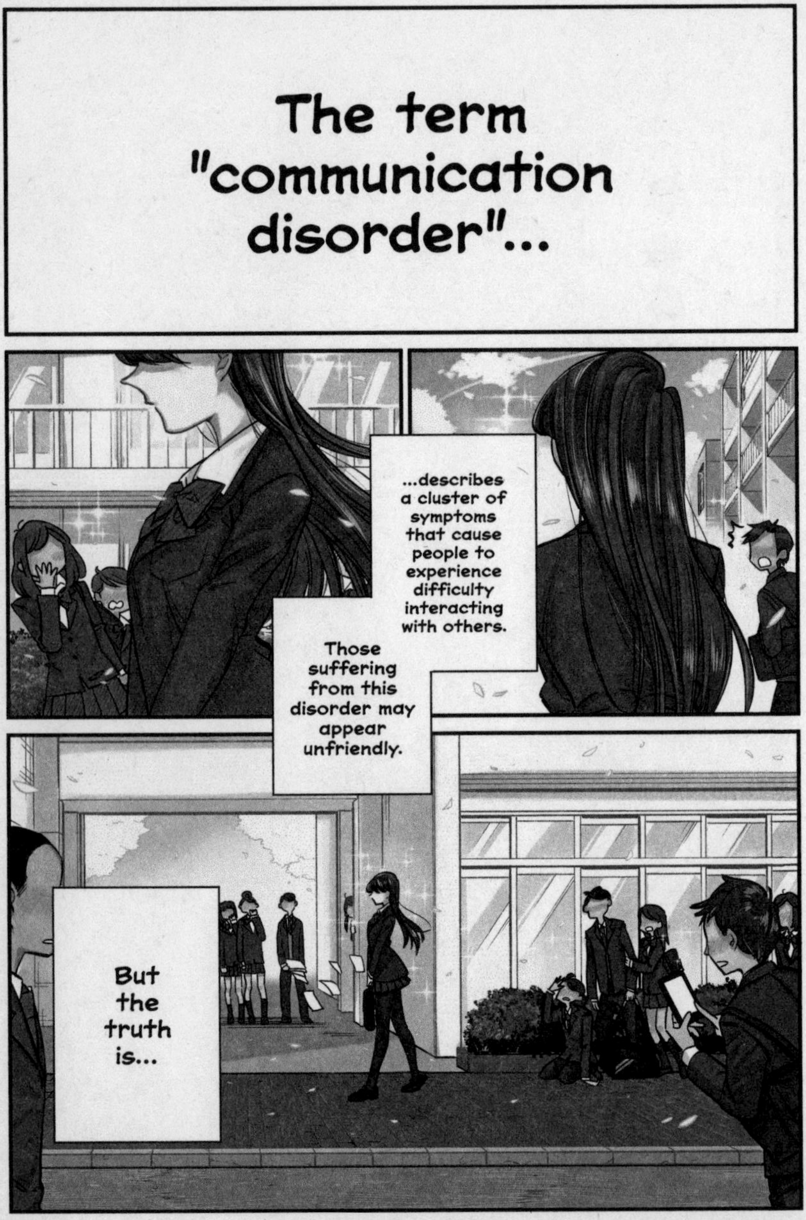
The term "communication disorder"...
...describes a cluster of symptoms that cause people to experience difficulty interacting with others.
Those suffering from this disorder may appear unfriendly.
But the truth is...

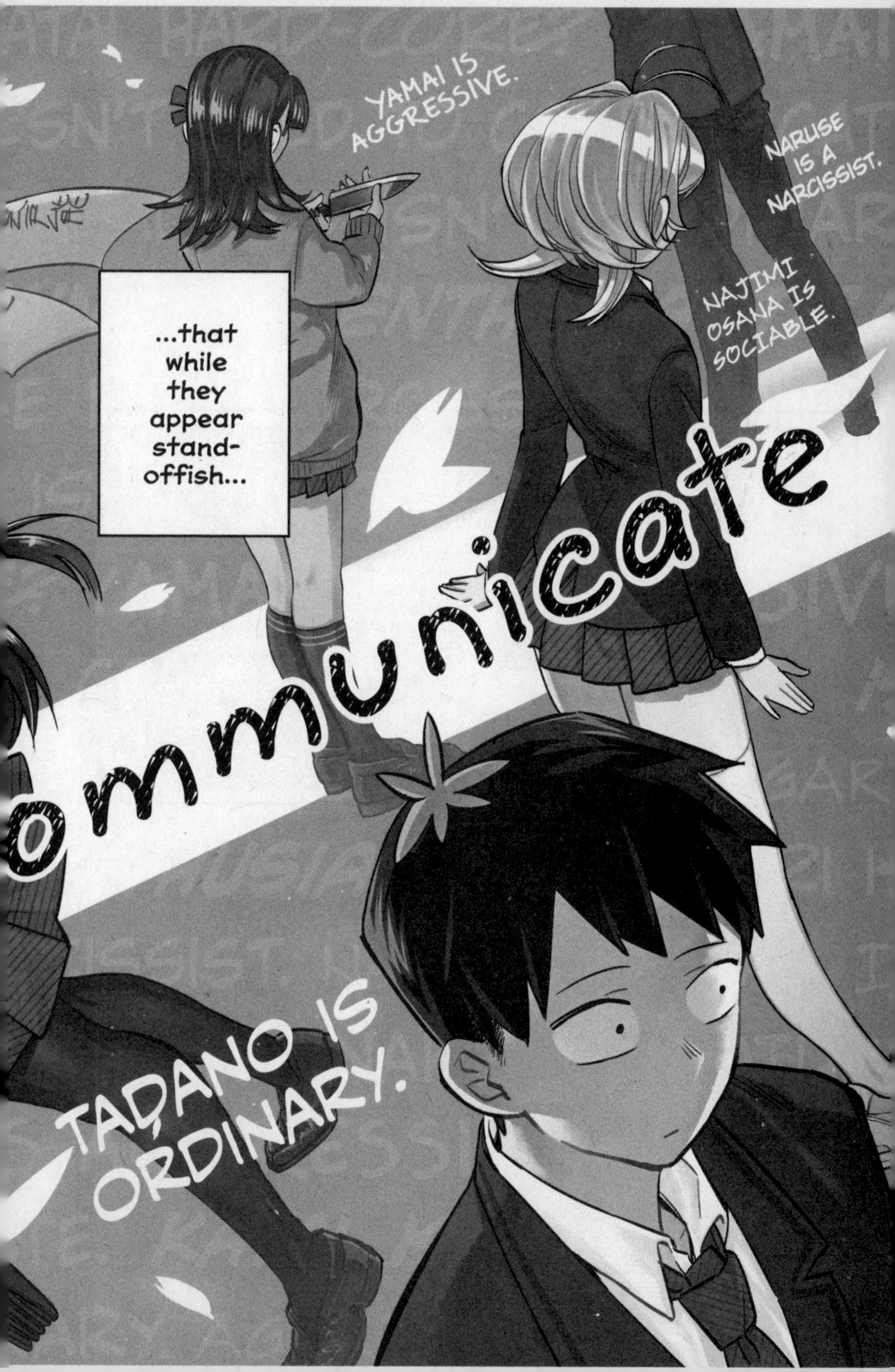
YAMAI IS AGGRESSIVE.
NARUSE IS A NARCISSIST.
NAJIMI OSANA IS SOCIABLE.
...that while they appear stand-offish...
ommunicate
TADANO IS ORDINARY.

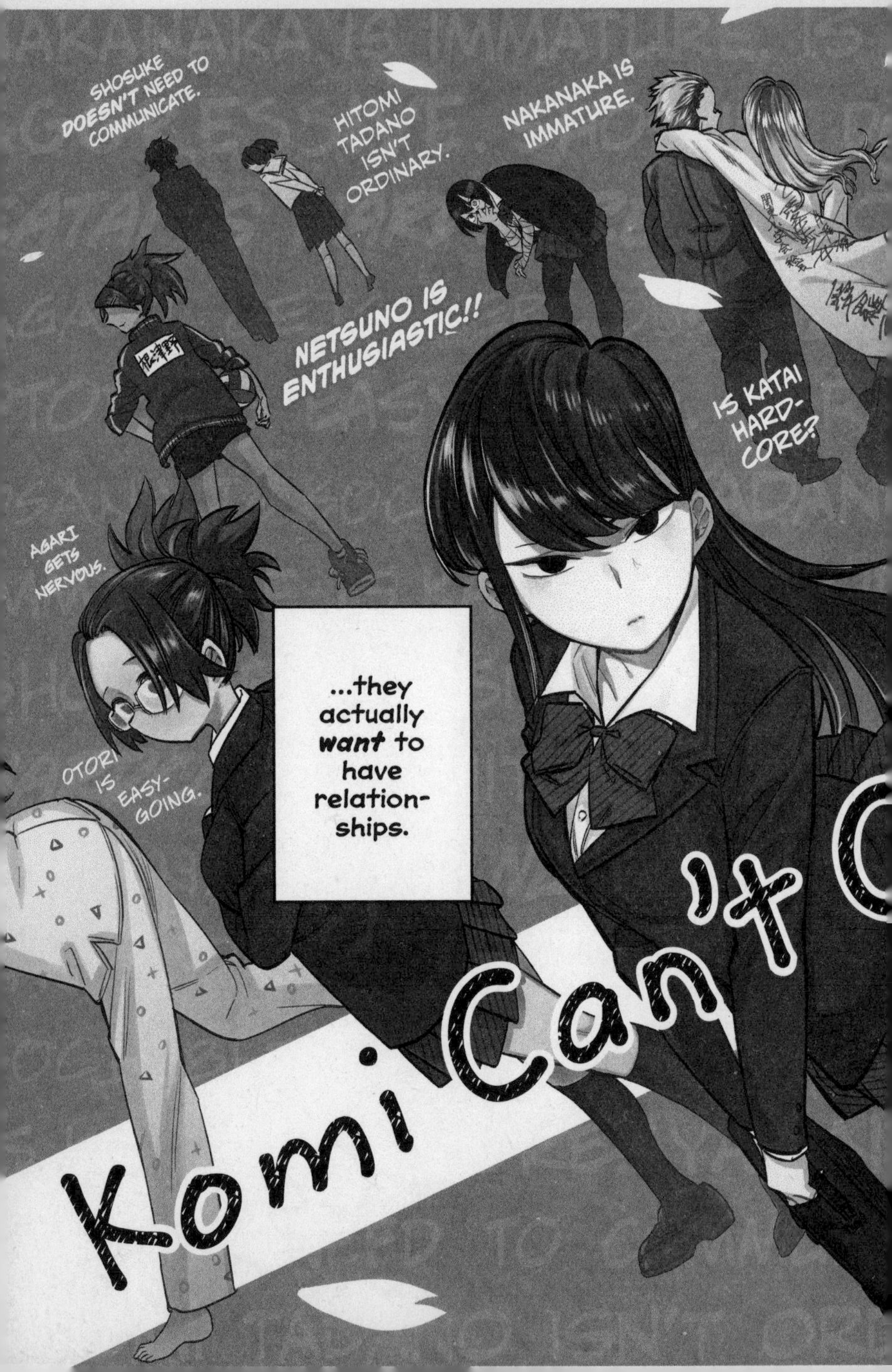
SHOSUKE DOESN'T NEED TO COMMUNICATE.
HITOMI TADANO ISN'T ORDINARY.
NAKANAKA IS IMMATURE.
NETSUNO IS ENTHUSIASTIC!!
IS KATAI HARD-CORE?
AGARI GETS NERVOUS.
OTORI IS EASY-GOING.
...they actually want to have relationships.
Komi Can't C

Komi Can't
Communicate

Communication 1: Totally Normal

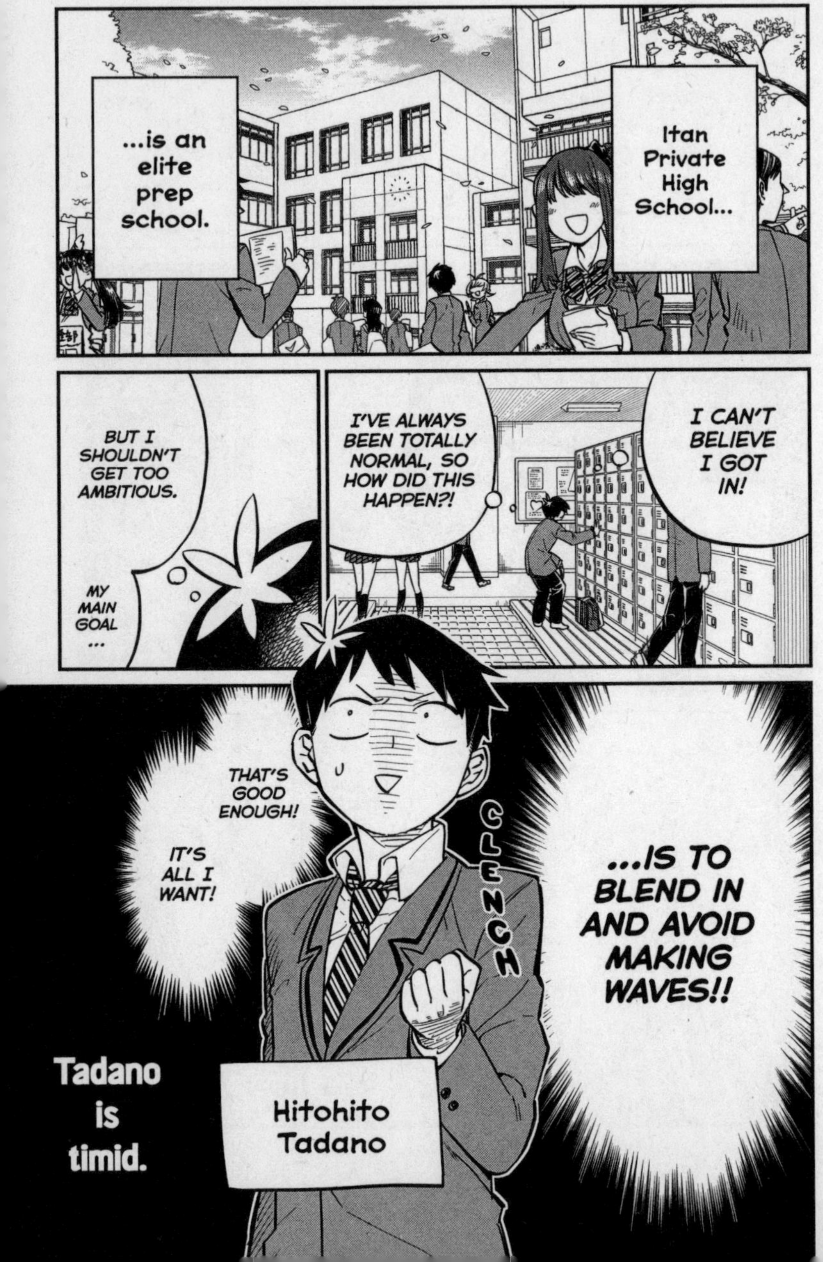
Itan Private High School...
...is an elite prep school.
I CAN'T BELIEVE I GOT IN!
I'VE ALWAYS BEEN TOTALLY NORMAL, SO HOW DID THIS HAPPEN?!
BUT I SHOULDN'T GET TOO AMBITIOUS.
MY MAIN GOAL...
...IS TO BLEND IN AND AVOID MAKING WAVES!!
CLENCH
THAT'S GOOD ENOUGH!
IT'S ALL I WANT!
Hitohito Tadano
Tadano is timid.

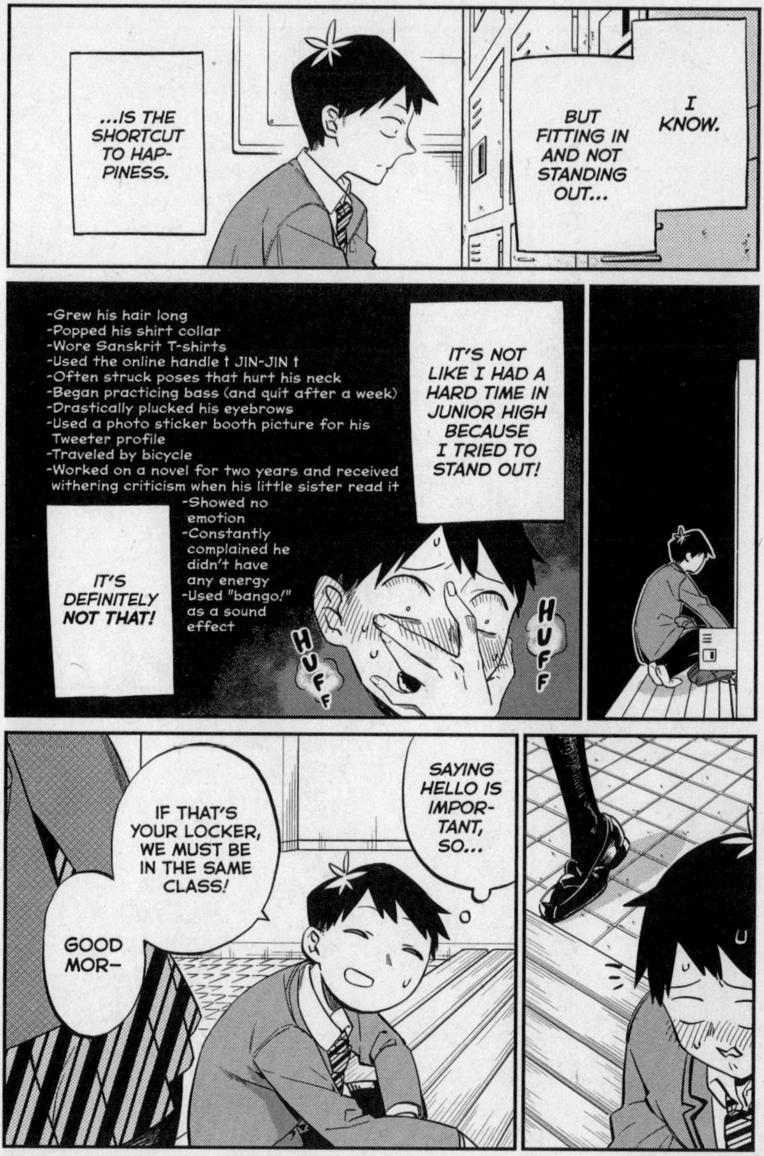
I KNOW.
BUT FITTING IN AND NOT STANDING OUT...
...IS THE SHORTCUT TO HAPPINESS.
IT'S NOT LIKE I HAD A HARD TIME IN JUNIOR HIGH BECAUSE I TRIED TO STAND OUT!
-Grew his hair long
-Popped his shirt collar
-Wore Sanskrit T-shirts
-Used the online handle † JIN-JIN †
-Often struck poses that hurt his neck
-Began practicing bass (and quit after a week)
-Drastically plucked his eyebrows
-Used a photo sticker booth picture for his Tweeter profile
-Traveled by bicycle
-Worked on a novel for two years and received withering criticism when his little sister read it
-Showed no emotion
-Constantly complained he didn't have any energy
-Used "bango!" as a sound effect
HUFF
HUFF
IT'S DEFINITELY NOT THAT!
SAYING HELLO IS IMPORTANT, SO...
IF THAT'S YOUR LOCKER, WE MUST BE IN THE SAME CLASS!
GOOD MOR-

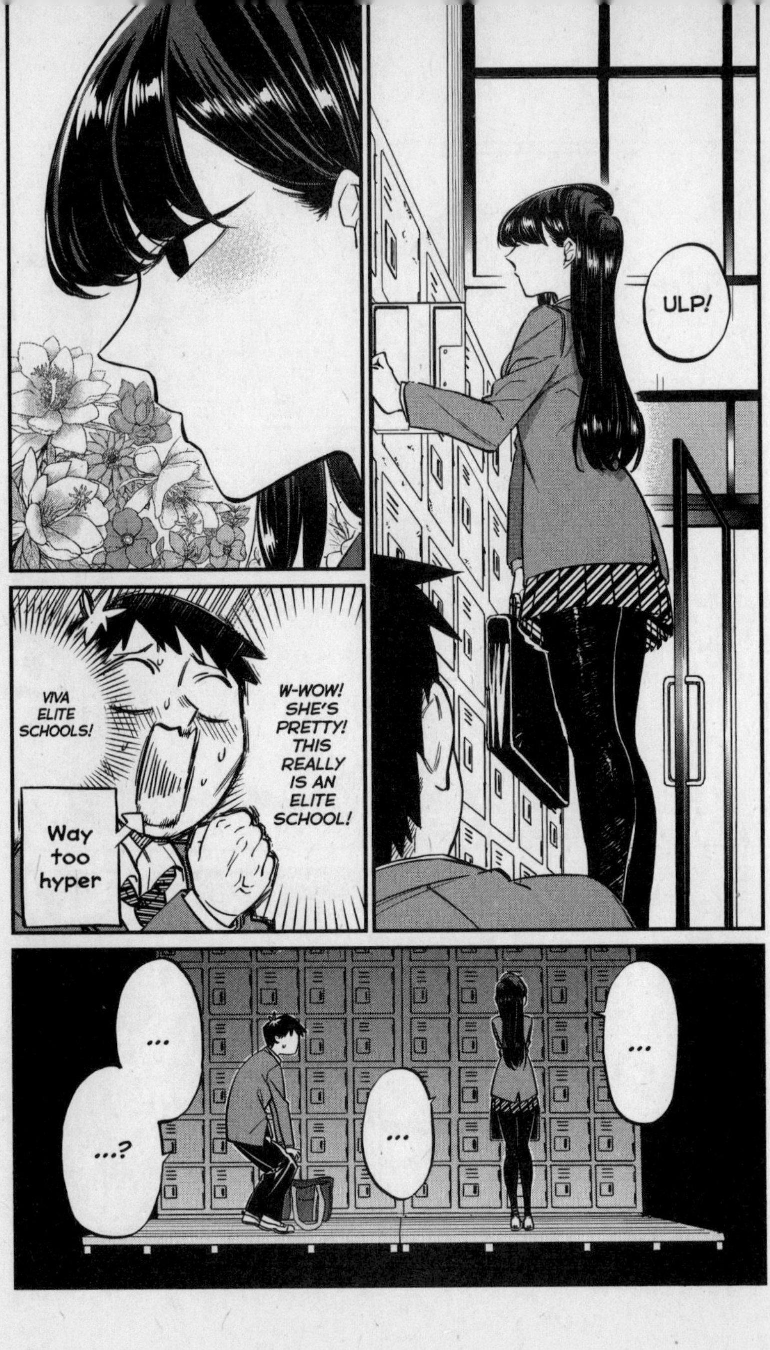
ULP!
W-WOW! SHE'S PRETTY! THIS REALLY IS AN ELITE SCHOOL!
VIVA ELITE SCHOOLS!
Way too hyper
...
...
...
...?

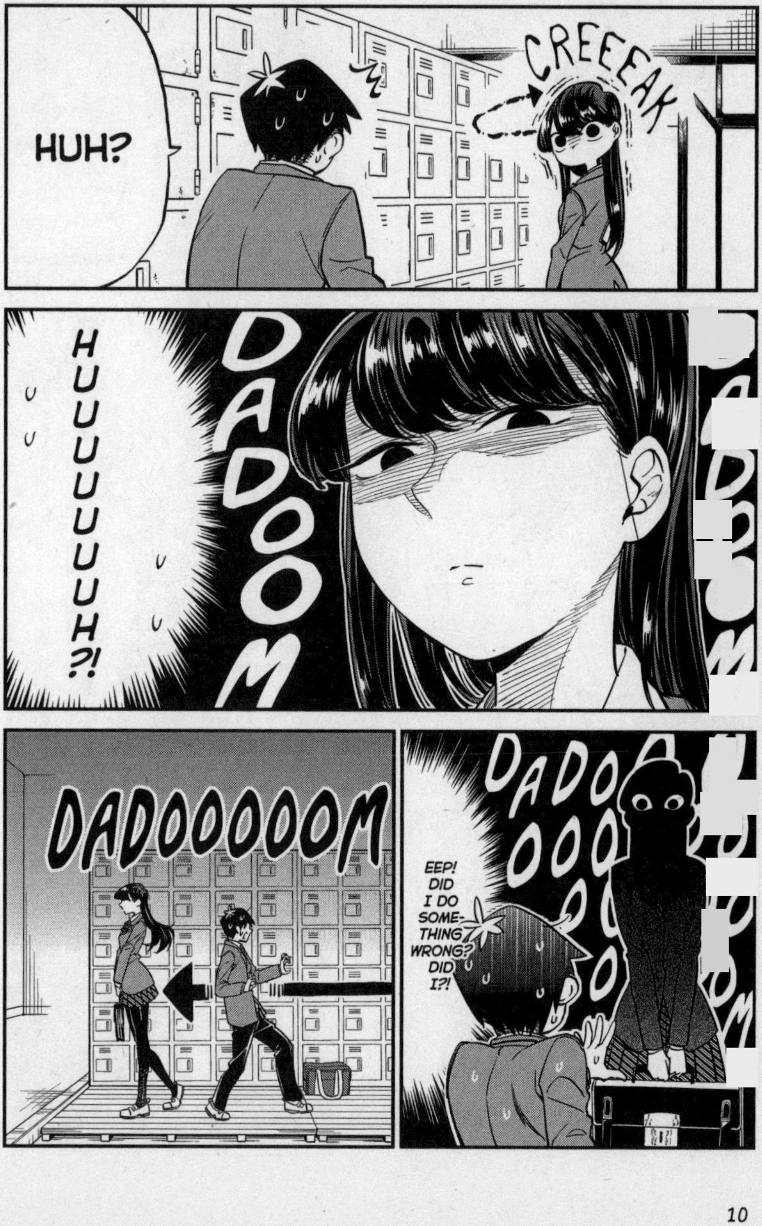
CREEEAK
HUH?
DADOOOM
HUUUUUUUH?!
EEP! DID I DO SOME-THING WRONG? DID I?!
DADOOOOOM

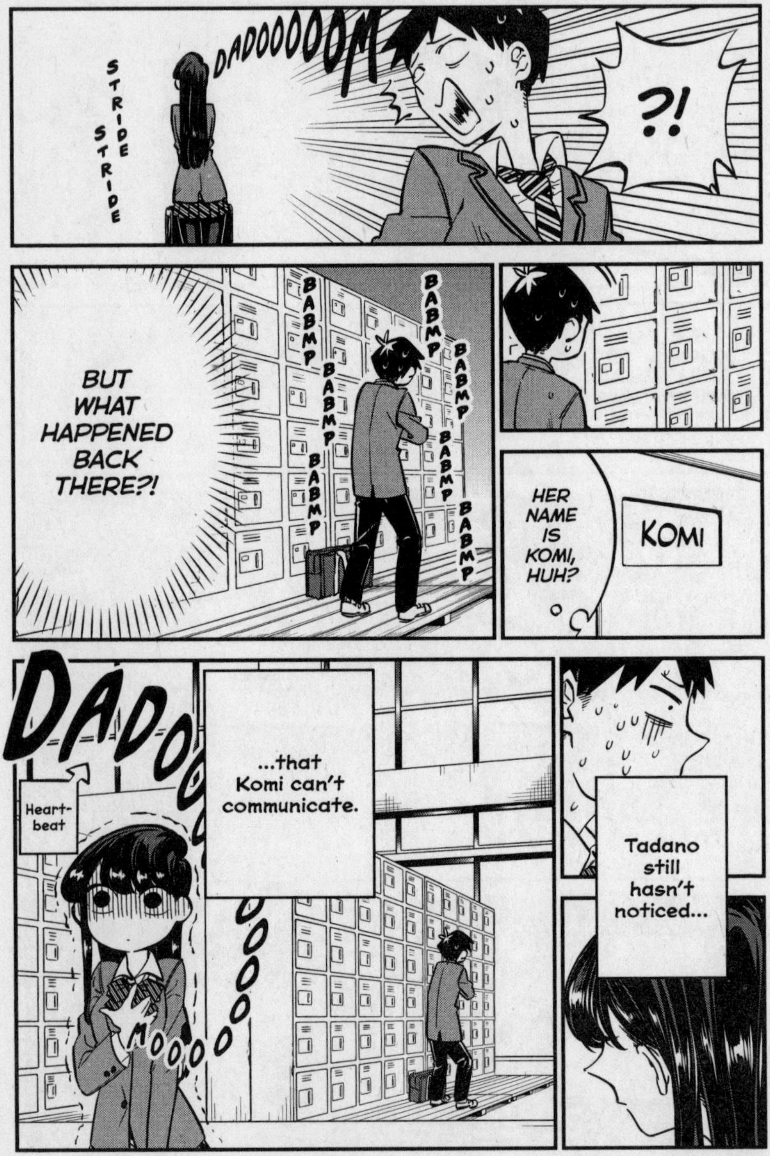
?!
DADOOOOOOM
STRIDE STRIDE
SIGN: KOMI
HER NAME IS KOMI, HUH?
BABMP BABMP BABMP BABMP BABMP BABMP BABMP
BUT WHAT HAPPENED BACK THERE?!
Tadano still hasn't noticed...
...that Komi can't communicate.
DADOOOOOOOOOOMOOOOO
Heart-beat

Communication 1 — The End

Communication 2: Peaceful

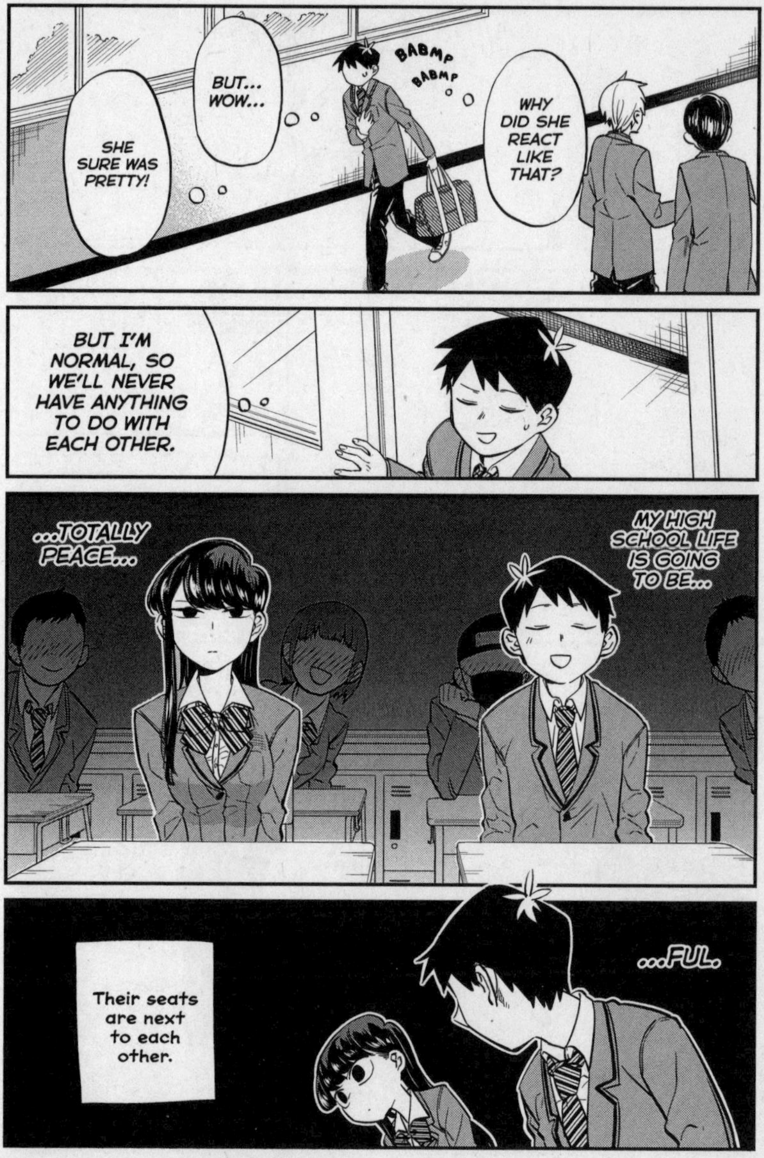
WHY DID SHE REACT LIKE THAT?
BABMP BABMP
BUT... WOW...
SHE SURE WAS PRETTY!
BUT I'M NORMAL, SO WE'LL NEVER HAVE ANYTHING TO DO WITH EACH OTHER.
MY HIGH SCHOOL LIFE IS GOING TO BE...
...TOTALLY PEACE...
...FUL.
Their seats are next to each other.

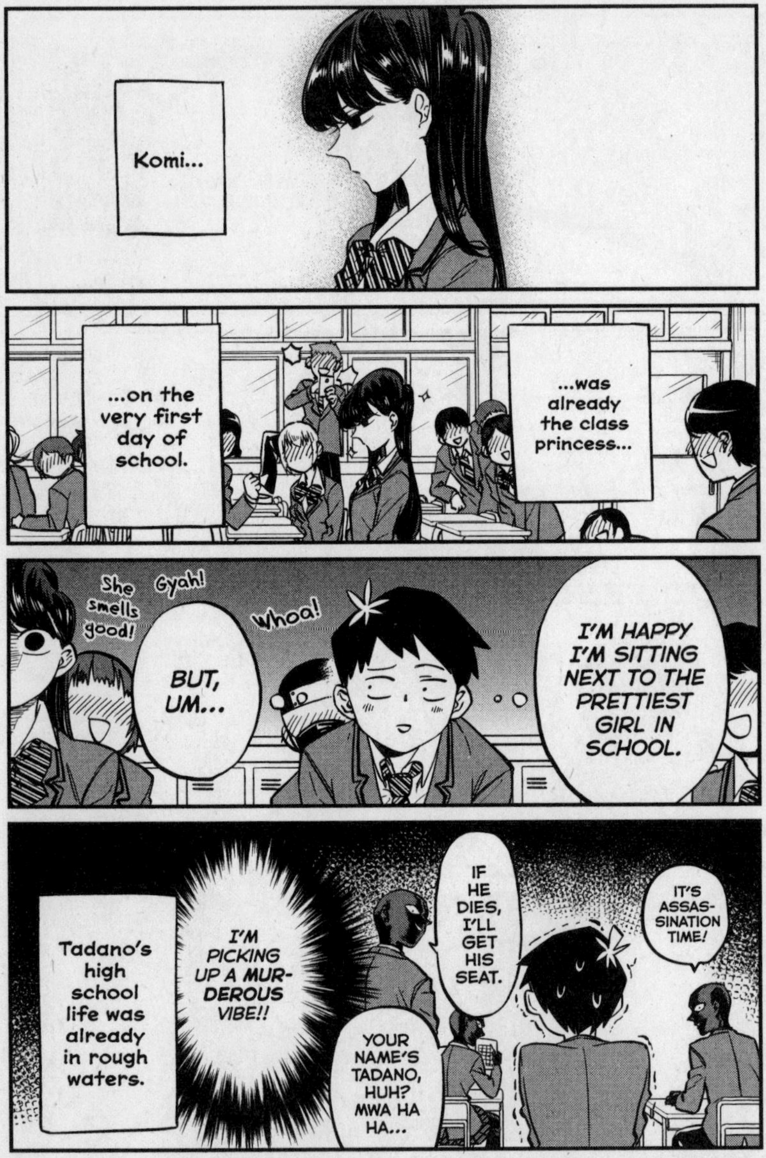
Komi...
...was already the class princess...
...on the very first day of school.
I'M HAPPY I'M SITTING NEXT TO THE PRETTIEST GIRL IN SCHOOL.
BUT, UM...
Whoa!
Gyah!
She smells good!
IT'S ASSAS-SINATION TIME!
IF HE DIES, I'LL GET HIS SEAT.
YOUR NAME'S TADANO, HUH? MWA HA HA...
I'M PICKING UP A MUR-DEROUS VIBE!!
Tadano's high school life was already in rough waters.

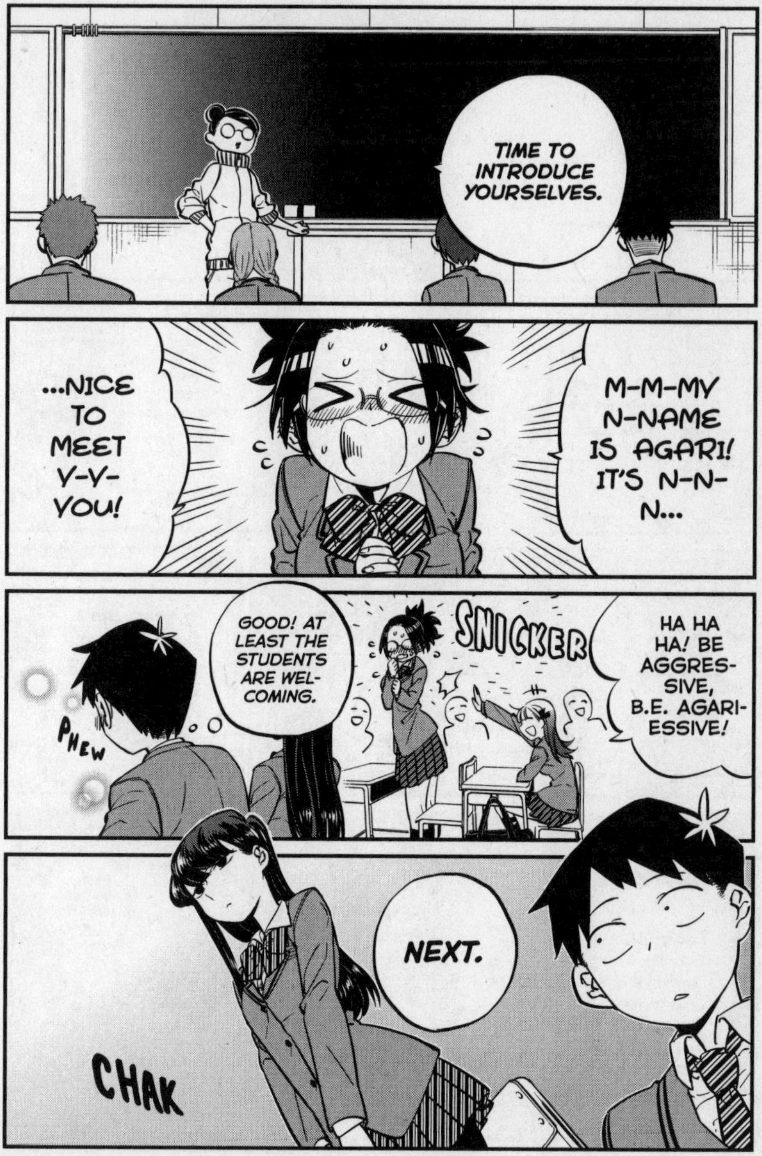
TIME TO INTRODUCE YOURSELVES.
M-M-MY N-NAME IS AGARI! IT'S N-N-N...
...NICE TO MEET Y-Y-YOU!
HA HA HA! BE AGGRES-SIVE, B.E. AGARI-ESSIVE!
SNICKER
GOOD! AT LEAST THE STUDENTS ARE WEL-COMING.
PHEW
NEXT.
CHAK

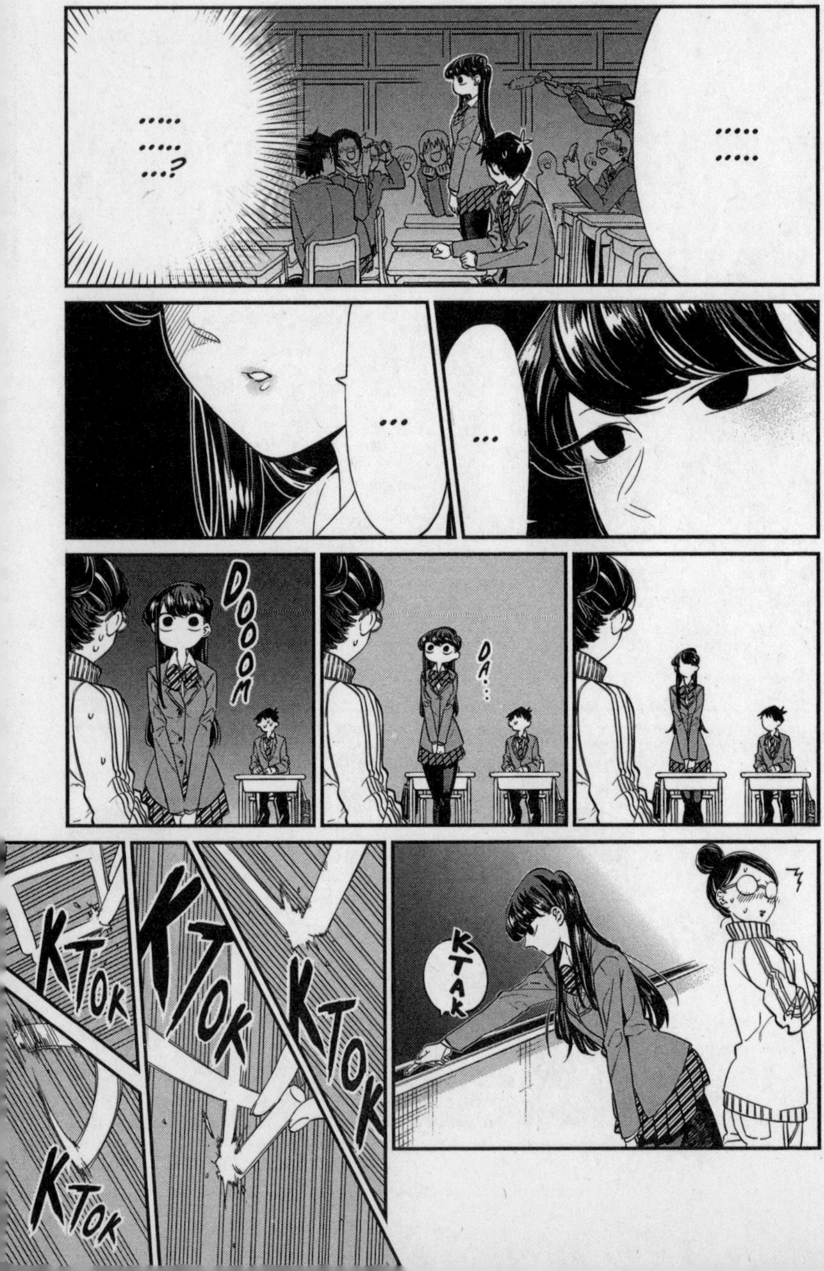
.....
.....
.....
.....
...?
...
...
DA...
DOOOOM
KTAK
KTOK
KTOK
KTOK
KTOK

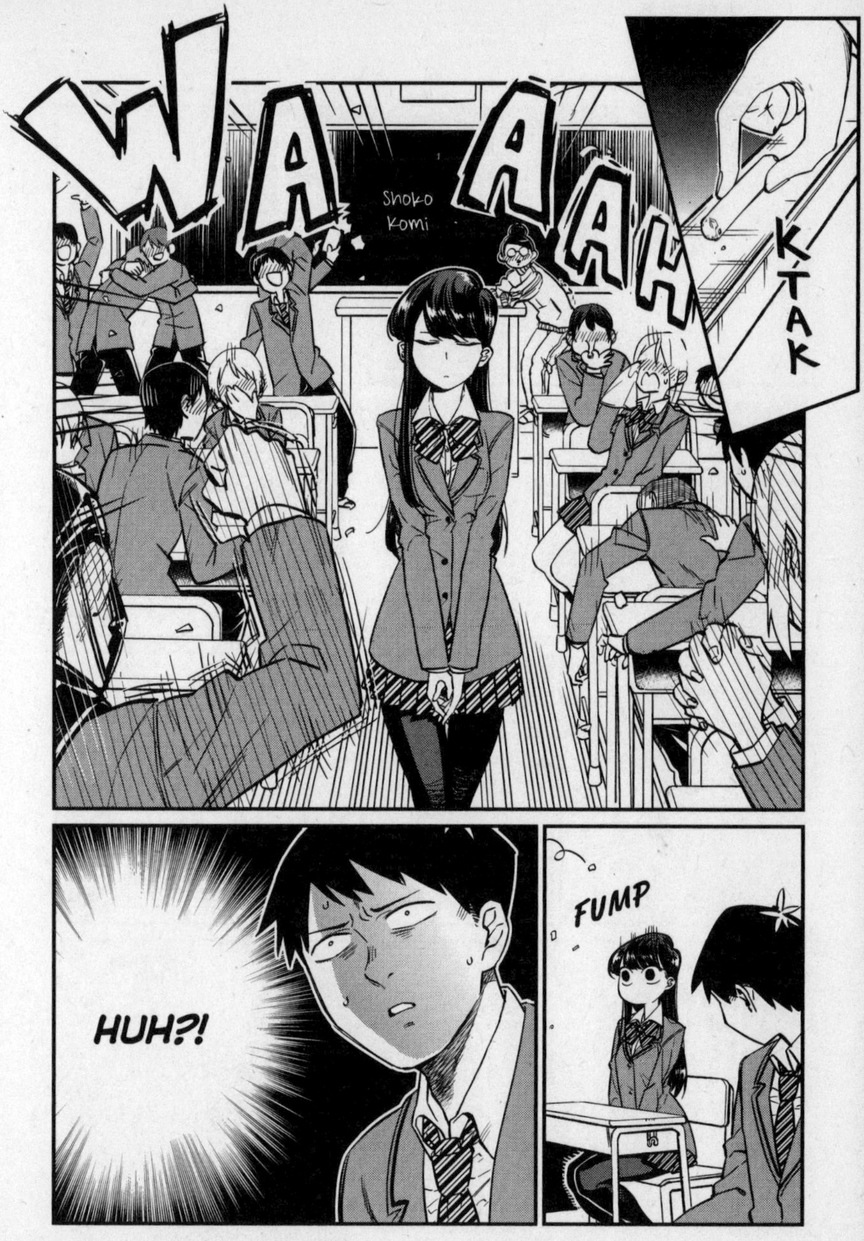
KTAK
WAAAH
Shoko Komi
FUMP
HUH?!

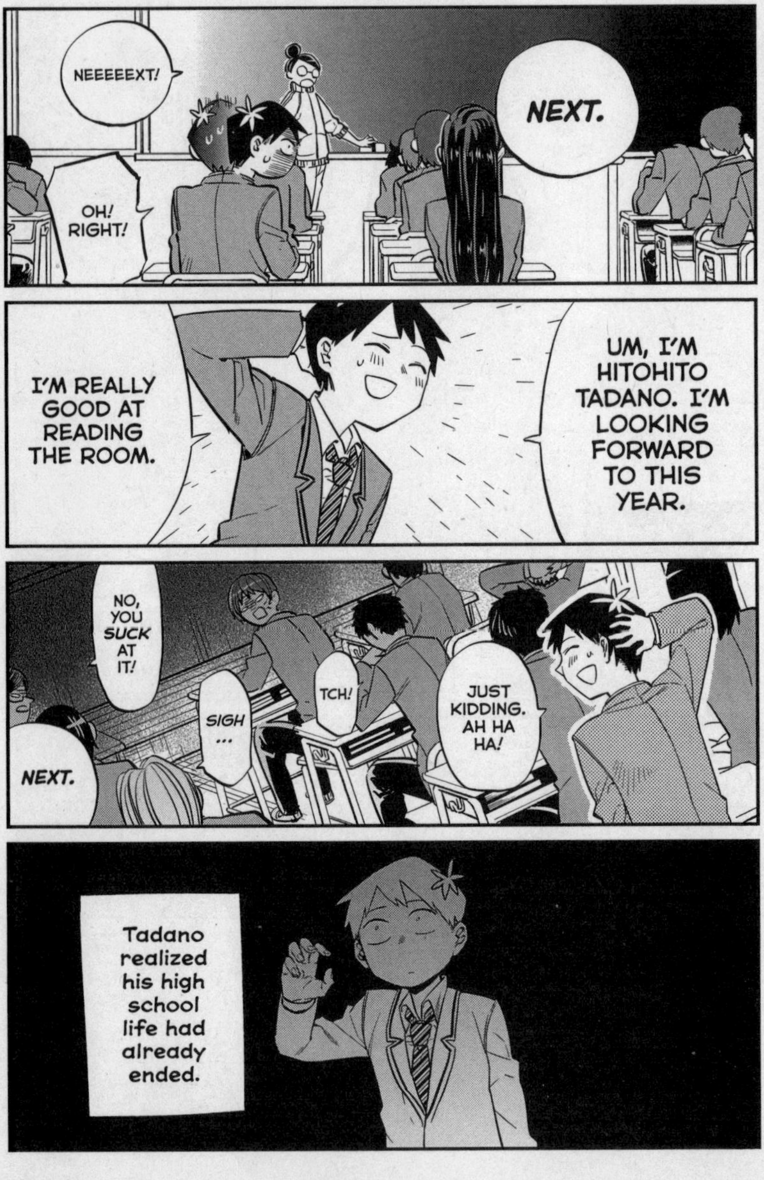
NEXT.
NEEEEEXT!
OH! RIGHT!
UM, I'M HITOHITO TADANO. I'M LOOKING FORWARD TO THIS YEAR.
I'M REALLY GOOD AT READING THE ROOM.
JUST KIDDING. AH HA HA!
TCH!
SIGH...
NO, YOU SUCK AT IT!
NEXT.
Tadano realized his high school life had already ended.

Communication 2 — The End

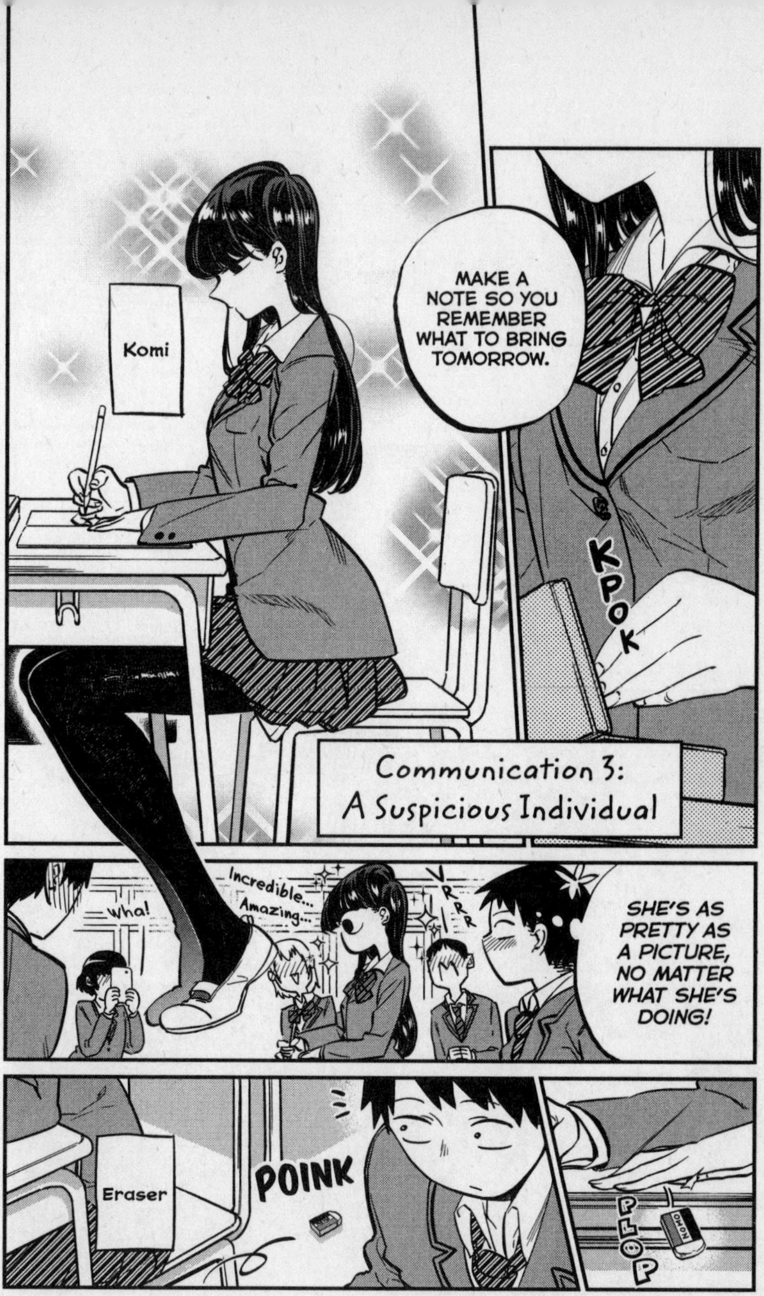
MAKE A NOTE SO YOU REMEMBER WHAT TO BRING TOMORROW.
KPOK
Komi
Communication 3: A Suspicious Individual
SHE'S AS PRETTY AS A PICTURE, NO MATTER WHAT SHE'S DOING!
VRRR
Incredible...
Amazing...
wha!
PLOP
POINK
Eraser

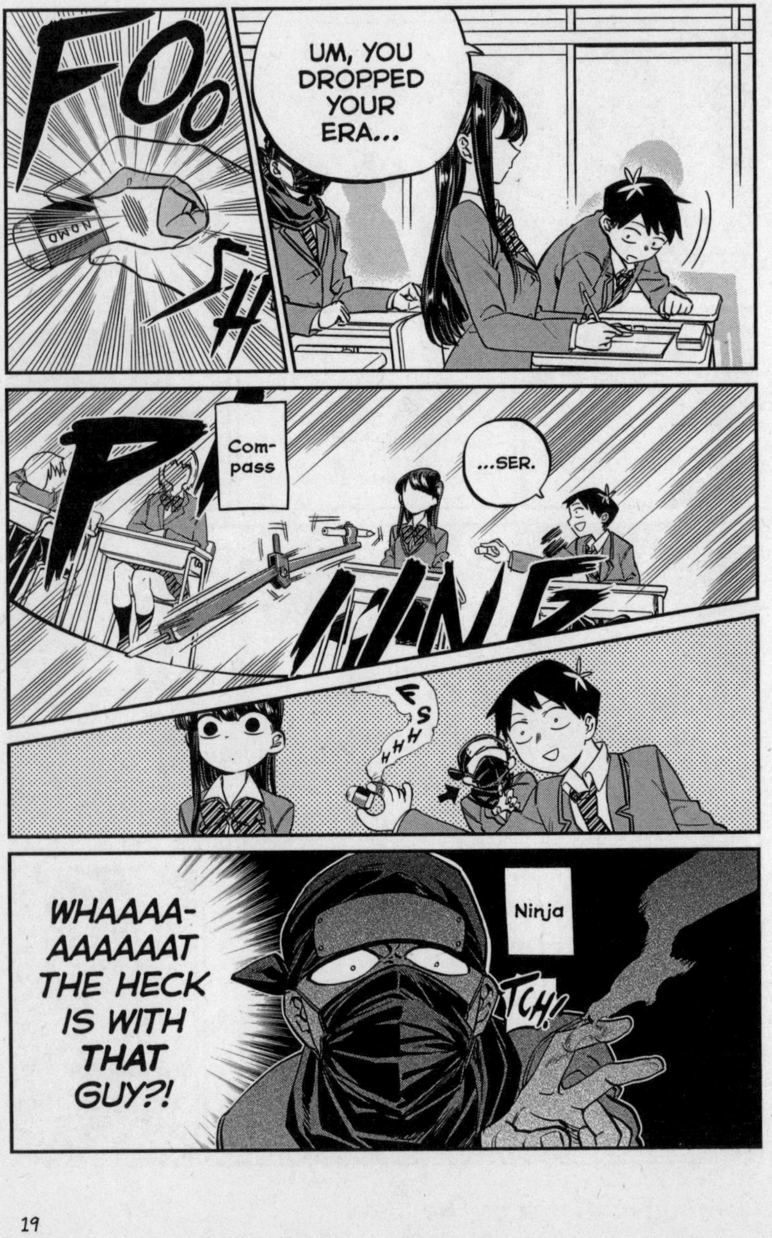
UM, YOU DROPPED YOUR ERA...
FOOSH
...SER.
Com-pass
PING
FSHHH
Ninja
WHAAAA-AAAAAAT THE HECK IS WITH THAT GUY?!
TCH!

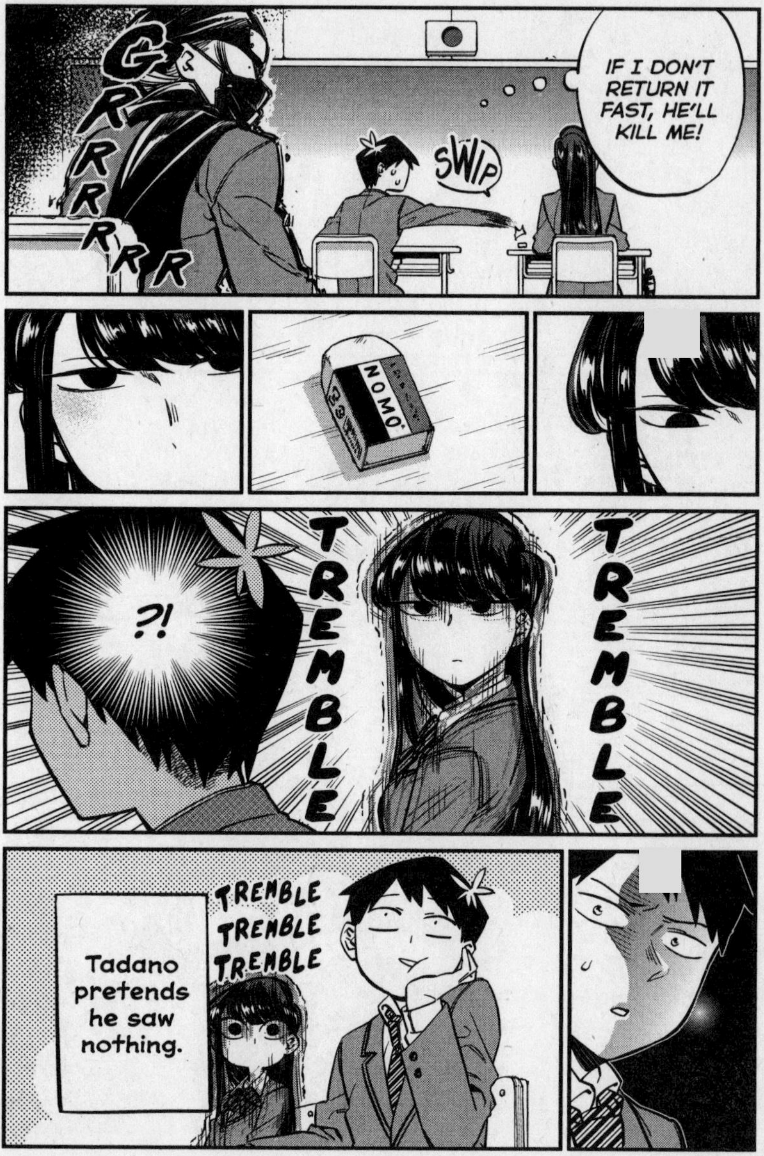
IF I DON'T RETURN IT FAST, HE'LL KILL ME!
SWIP
GRRRRRRR
TREMBLE
TREMBLE
?!
TREMBLE TREMBLE TREMBLE
Tadano pretends he saw nothing.

Communication 3 — The End

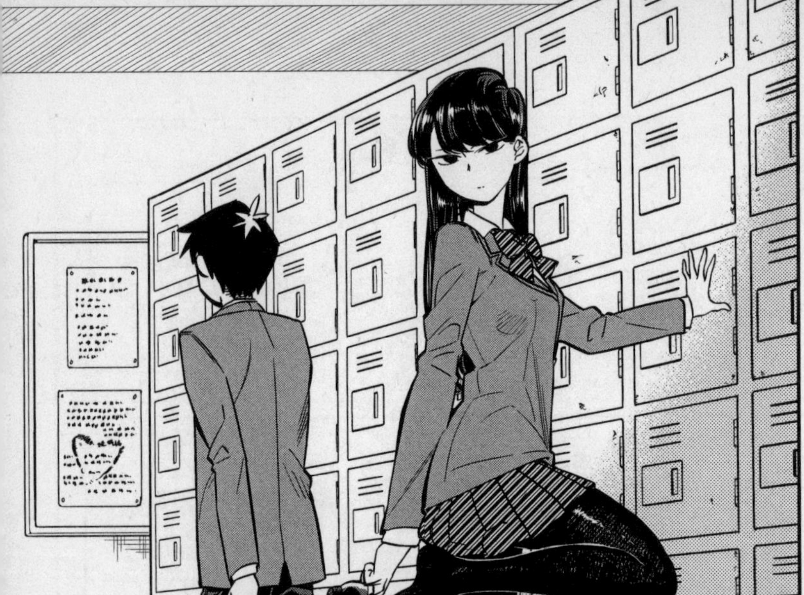
Komi Can't Communicate
Communication 4:
Not Very Good
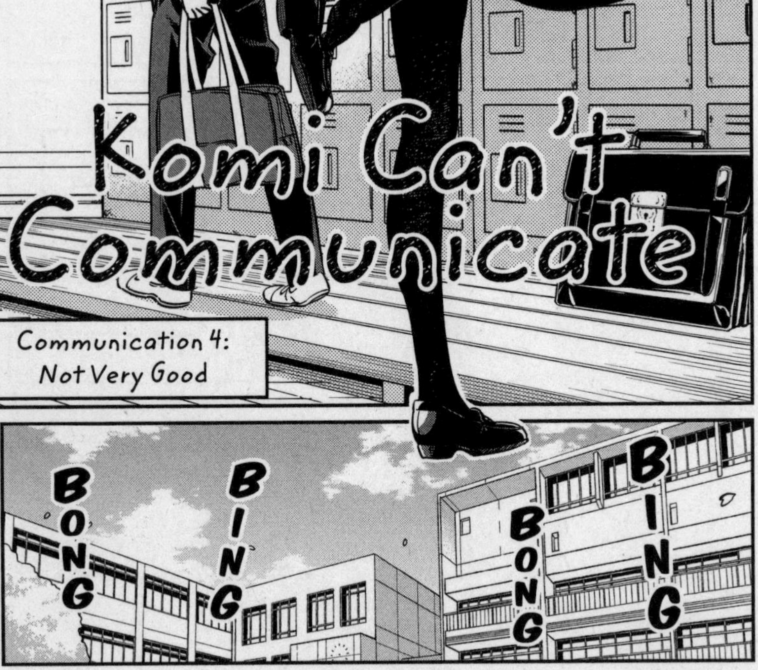
BING
BONG
BING
BONG

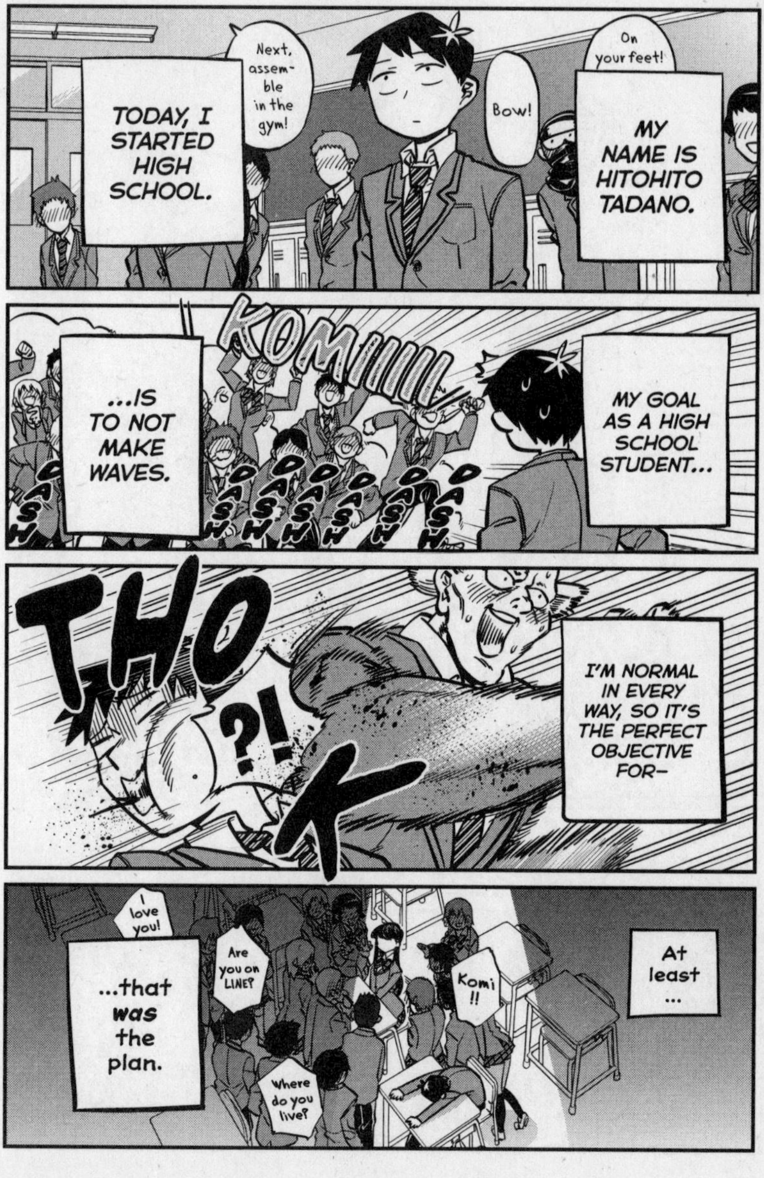
On your feet!
MY NAME IS HITOHITO TADANO.
Bow!
Next, assemble in the gym!
TODAY, I STARTED HIGH SCHOOL.
MY GOAL AS A HIGH SCHOOL STUDENT...
KOMIIIIII
DASH DASH DASH DASH DASH DASH DASH
...IS TO NOT MAKE WAVES.
I'M NORMAL IN EVERY WAY, SO IT'S THE PERFECT OBJECTIVE FOR–
?!
THOK
At least...
Komi!!
Are you on LINE?
I love you!
Where do you live?
...that *was* the plan.

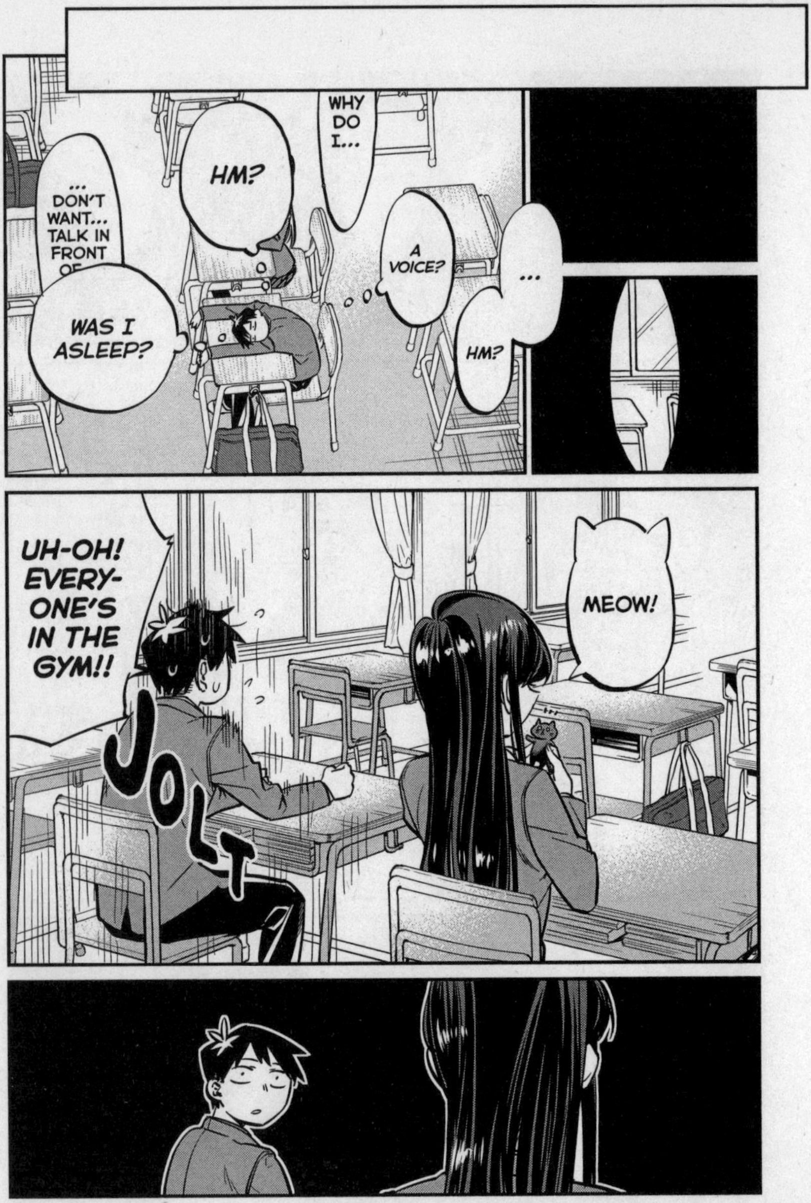
WHY DO I...
... DON'T WANT... TALK IN FRONT OF
HM?
WAS I ASLEEP?
A VOICE?
...
HM?
MEOW!
UH-OH! EVERYONE'S IN THE GYM!!
JOLT

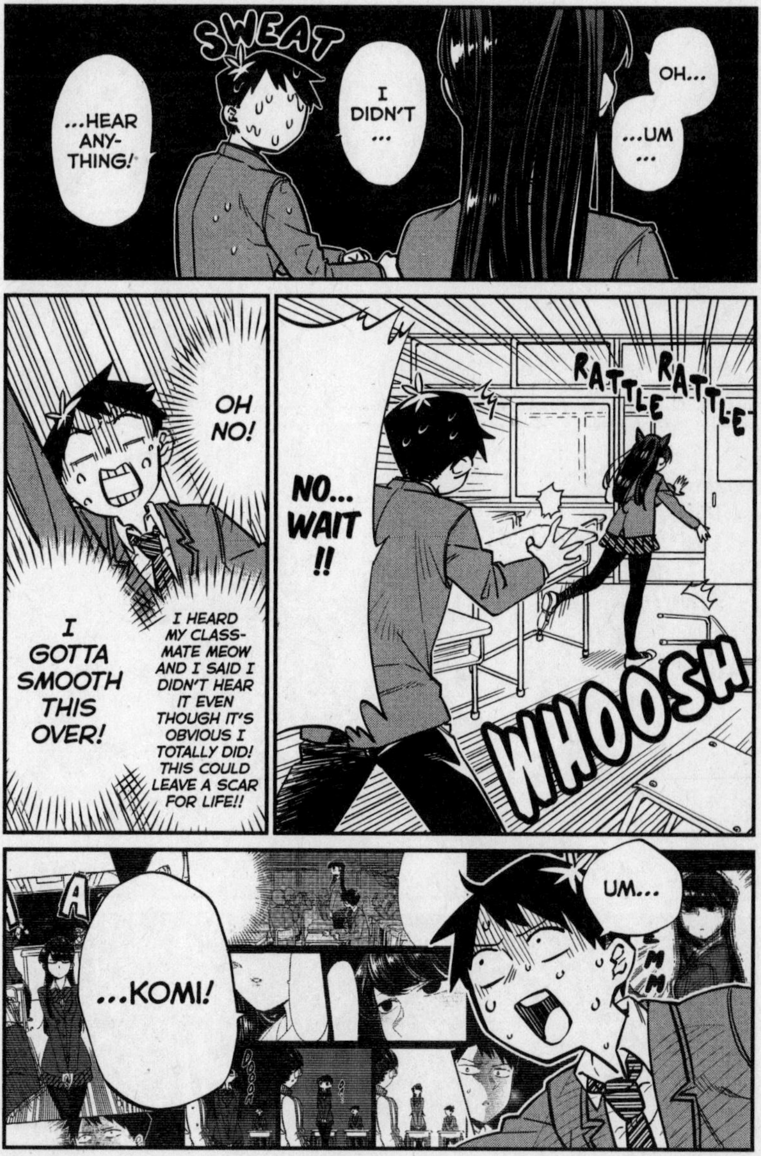
OH...
...UM ...
SWEAT
I DIDN'T ...
...HEAR ANYTHING!
RATTLE RATTLE
NO... WAIT!!
WHOOSH
OH NO!
I GOTTA SMOOTH THIS OVER!
I HEARD MY CLASSMATE MEOW AND I SAID I DIDN'T HEAR IT EVEN THOUGH IT'S OBVIOUS I TOTALLY DID! THIS COULD LEAVE A SCAR FOR LIFE!!
UM...
...KOMI!

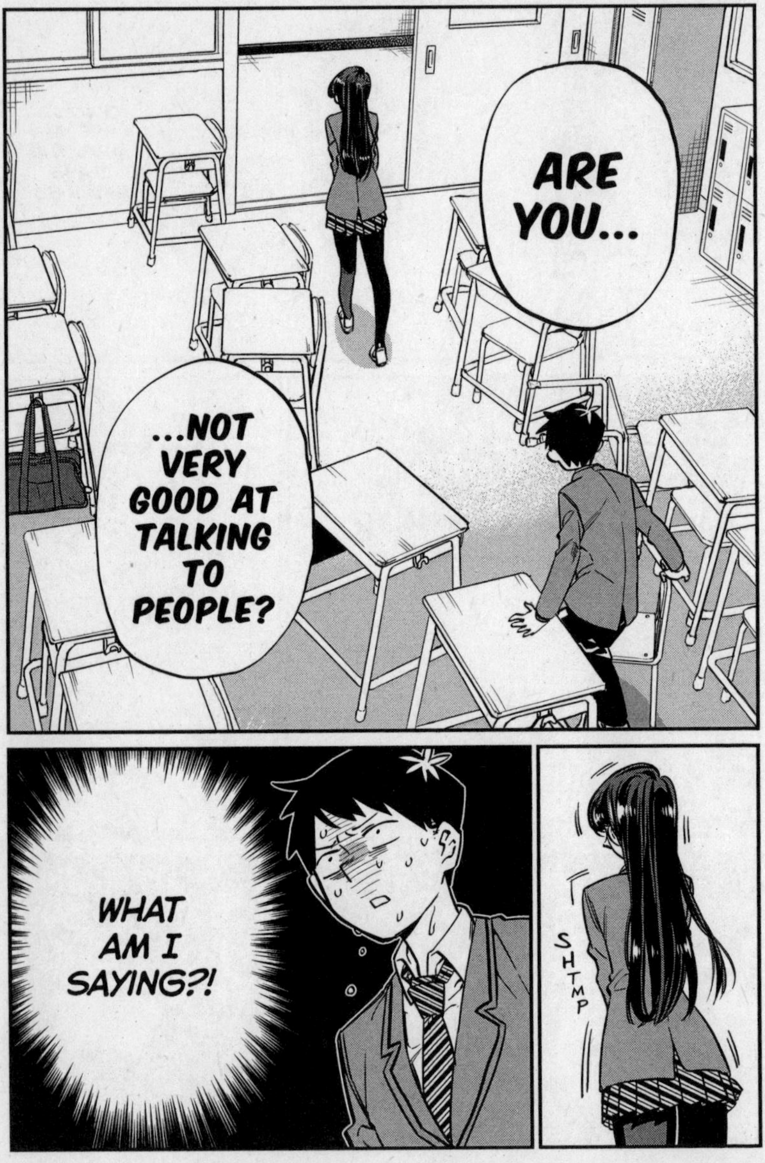
ARE YOU...
...NOT VERY GOOD AT TALKING TO PEOPLE?
SHTMP
WHAT AM I SAYING?!

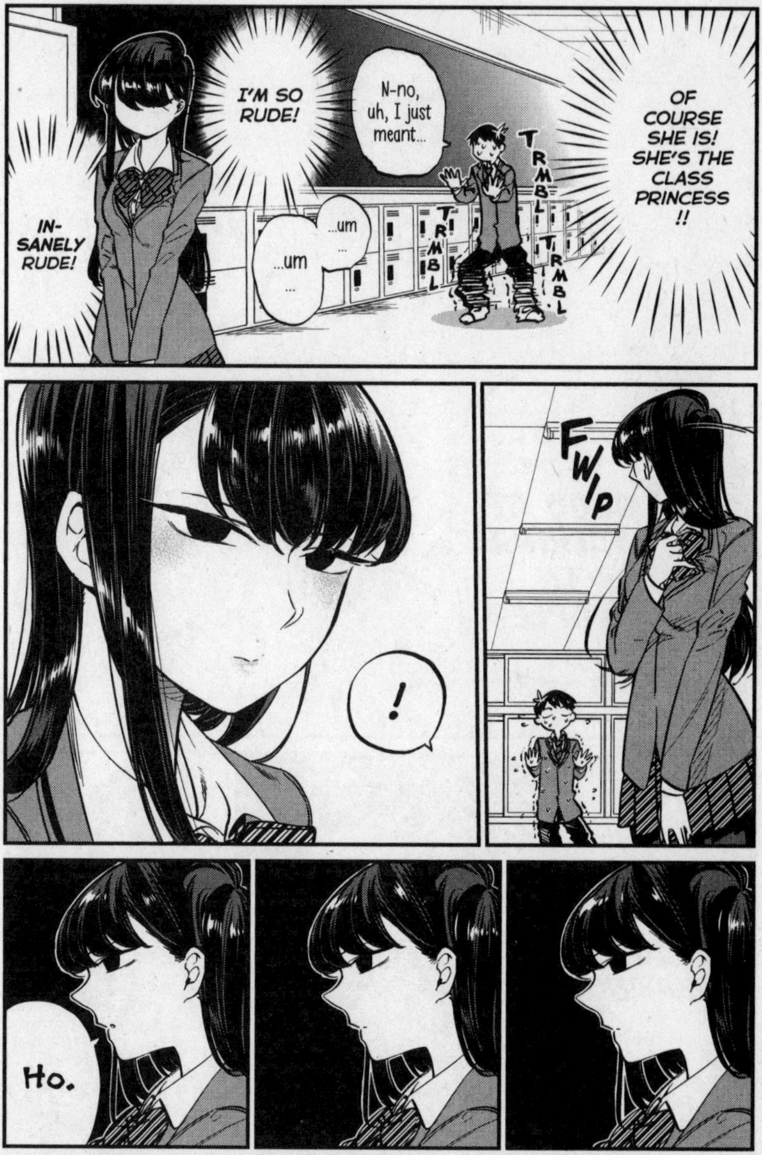
OF COURSE SHE IS! SHE'S THE CLASS PRINCESS!!
TRMBL
TRMBL
TRMBL
N-no, uh, I just meant...
I'M SO RUDE!
...um ...
...um ...
IN-SANELY RUDE!
FWIP
!
Ho.

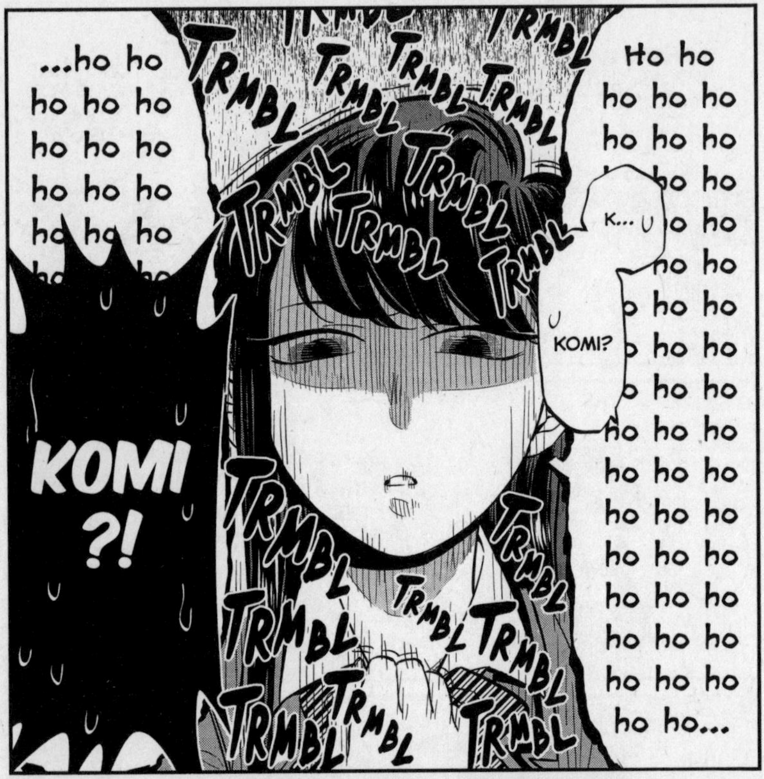
Ho ho ho ho ho ho ho ho ho ho ho ho ho ho ho ho ho ho ho ho ho ho ho ho ho ho ho ho ho ho ho ho ho ho ho ho ho ho ho ho ho ho ho ho ho ho ho ho ho ho ho...
K...
KOMI?
TRMBL TRMBL TRMBL TRMBL TRMBL TRMBL TRMBL TRMBL TRMBL TRMBL TRMBL TRMBL TRMBL TRMBL TRMBL
...ho ho ho ho ho ho ho ho ho ho ho ho ho ho ho
KOMI ?!

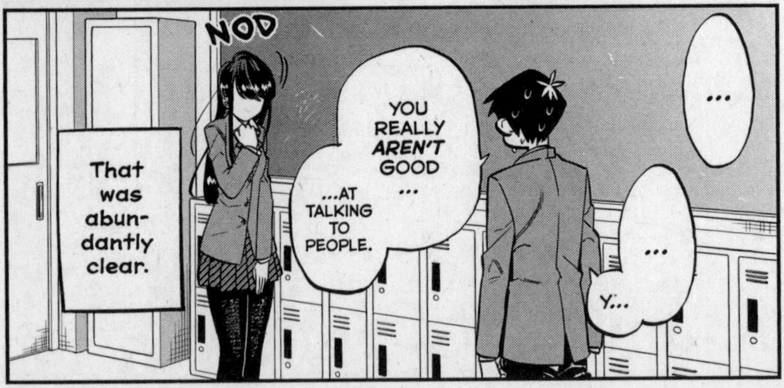
...
...
Y...
YOU REALLY AREN'T GOOD ...
...AT TALKING TO PEOPLE.
NOD
That was abundantly clear.

Communication 4 — The End

Communication 5: Wanting to Talk

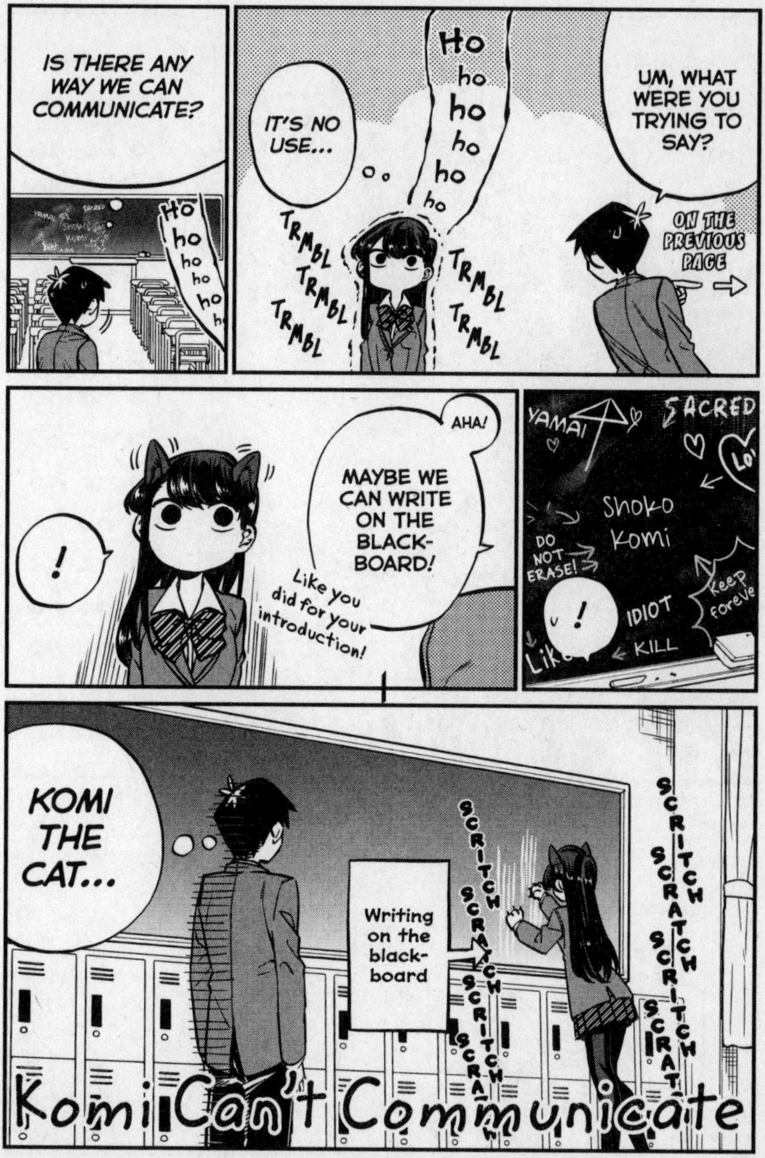
UM, WHAT WERE YOU TRYING TO SAY?
ON THE PREVIOUS PAGE
Ho ho ho ho ho ho
IT'S NO USE...
TRMBL TRMBL TRMBL
TRMBL TRMBL
IS THERE ANY WAY WE CAN COMMUNICATE?
Ho ho ho ho ho
YAMAI
SACRED
Shoko Komi
DO NOT ERASE!
Keep foreve
!
IDIOT
KILL
AHA!
MAYBE WE CAN WRITE ON THE BLACKBOARD!
Like you did for your introduction!
!
SCRITCH SCRATCH SCRITCH SCRATCH
SCRITCH SCRATCH SCRITCH SCRATCH
Writing on the blackboard
KOMI THE CAT...
Komi Can't Communicate

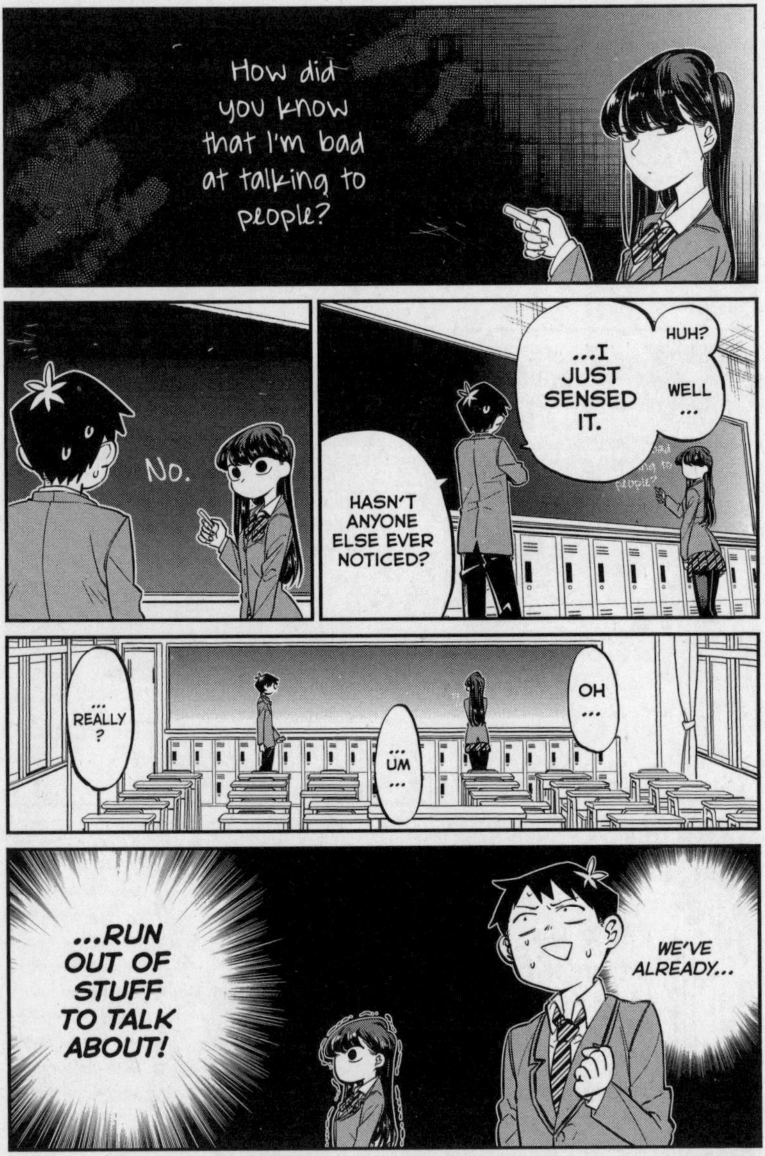
How did you know that I'm bad at talking to people?
HUH? WELL ...
...I JUST SENSED IT.
HASN'T ANYONE ELSE EVER NOTICED?
No.
OH ...
... UM ...
... REALLY ?
WE'VE ALREADY...
...RUN OUT OF STUFF TO TALK ABOUT!

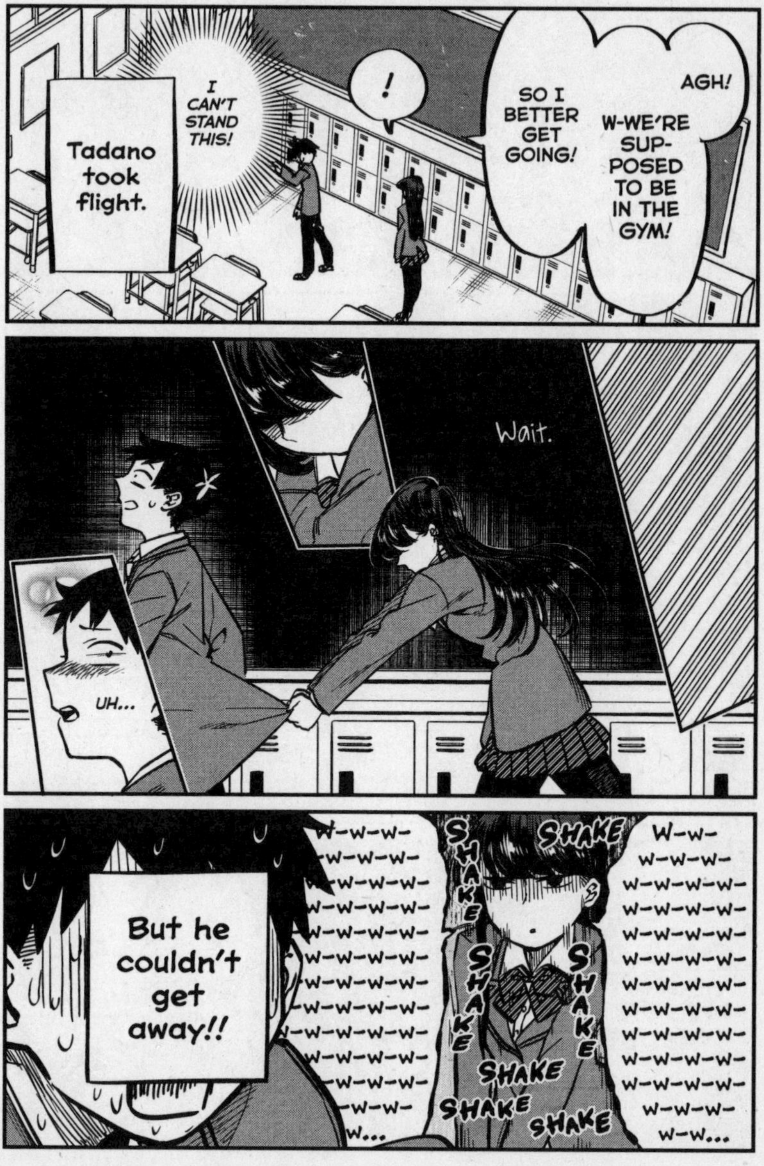
AGH! W-WE'RE SUPPOSED TO BE IN THE GYM!
SO I BETTER GET GOING!
!
I CAN'T STAND THIS!
Tadano took flight.
Wait.
UH...
W-w-
w-w-w-
w-w-w-w-
w-w-w-w-
w-w-w-w-
w-w-w-w-
w-w-w-w-
w-w-w-w-
w-w-w-w-
w-w-w-w-
w-w-w-w-
w-w-w-
w-w...
SHAKE SHAKE SHAKE SHAKE SHAKE SHAKE SHAKE SHAKE
But he couldn't get away!!
W-w-w-
-w-w-w-
-w-w-w-w-
-w-w-w-w-
-w-w-w-w-
-w-w-w-w-
-w-w-w-w-
-w-w-w-w-
-w-w-w-w-
-w-w-w-w-
-w-w-w-w-
-w-w-
w...

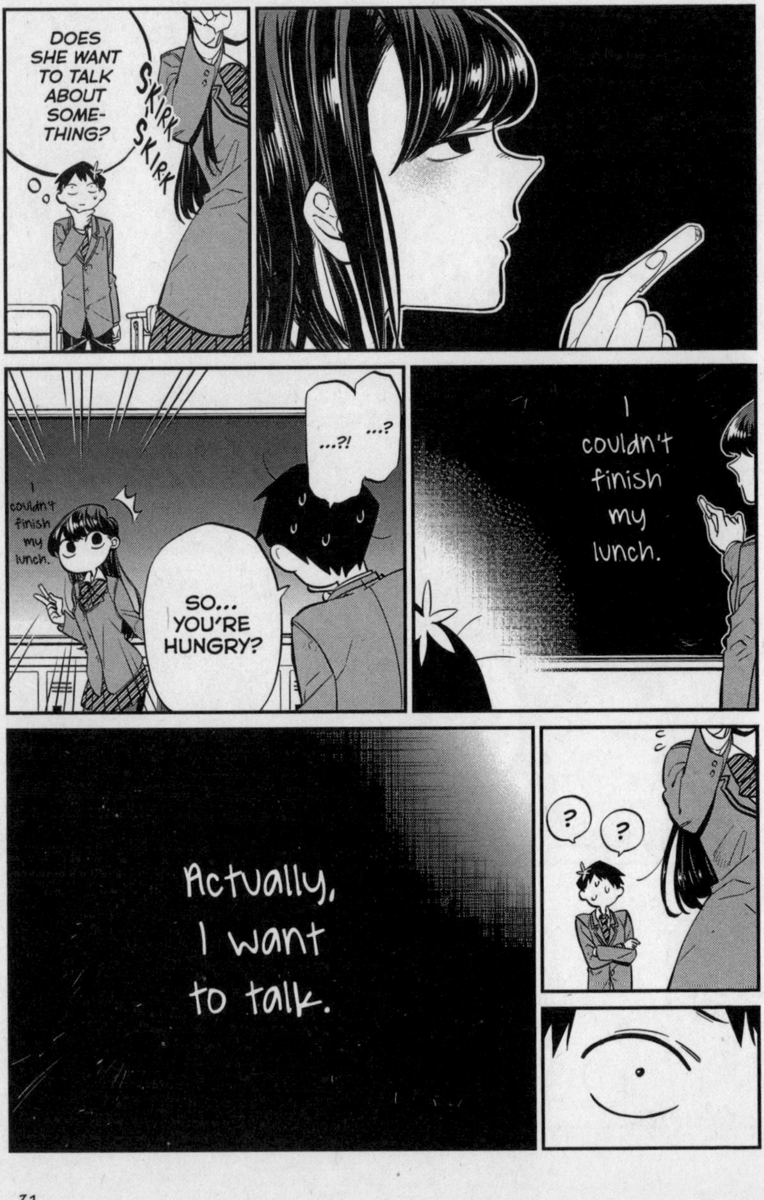
DOES SHE WANT TO TALK ABOUT SOME-THING?
SKIRK SKIRK
I couldn't finish my lunch.
...?
...?!
I couldn't finish my lunch.
SO... YOU'RE HUNGRY?
?
?
Actually, I want to talk.

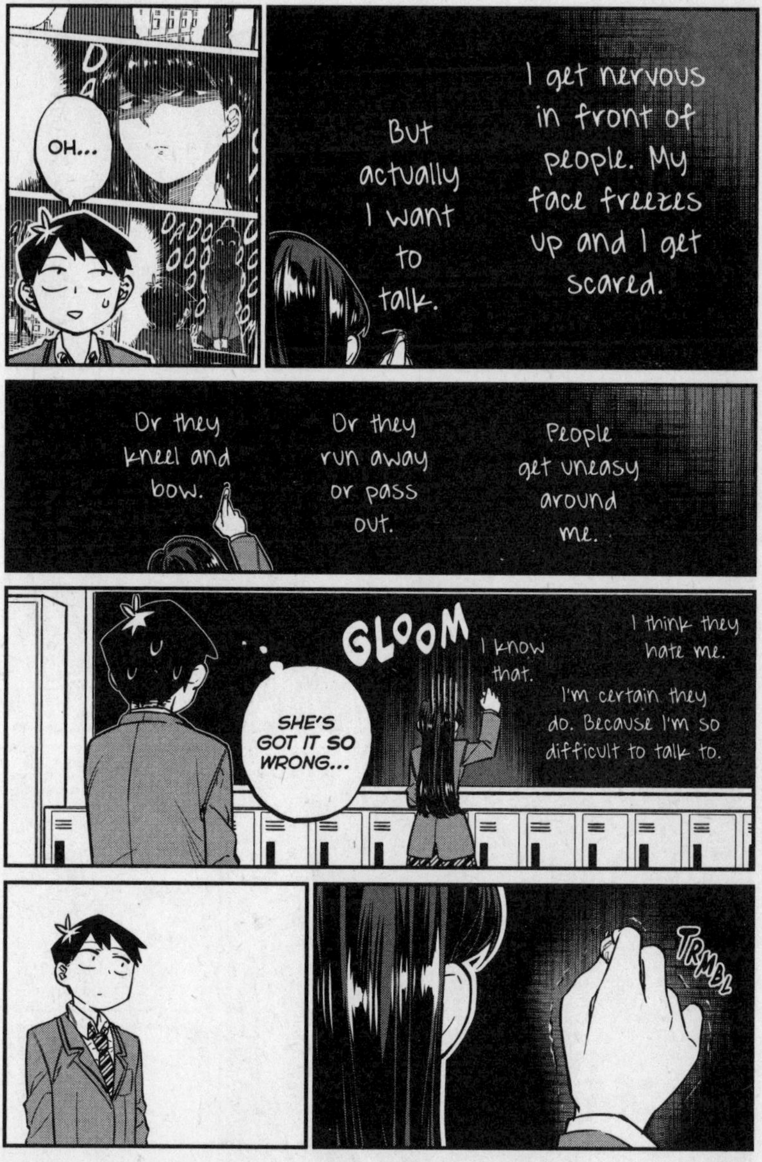
I get nervous in front of people. My face freezes up and I get scared.
But actually I want to talk.
OH...
People get uneasy around me.
Or they run away or pass out.
Or they kneel and bow.
I think they hate me.
I know that.
I'm certain they do. Because I'm so difficult to talk to.
GLOOM
SHE'S GOT IT SO WRONG...
TRMBL

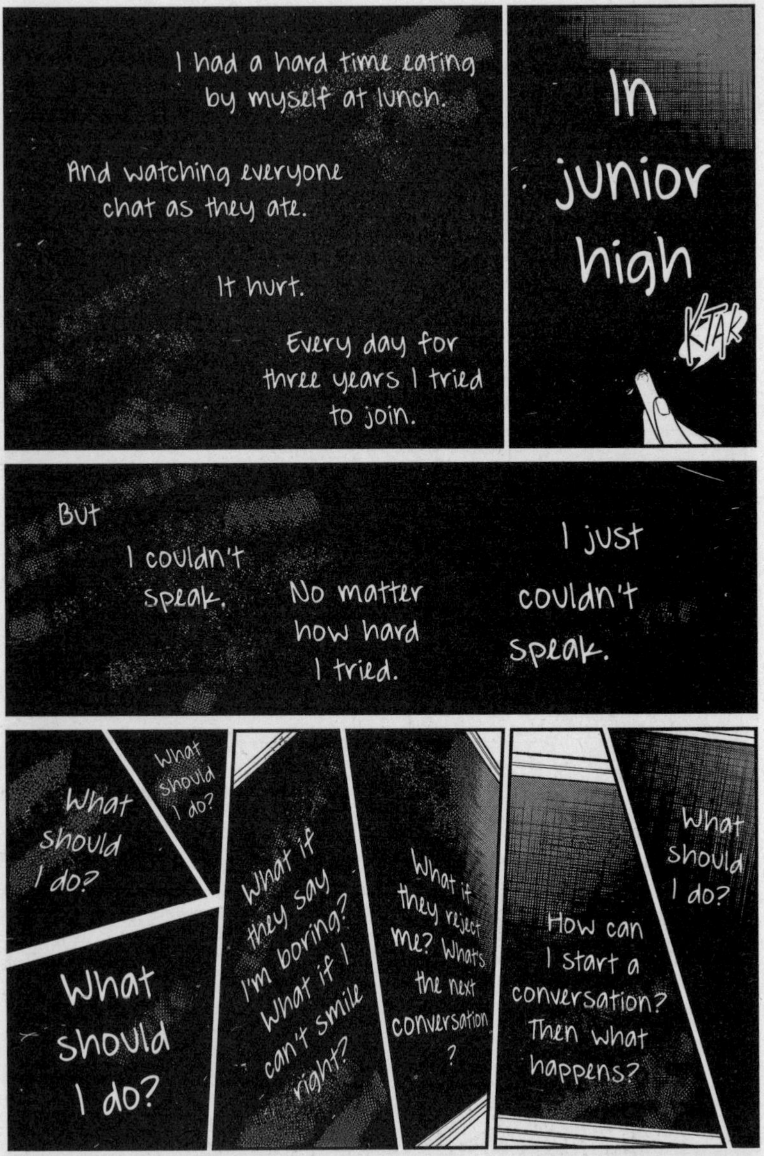
In junior high
KTAK
I had a hard time eating by myself at lunch.
And watching everyone chat as they ate.
It hurt.
Every day for three years I tried to join.
I just couldn't speak.
No matter how hard I tried.
But I couldn't speak.
What should I do?
How can I start a conversation? Then what happens?
What if they reject me? What's the next conversation?
What if they say I'm boring? What if I can't smile right?
What should I do?
What should I do?
What should I do?

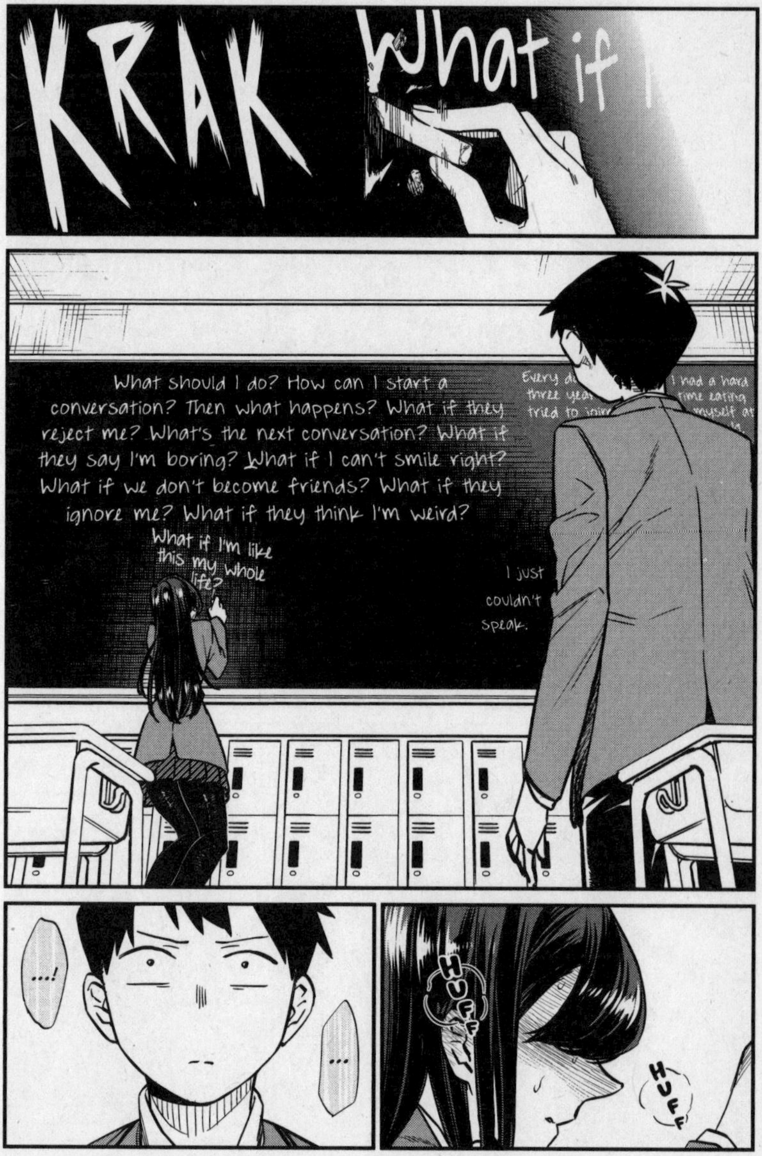
KRAK
What if I
What should I do? How can I start a conversation? Then what happens? What if they reject me? What's the next conversation? What if they say I'm boring? What if I can't smile right? What if we don't become friends? What if they ignore me? What if they think I'm weird?
What if I'm like this my whole life?
I just couldn't speak.
HUFF
HUFF
...!
...

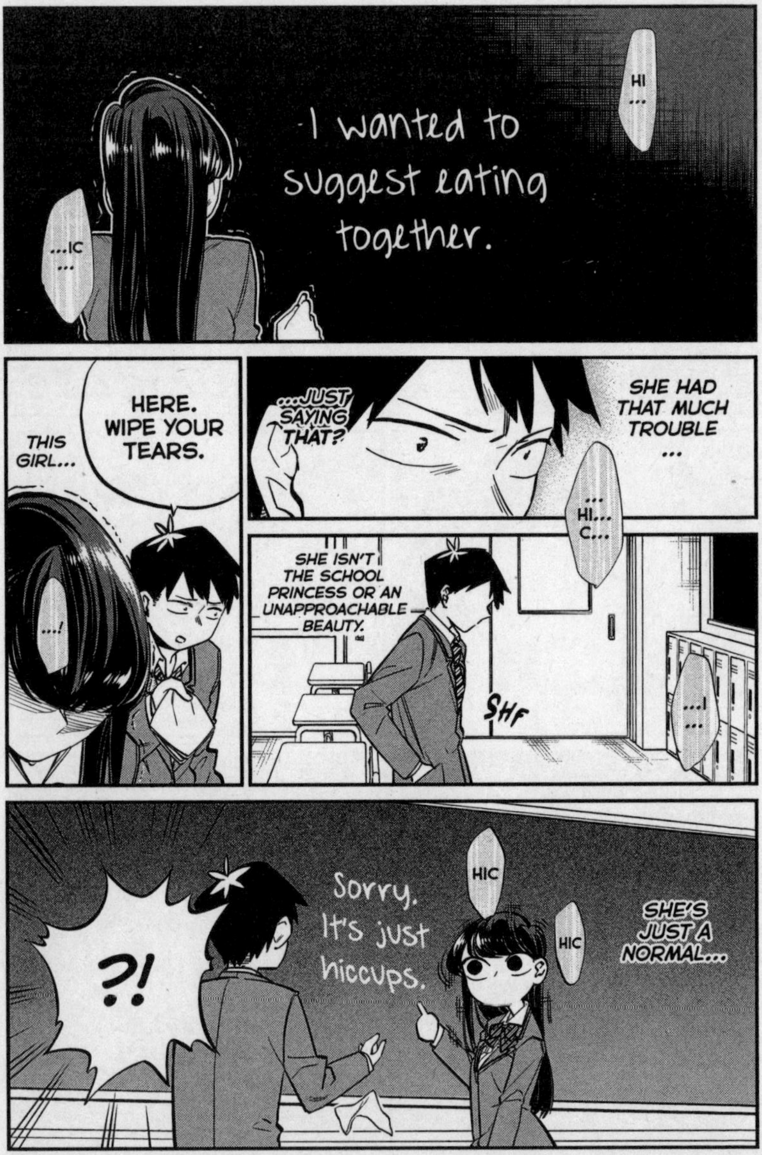
HI ...
I wanted to suggest eating together.
...IC ...
SHE HAD THAT MUCH TROUBLE ...
... HI... C...
...JUST SAYING THAT?
...I ...
SHF
SHE ISN'T THE SCHOOL PRINCESS OR AN UNAPPROACHABLE BEAUTY.
HERE. WIPE YOUR TEARS.
THIS GIRL...
...!
SHE'S JUST A NORMAL...
HIC
HIC
Sorry. It's just hiccups.
?!

Communication 5 — The End

Communication 6: Wanting to Apologize

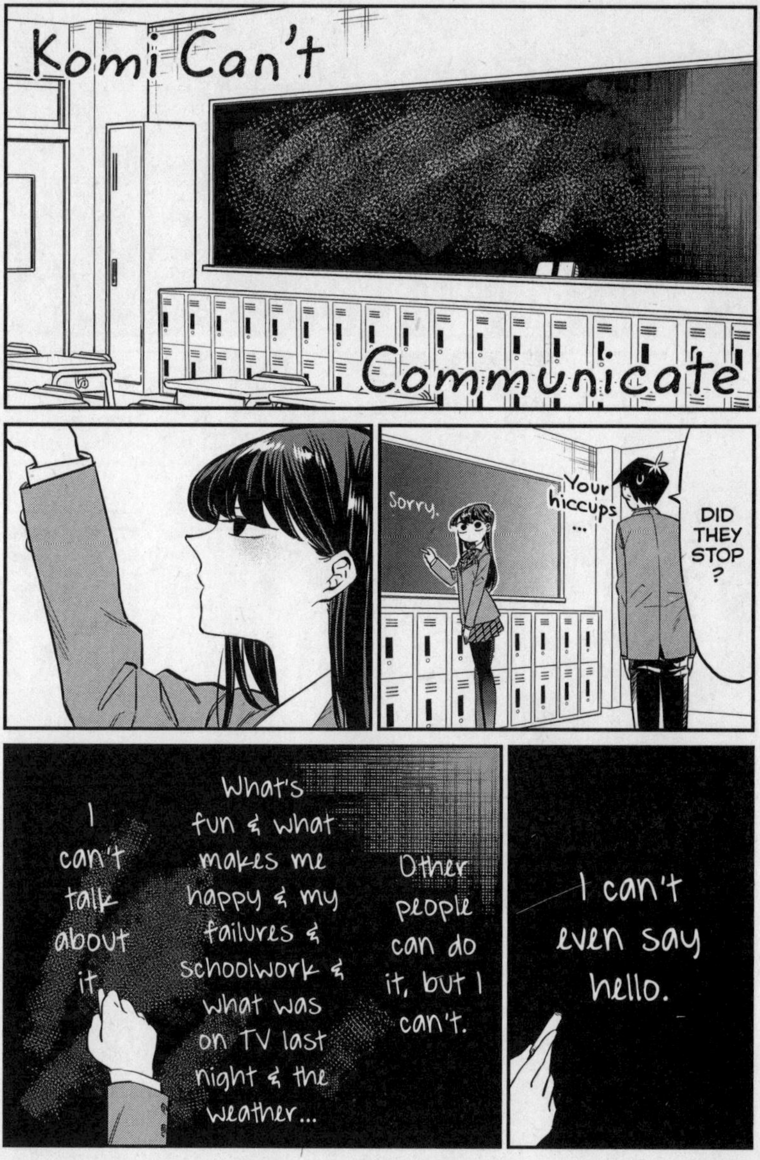

Komi Can't Communicate
Your hiccups...
DID THEY STOP?
Sorry.
I can't even say hello.
Other people can do it, but I can't.
What's fun & what makes me happy & my failures & schoolwork & what was on TV last night & the weather...
I can't talk about it.

↓ Sorta happy

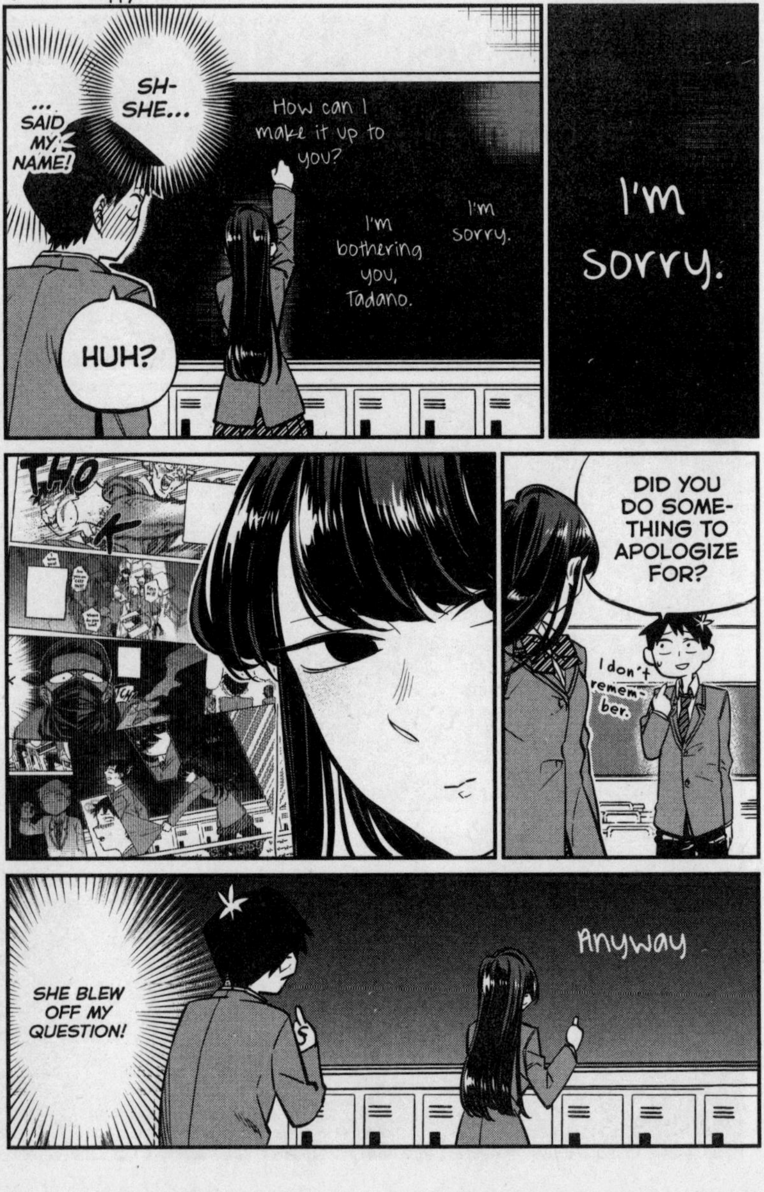
I'm sorry.
How can I make it up to you?
I'm sorry.
I'm bothering you, Tadano.
SH-SHE...
...SAID MY NAME!
HUH?
DID YOU DO SOMETHING TO APOLOGIZE FOR?
I don't remember.
THOK
Anyway
SHE BLEW OFF MY QUESTION!

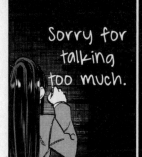 Sorry for talking too much.

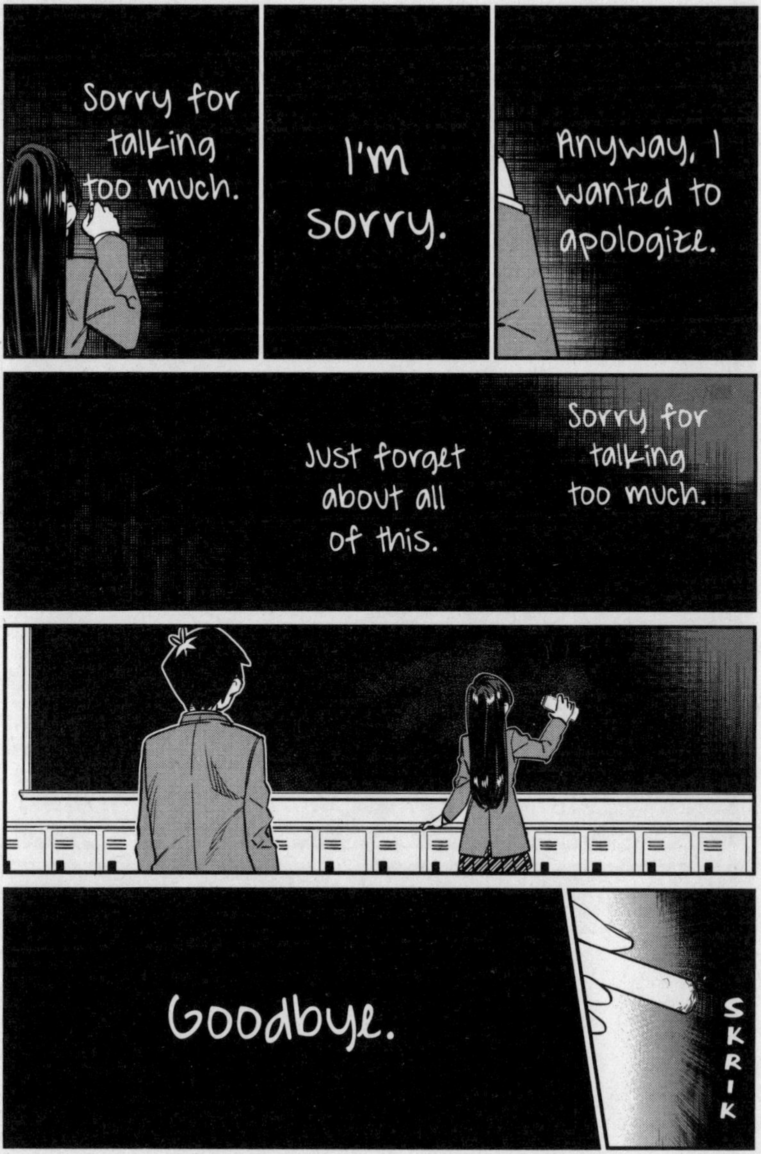

I'm sorry.

 Anyway, I wanted to apologize.

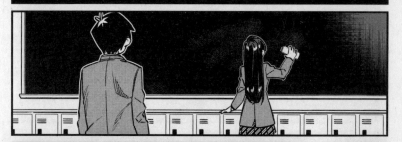 Just forget about all of this.

Sorry for talking too much.

Goodbye.

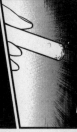 SKRIK

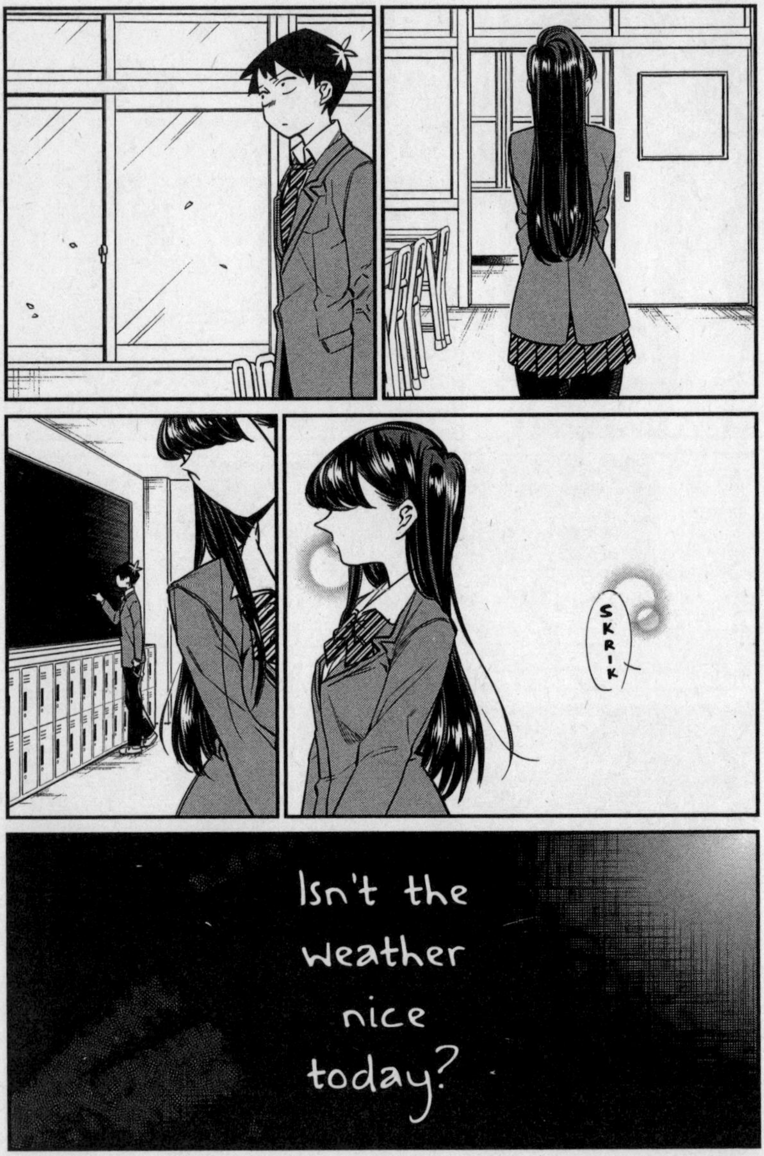
SKRIK
Isn't the weather nice today?

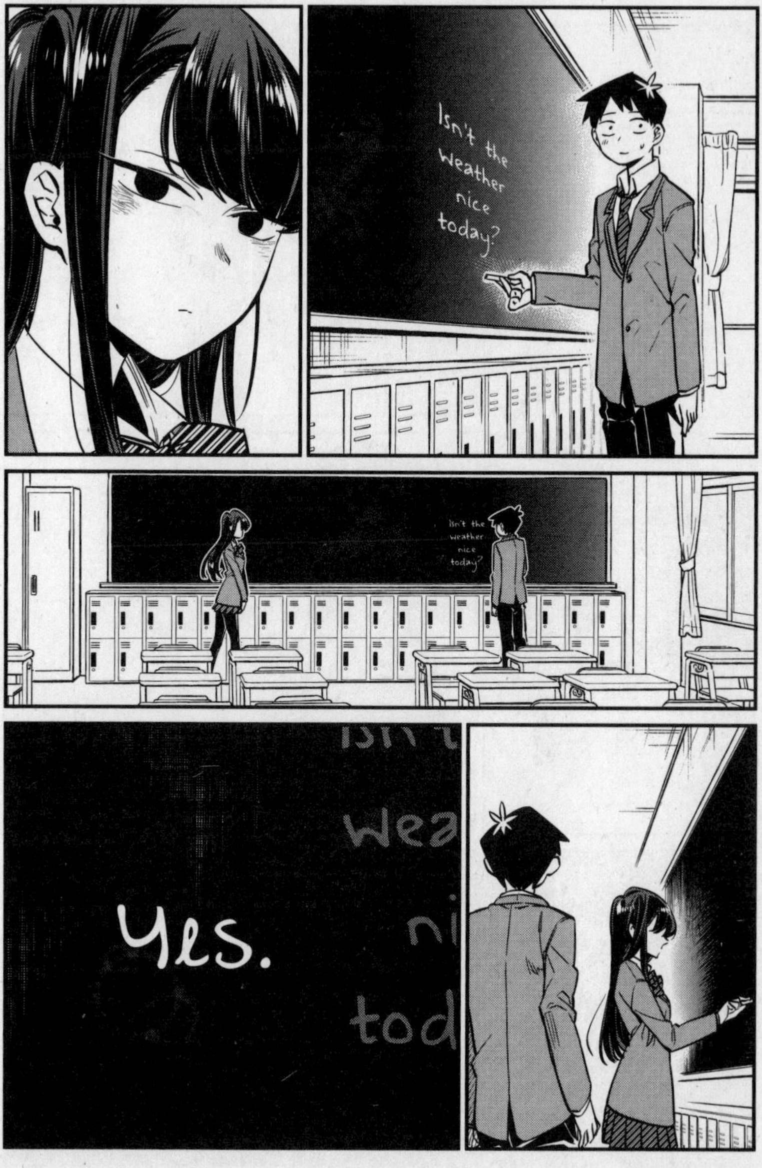
Isn't the weather nice today?
Isn't the weather nice today?
Yes.

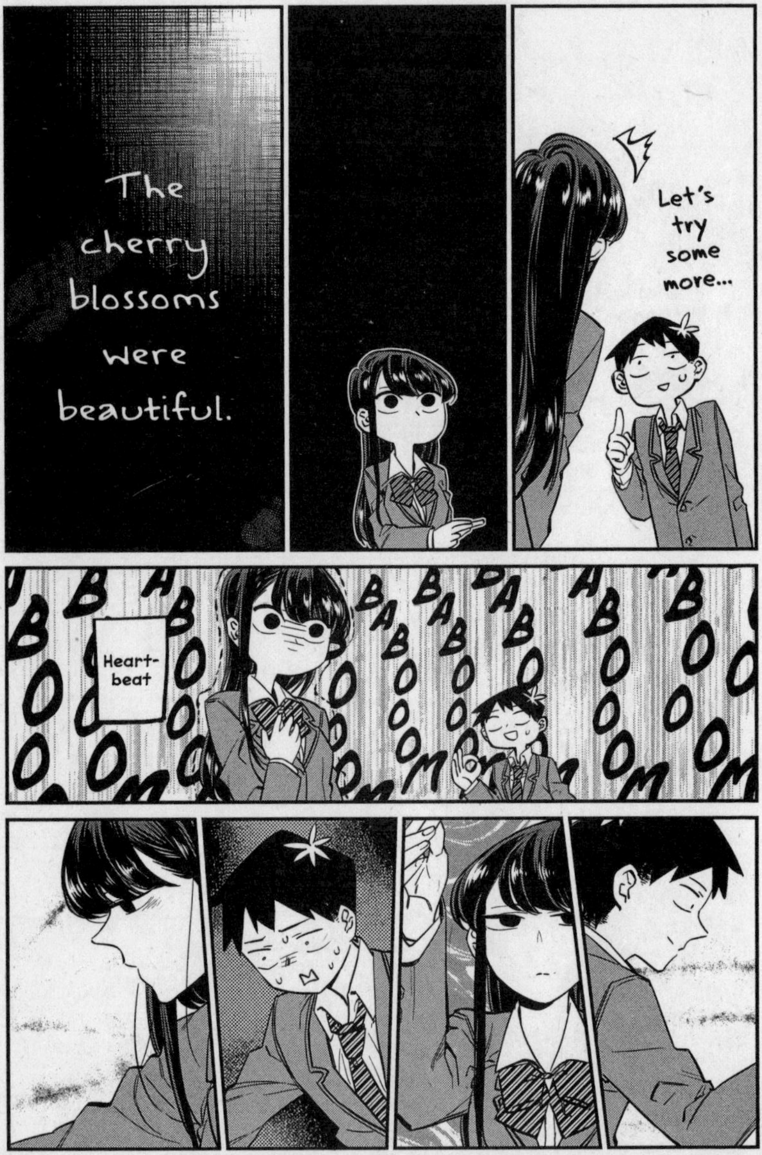
The cherry blossoms were beautiful.
Let's try some more...
Heart-beat
BABOOOOM

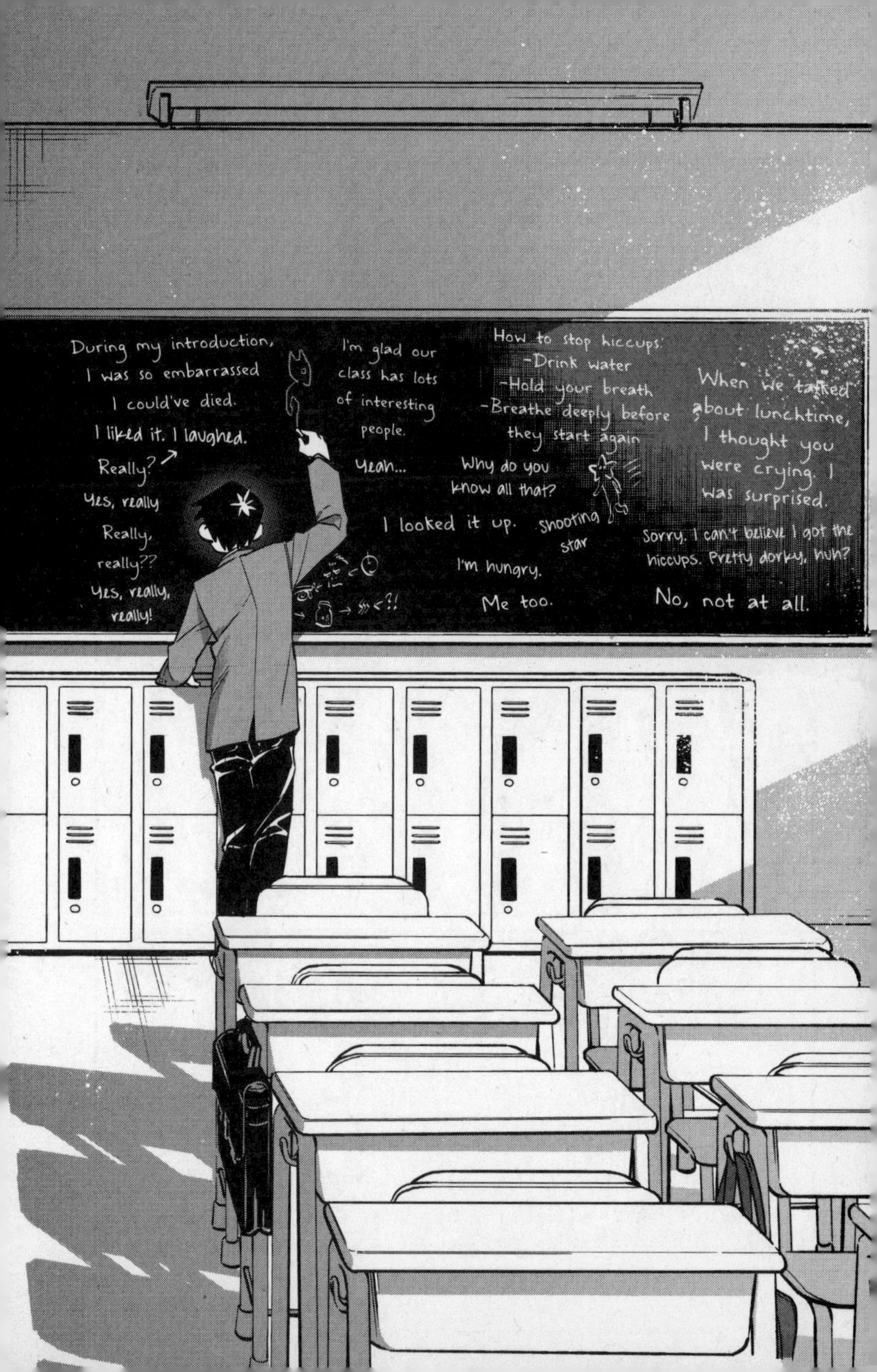
During my introduction, I was so embarrassed I could've died.
I liked it. I laughed.
Really?
Yes, really
Really, really??
Yes, really, really!
I'm glad our class has lots of interesting people.
Yeah...
How to stop hiccups:
-Drink water
-Hold your breath
-Breathe deeply before they start again
Why do you know all that?
I looked it up.
Shooting star
I'm hungry.
Me too.
When we talked about lunchtime, I thought you were crying. I was surprised.
Sorry. I can't believe I got the hiccups. Pretty dorky, huh?
No, not at all.

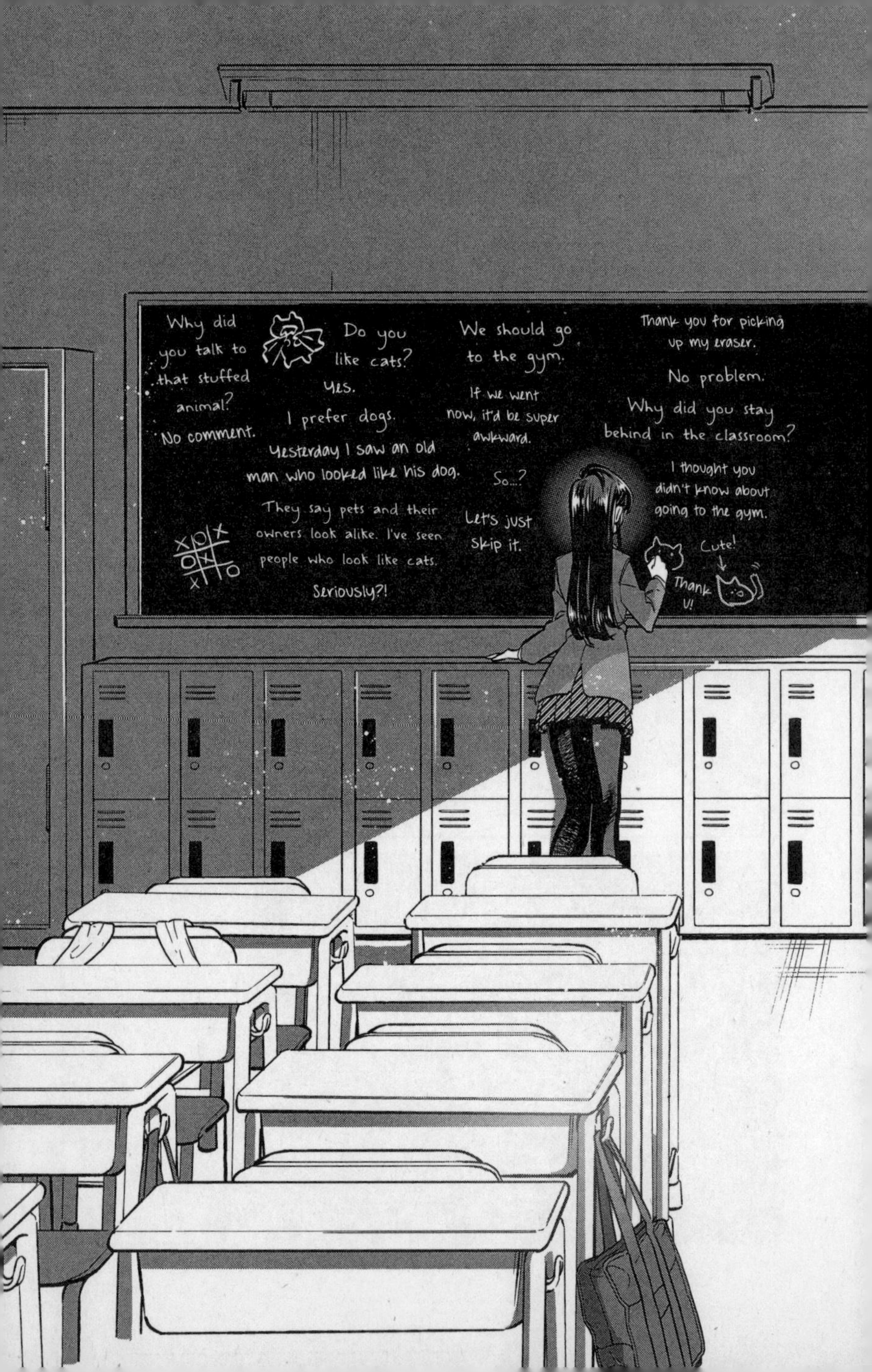
Thank you for picking up my eraser.
No problem.
Why did you stay behind in the classroom?
I thought you didn't know about going to the gym.
Cute!
Thank U!
We should go to the gym.
If we went now, it'd be super awkward.
So...?
Let's just skip it.
Do you like cats?
Yes.
I prefer dogs.
Yesterday I saw an old man who looked like his dog.
They say pets and their owners look alike. I've seen people who look like cats.
Seriously?!
Why did you talk to that stuffed animal?
No comment.

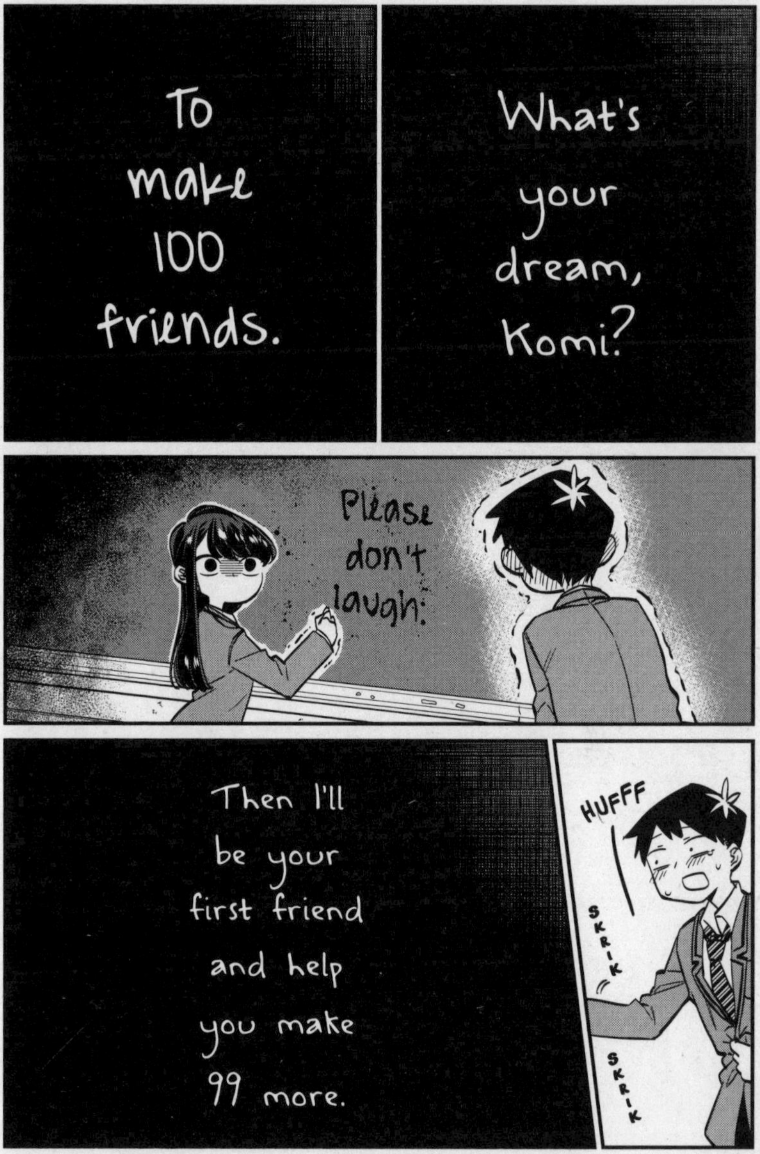
What's your dream, Komi?
To make 100 friends.
Please don't laugh.
HUFFF
SKRIK
SKRIK
Then I'll be your first friend and help you make 99 more.

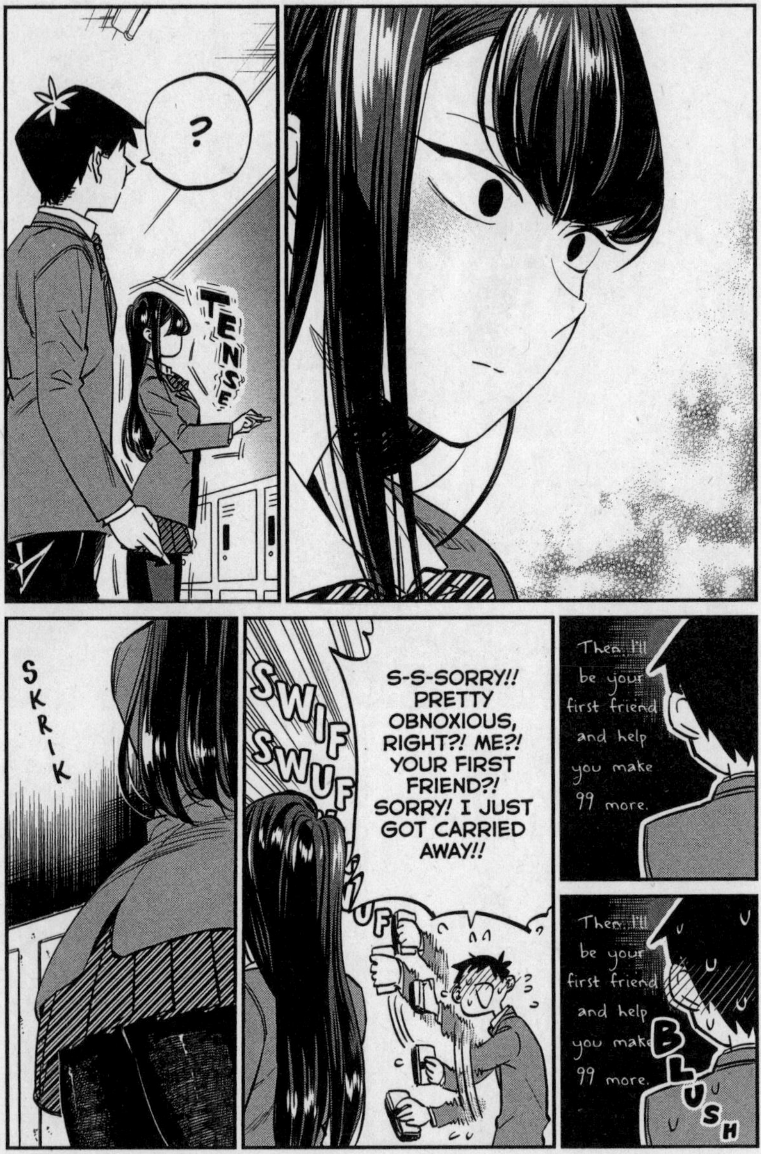
?
TENSE
Then, I'll be your first friend and help you make 99 more.
Then, I'll be your first friend and help you make 99 more.
BLUSH
SWIF
SWUF
S-S-SORRY!! PRETTY OBNOXIOUS, RIGHT?! ME?! YOUR FIRST FRIEND?! SORRY! I JUST GOT CARRIED AWAY!!
SKRIK

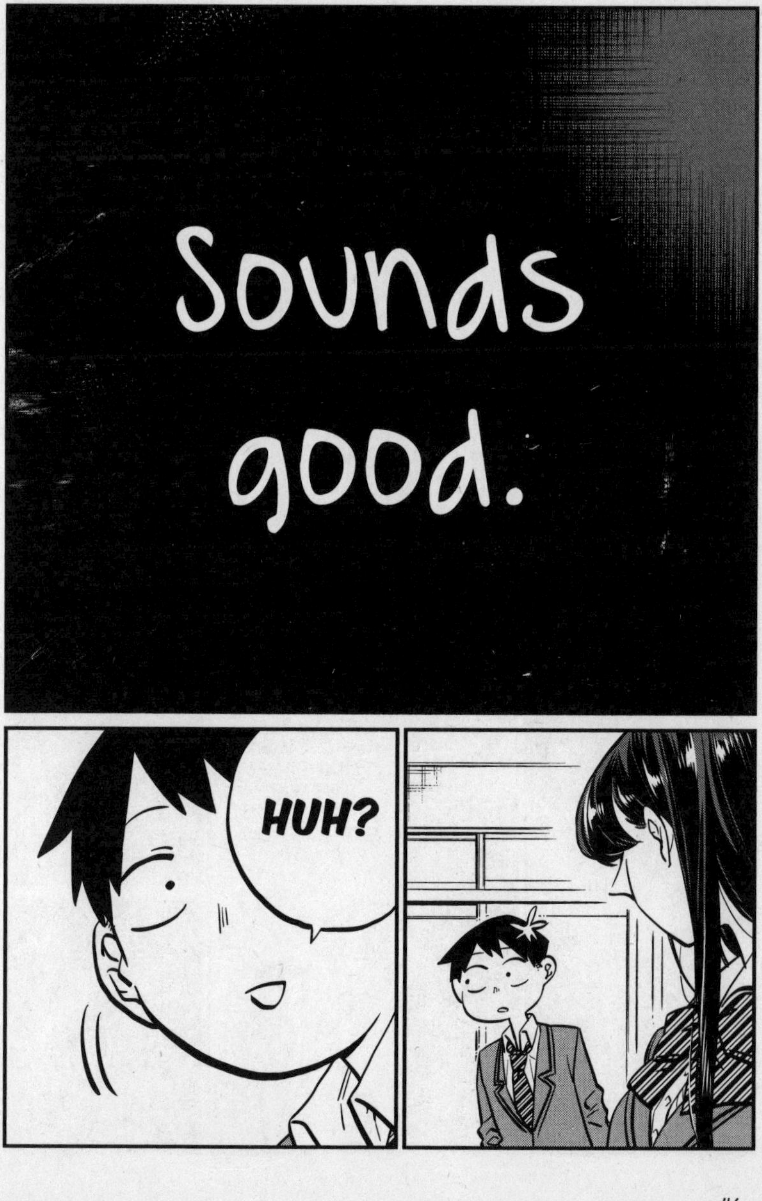
Sounds good.
HUH?

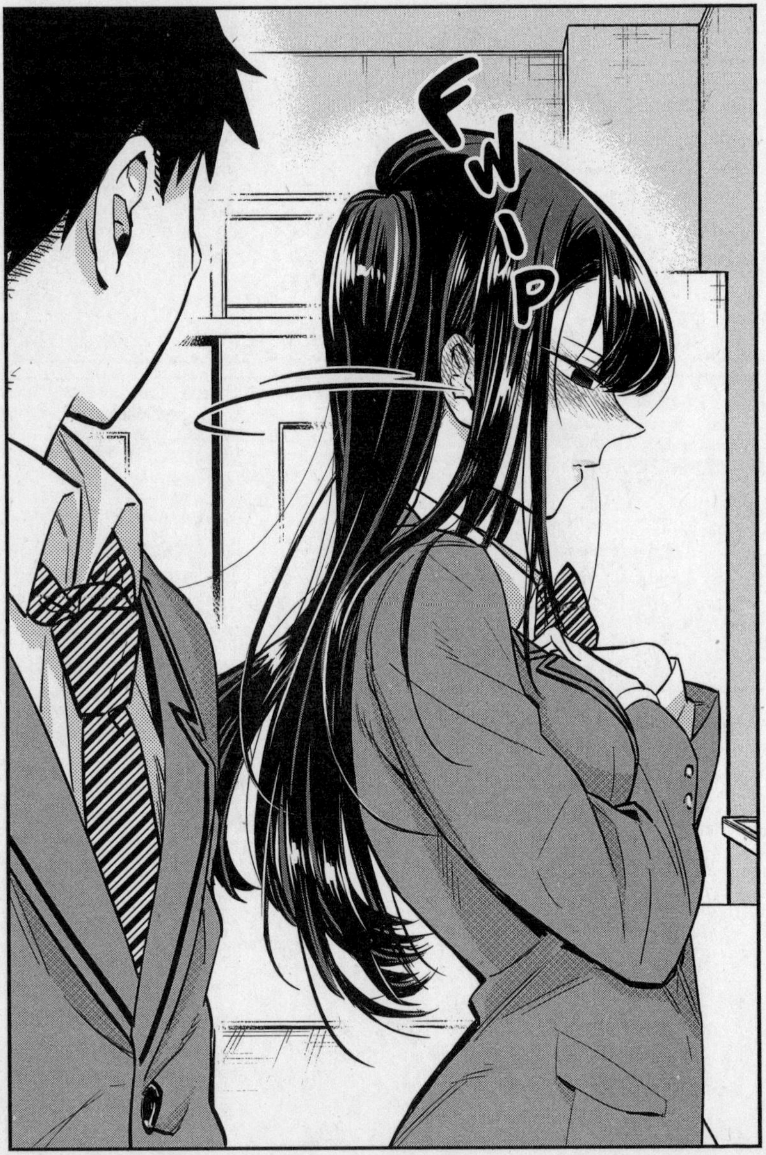
FWIP

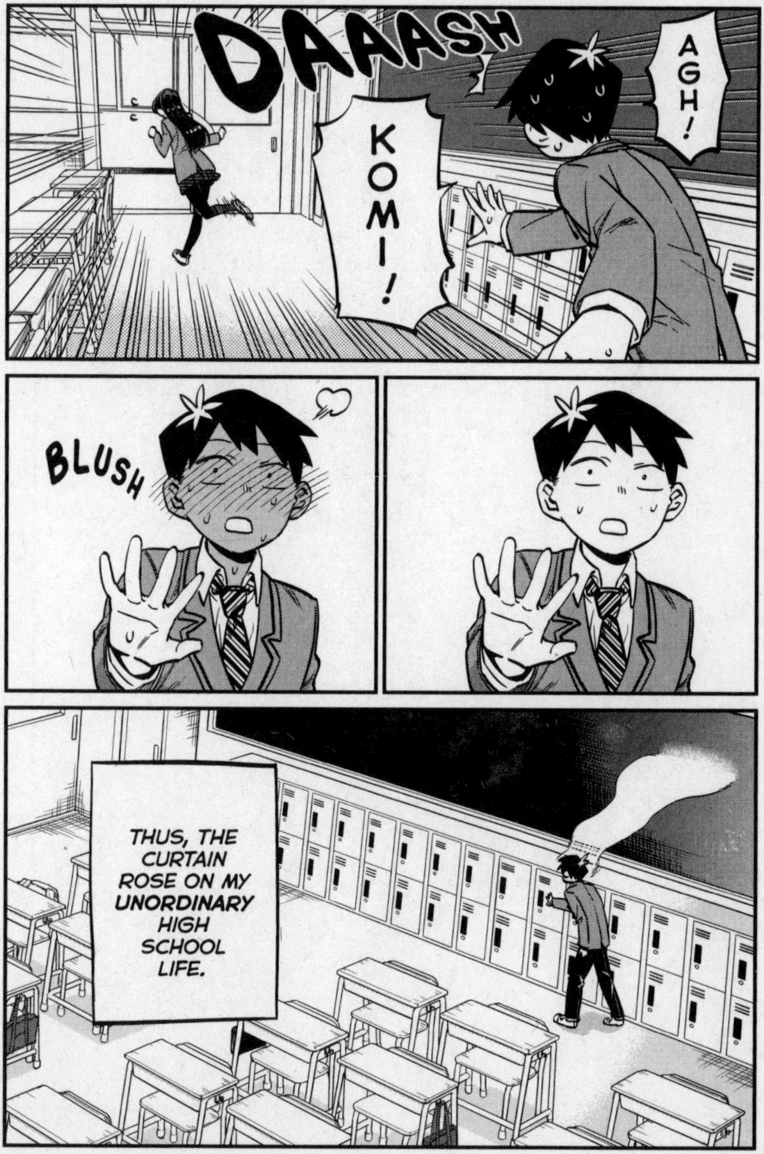
AGH!
KOMI!
DAAASH
BLUSH
THUS, THE CURTAIN ROSE ON MY UNORDINARY HIGH SCHOOL LIFE.

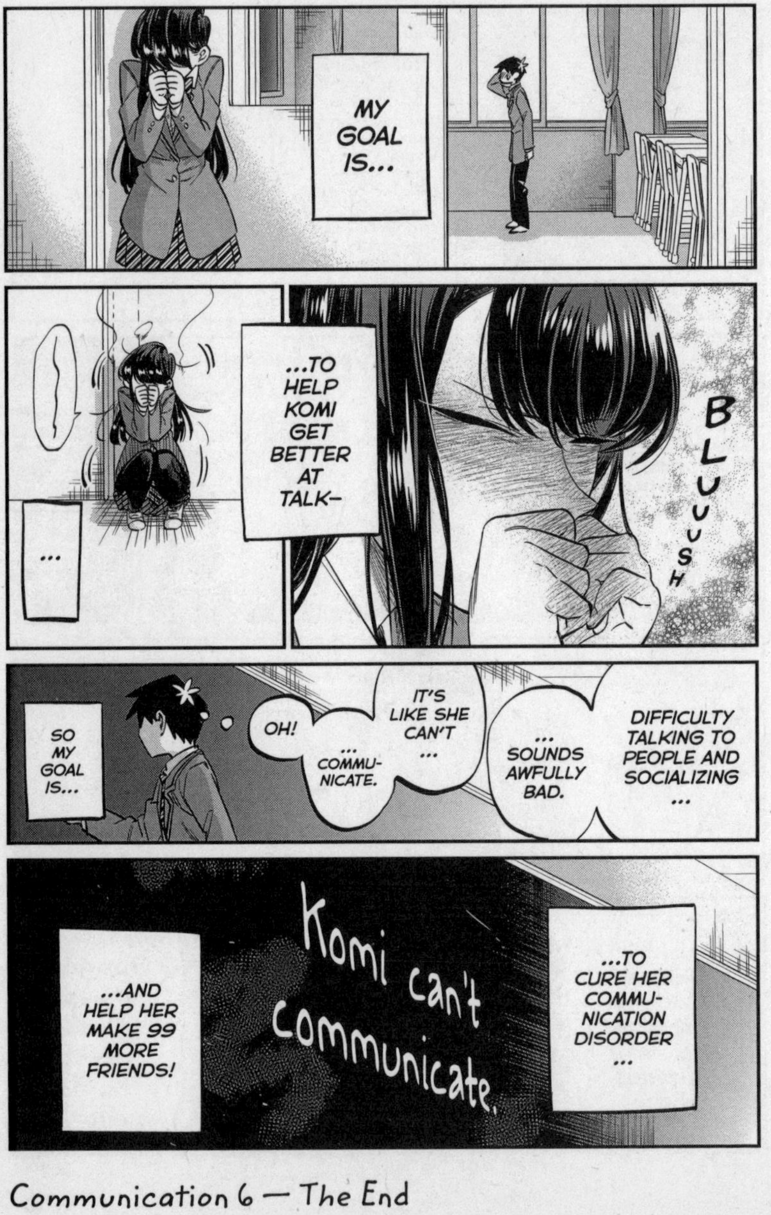
MY GOAL IS...
...TO HELP KOMI GET BETTER AT TALK—
BLUUUUSH
...
DIFFICULTY TALKING TO PEOPLE AND SOCIALIZING...
...SOUNDS AWFULLY BAD.
IT'S LIKE SHE CAN'T...
...COMMUNICATE.
OH!
SO MY GOAL IS...
...TO CURE HER COMMUNICATION DISORDER...
Komi can't communicate.
...AND HELP HER MAKE 99 MORE FRIENDS!

Communication 6 — The End

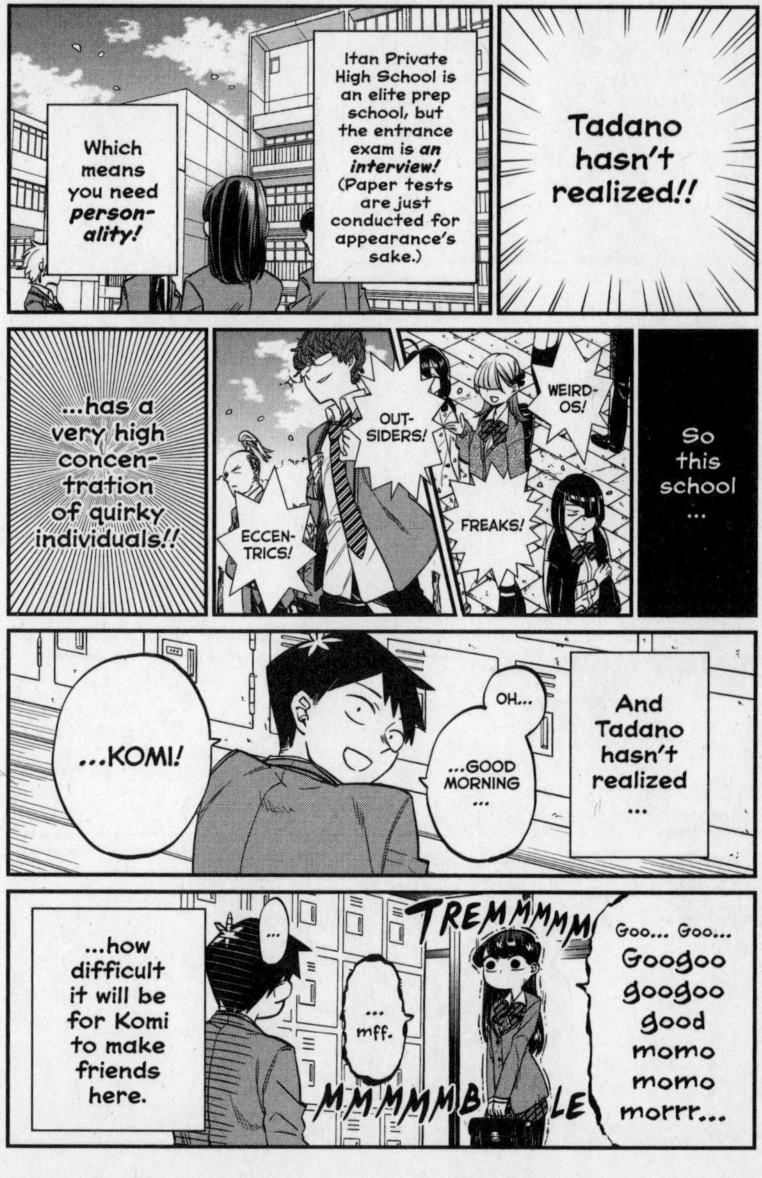
Tadano hasn't realized!!
Itan Private High School is an elite prep school, but the entrance exam is *an interview!* (Paper tests are just conducted for appearance's sake.)
Which means you need *personality!*
So this school ...
WEIRD-OS!
OUT-SIDERS!
FREAKS!
ECCEN-TRICS!
...has a very high concentration of quirky individuals!!
And Tadano hasn't realized ...
OH...
...GOOD MORNING ...
...KOMI!
Goo... Goo... Googoo googoo good momo momo morrr...
TREMMMMM
MMMMMMBLE
...
... mff.
...how difficult it will be for Komi to make friends here.

Komi Can't Communicate

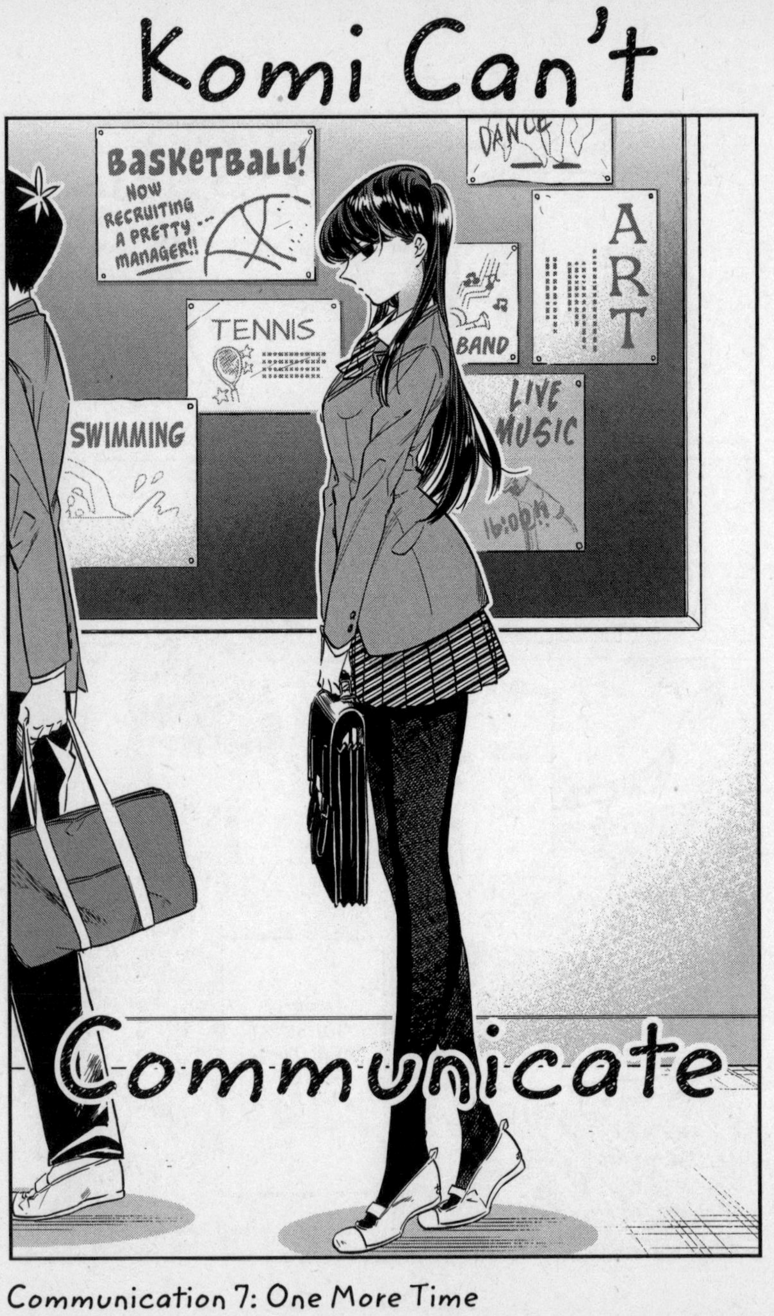
DANCE
BASKETBALL! NOW RECRUITING A PRETTY MANAGER!!
ART
TENNIS
BAND
LIVE MUSIC
SWIMMING

Communication 7: One More Time

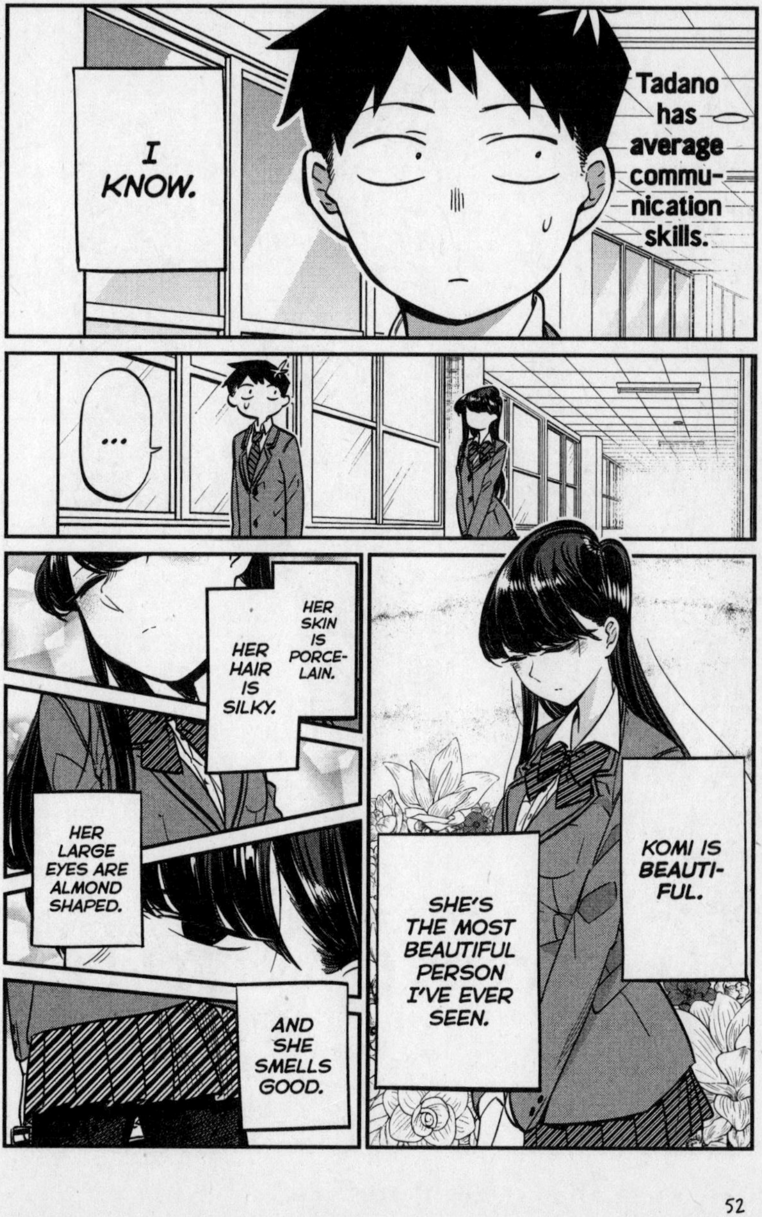
Tadano has average communication skills.
I KNOW.
...
KOMI IS BEAUTIFUL.
SHE'S THE MOST BEAUTIFUL PERSON I'VE EVER SEEN.
HER SKIN IS PORCELAIN.
HER HAIR IS SILKY.
HER LARGE EYES ARE ALMOND SHAPED.
AND SHE SMELLS GOOD.

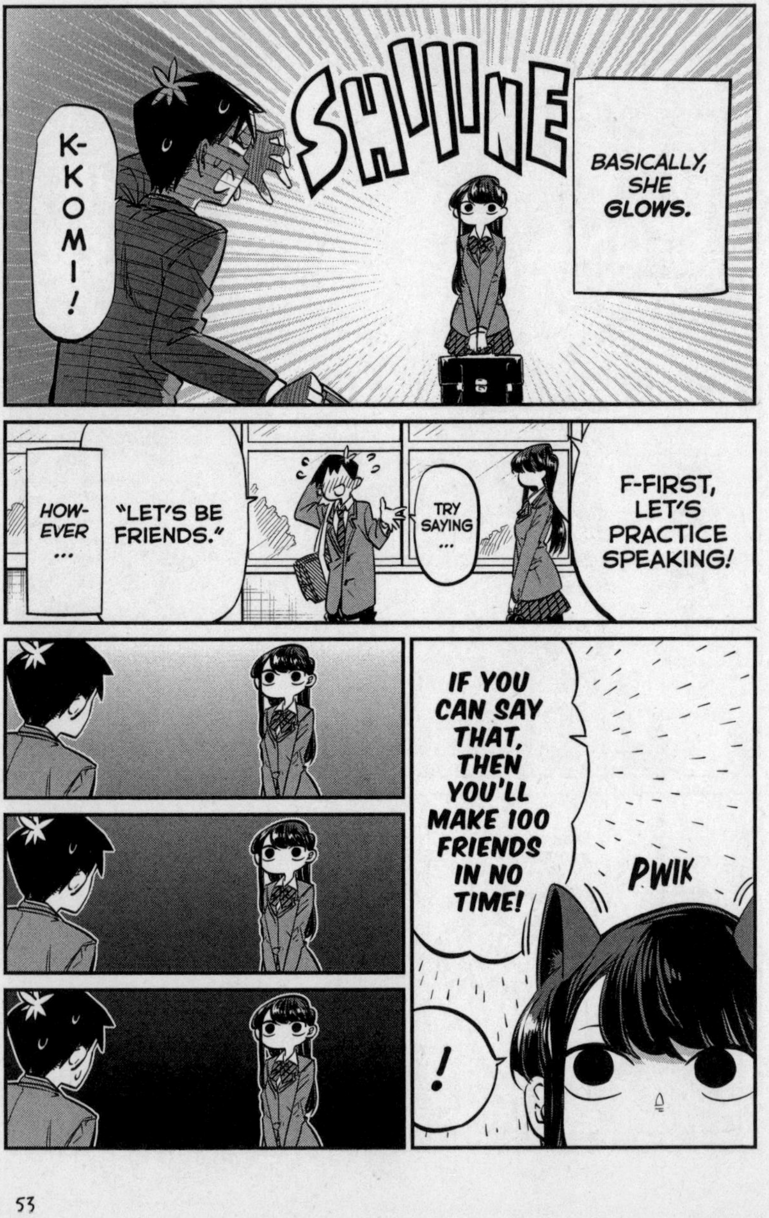
BASICALLY, SHE GLOWS.
SHIIINE
K-KOMI!
F-FIRST, LET'S PRACTICE SPEAKING!
TRY SAYING ...
"LET'S BE FRIENDS."
HOW-EVER ...
IF YOU CAN SAY THAT, THEN YOU'LL MAKE 100 FRIENDS IN NO TIME!
PWIK
!

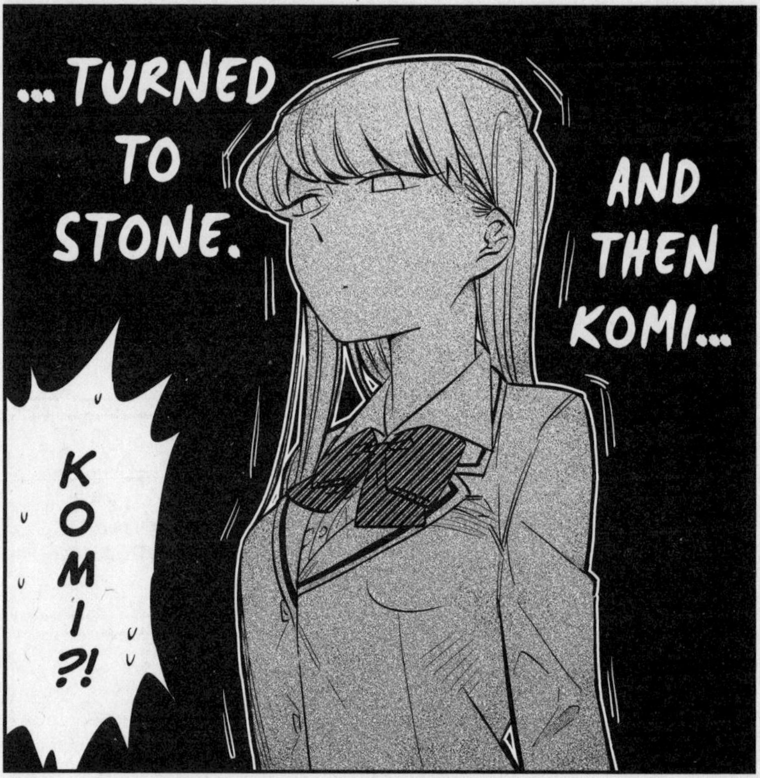
AND THEN KOMI...
...TURNED TO STONE.
KOMI?!

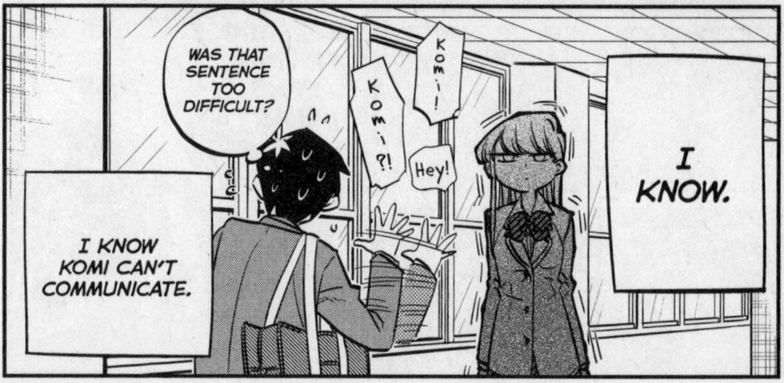
I KNOW.
Komi!
Komi?!
Hey!
WAS THAT SENTENCE TOO DIFFICULT?
I KNOW KOMI CAN'T COMMUNICATE.

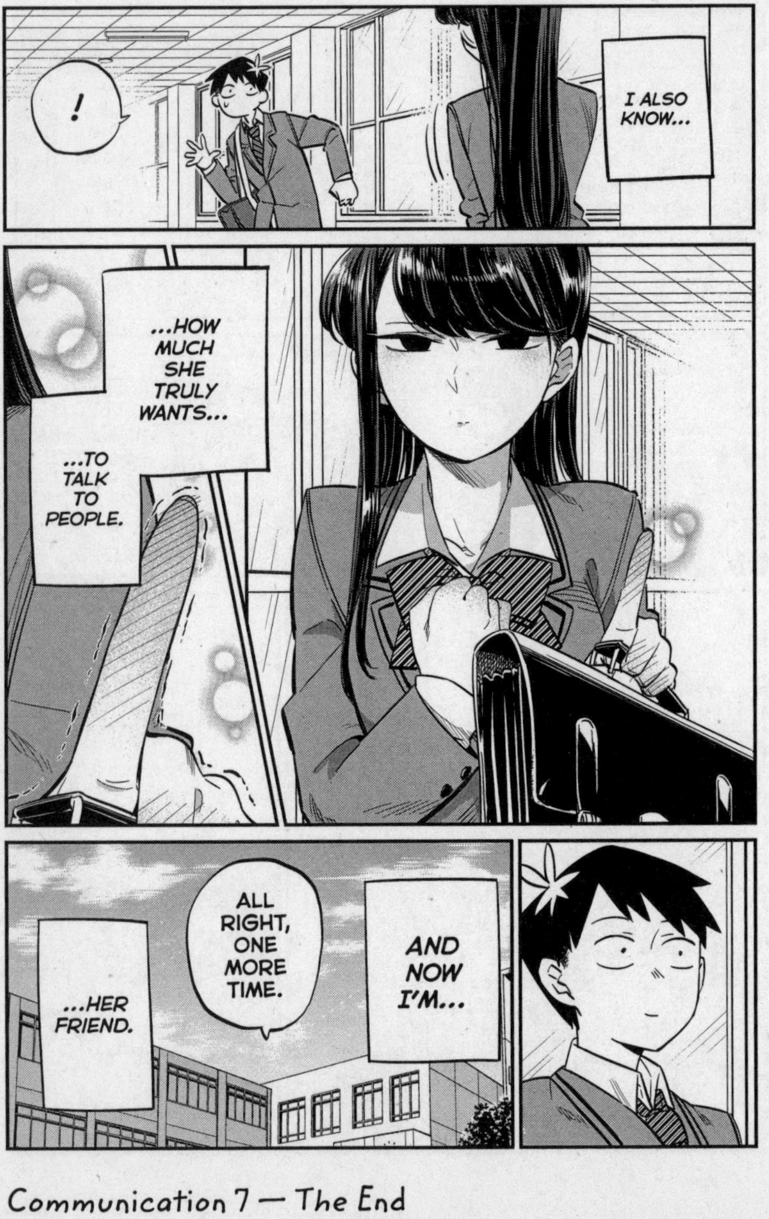
I ALSO KNOW...
!
...HOW MUCH SHE TRULY WANTS...
...TO TALK TO PEOPLE.
AND NOW I'M...
ALL RIGHT, ONE MORE TIME.
...HER FRIEND.

Communication 7 — The End

Communication 8: Scary

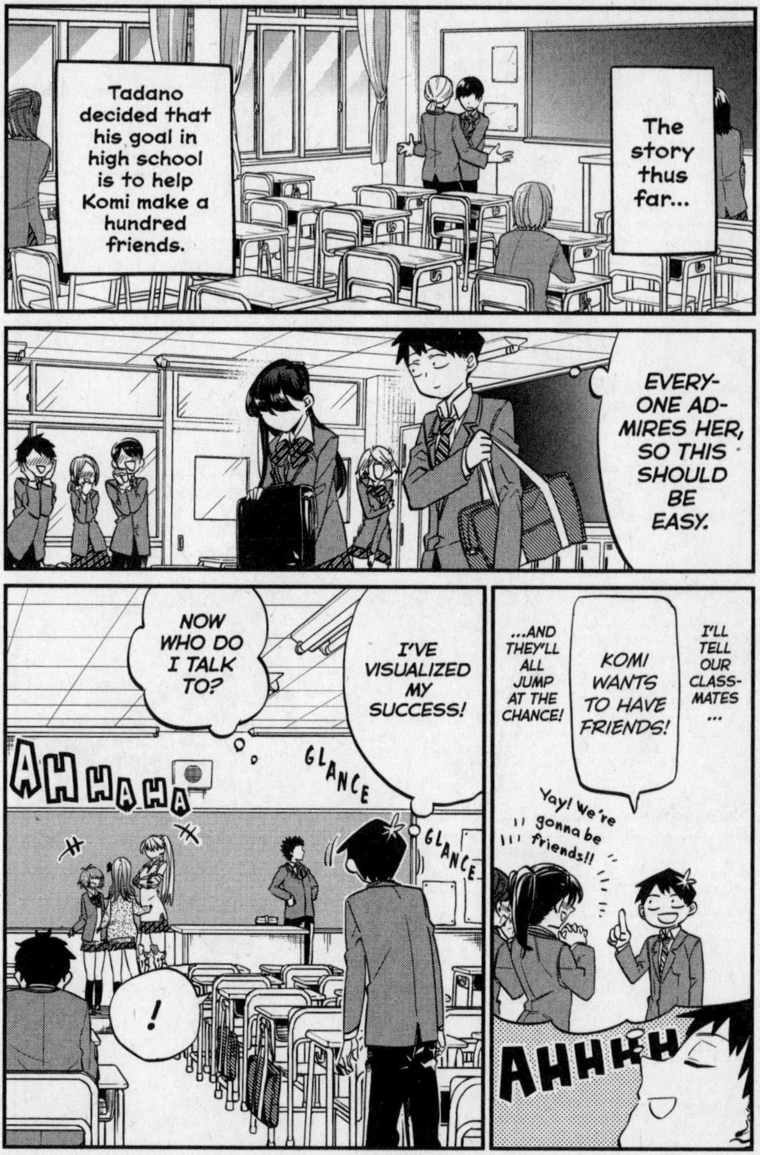
The story thus far...
Tadano decided that his goal in high school is to help Komi make a hundred friends.
EVERYONE ADMIRES HER, SO THIS SHOULD BE EASY.
I'LL TELL OUR CLASSMATES...
KOMI WANTS TO HAVE FRIENDS!
...AND THEY'LL ALL JUMP AT THE CHANCE!
Yay! We're gonna be friends!!
AHHHH
I'VE VISUALIZED MY SUCCESS!
NOW WHO DO I TALK TO?
GLANCE
GLANCE
AHHAHAHA
!

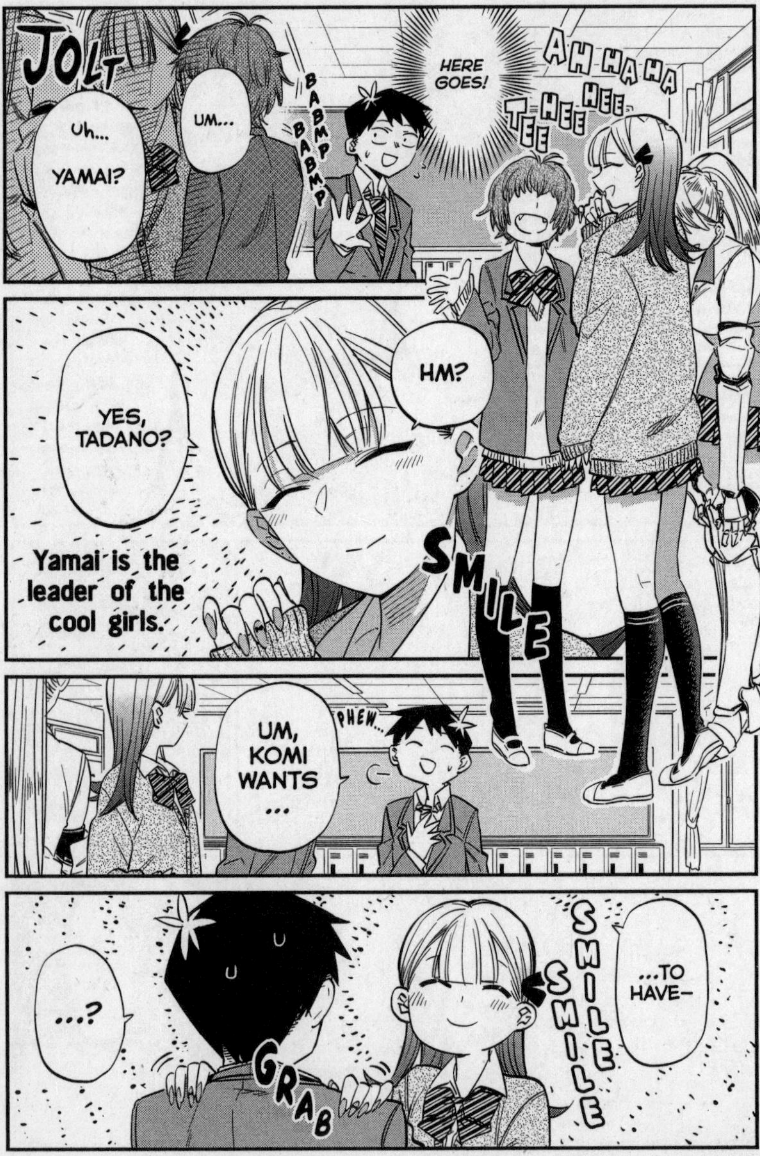
AH HA HA HA
TEE HEE HEE
HERE GOES!
BABMP BABMP
UM...
JOLT
Uh... YAMAI?
HM?
SMILE
YES, TADANO?
Yamai is the leader of the cool girls.
PHEW...
UM, KOMI WANTS ...
...TO HAVE—
SMILE SMILE
GRAB
...?

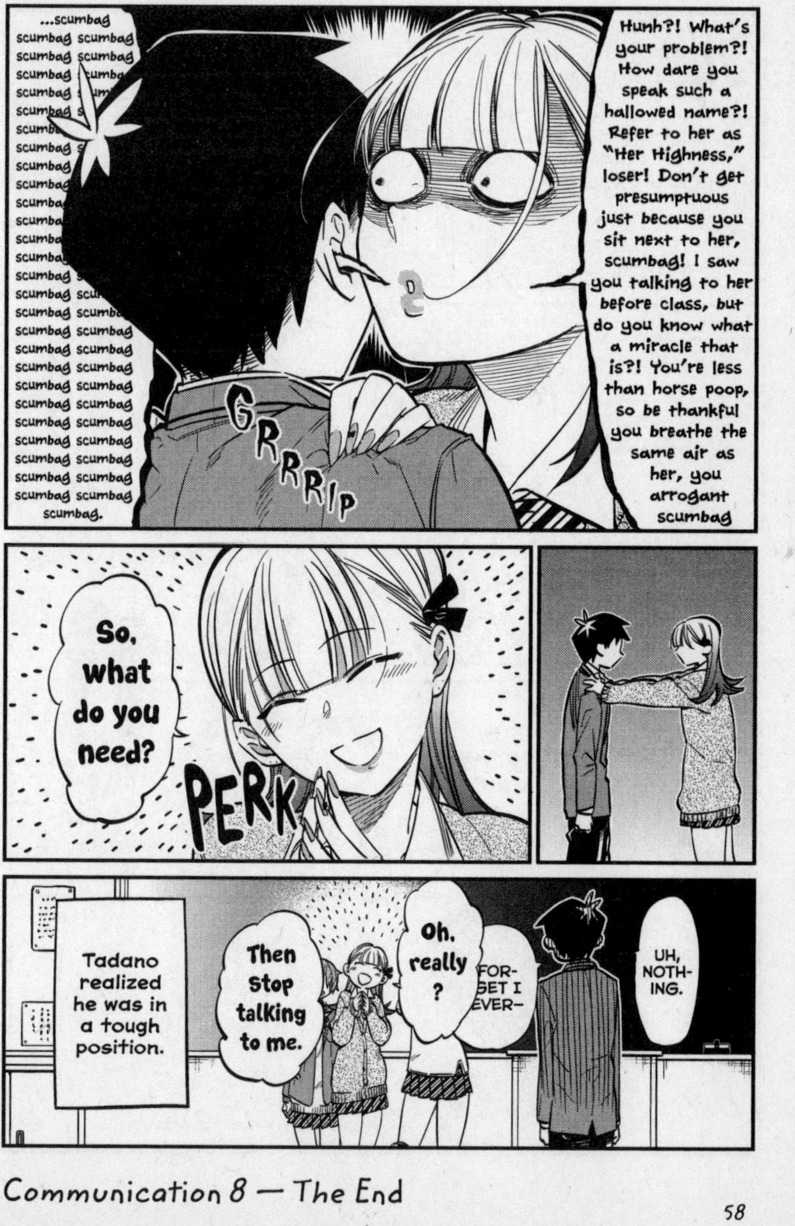
Hunh?! What's your problem?! How dare you speak such a hallowed name?! Refer to her as "Her Highness," loser! Don't get presumptuous just because you sit next to her, scumbag! I saw you talking to her before class, but do you know what a miracle that is?! You're less than horse poop, so be thankful you breathe the same air as her, you arrogant scumbag
GRRRIP
...scumbag scumbag.
So, what do you need?
PERK
UH, NOTHING.
FOR-GET I EVER—
Oh, really?
Then stop talking to me.
Tadano realized he was in a tough position.

Communication 8 — The End

Communication 9: Old Friends

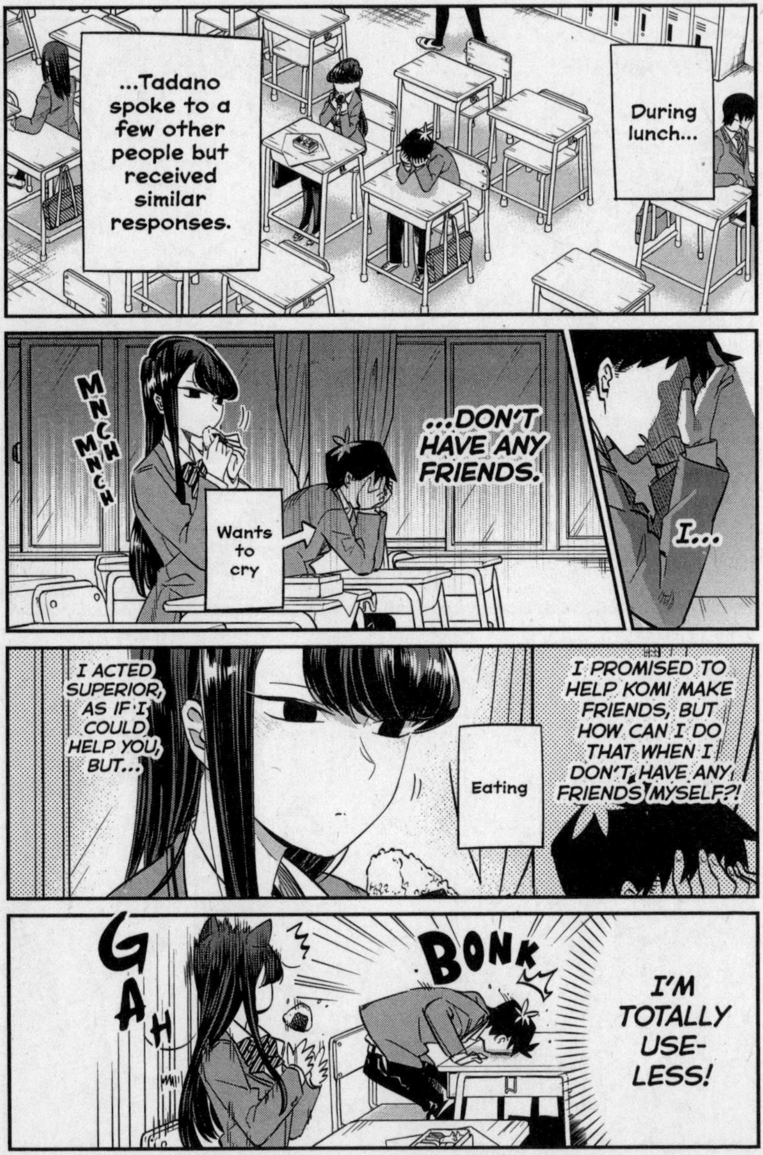
During lunch...
...Tadano spoke to a few other people but received similar responses.
I...
...DON'T HAVE ANY FRIENDS.
Wants to cry
MNCH MNCH MNCH
I PROMISED TO HELP KOMI MAKE FRIENDS, BUT HOW CAN I DO THAT WHEN I DON'T HAVE ANY FRIENDS MYSELF?!
Eating
I ACTED SUPERIOR, AS IF I COULD HELP YOU, BUT...
I'M TOTALLY USE-LESS!
BONK
GAH

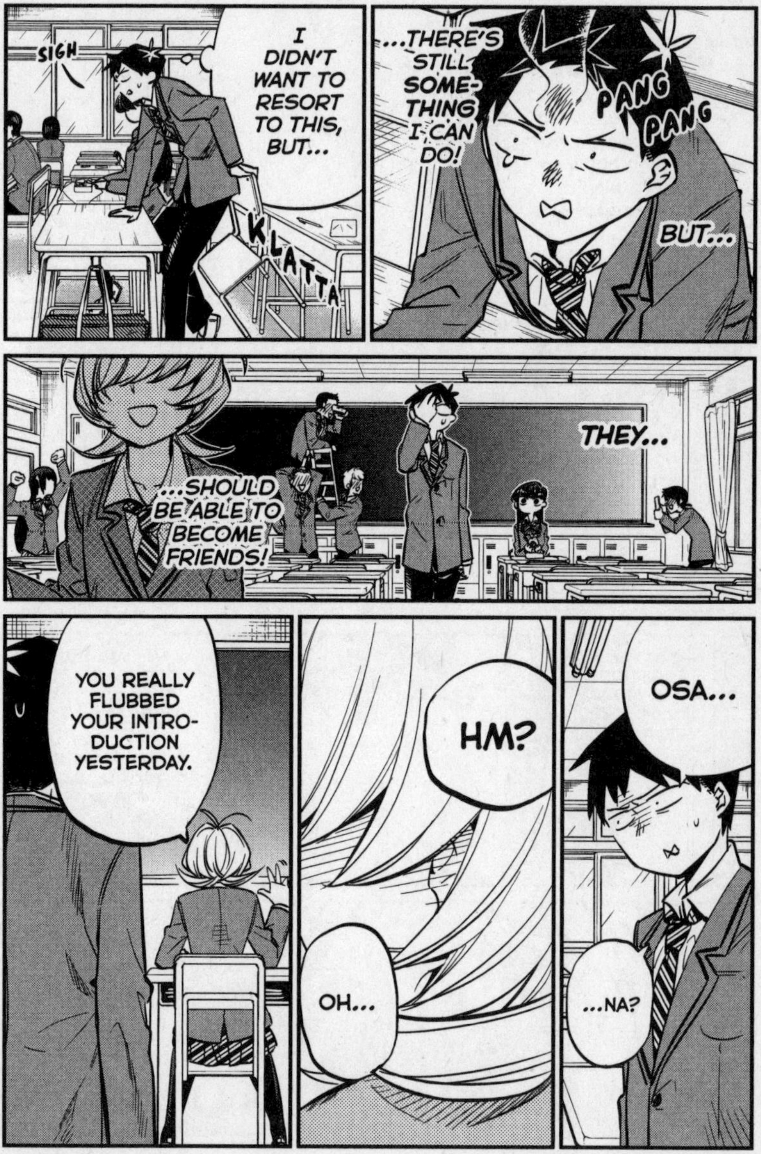
PANG PANG
BUT...
...THERE'S STILL SOME-THING I CAN DO!
SIGH
I DIDN'T WANT TO RESORT TO THIS, BUT...
KLATTA
THEY...
...SHOULD BE ABLE TO BECOME FRIENDS!
OSA...
...NA?
HM?
OH...
YOU REALLY FLUBBED YOUR INTRO-DUCTION YESTERDAY.

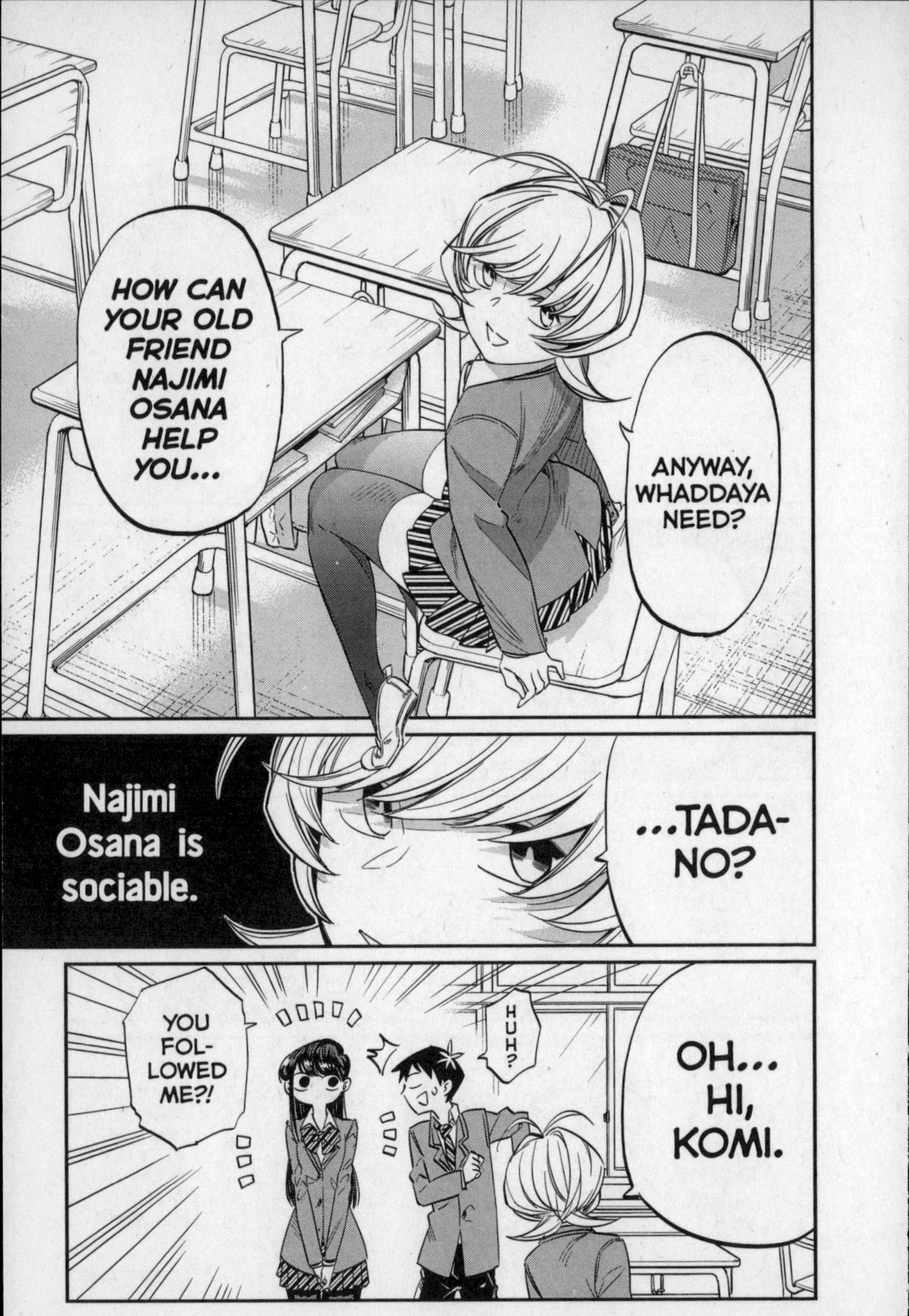
ANYWAY, WHADDAYA NEED?
HOW CAN YOUR OLD FRIEND NAJIMI OSANA HELP YOU...
...TADA-NO?
Najimi Osana is sociable.
OH... HI, KOMI.
HUH?
YOU FOL-LOWED ME?!

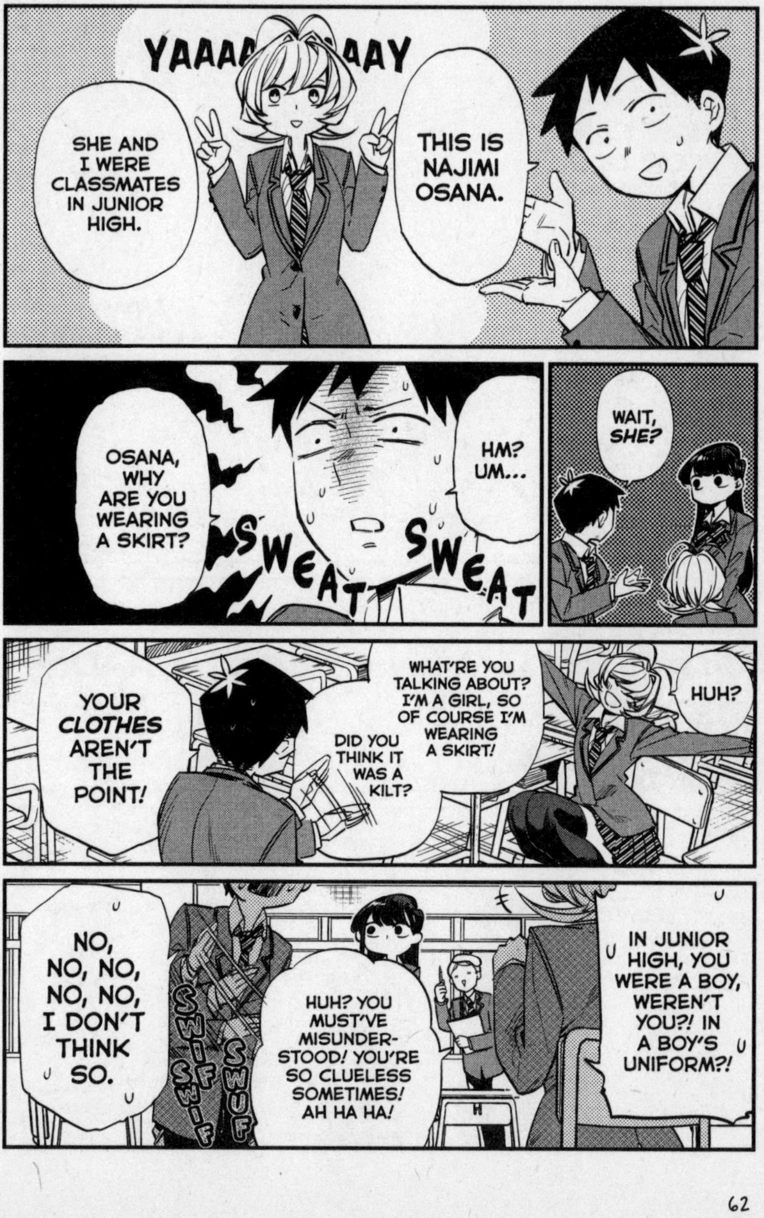
THIS IS NAJIMI OSANA.
SHE AND I WERE CLASSMATES IN JUNIOR HIGH.
WAIT, *SHE?*
HM? UM...
SWEAT SWEAT
OSANA, WHY ARE YOU WEARING A SKIRT?
HUH?
WHAT'RE YOU TALKING ABOUT? I'M A GIRL, SO OF COURSE I'M WEARING A SKIRT!
DID YOU THINK IT WAS A KILT?
YOUR *CLOTHES* AREN'T THE POINT!
IN JUNIOR HIGH, YOU WERE A BOY, WEREN'T YOU?! IN A BOY'S UNIFORM?!
HUH? YOU MUST'VE MISUNDER-STOOD! YOU'RE SO CLUELESS SOMETIMES! AH HA HA!
SWUF
SWIF SWIF
NO, NO, NO, NO, NO, NO, NO, I DON'T THINK SO.

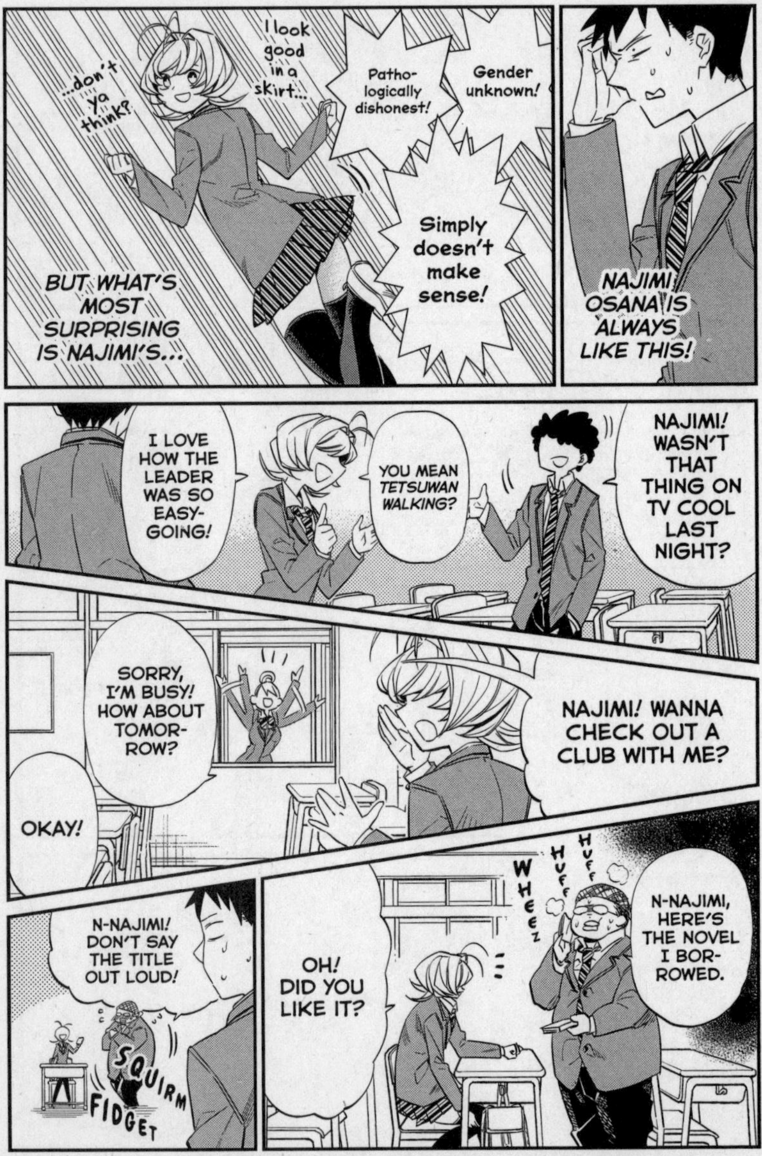
NAJIMI OSANA IS ALWAYS LIKE THIS!
BUT WHAT'S MOST SURPRISING IS NAJIMI'S...
Gender unknown!
Patho-logically dishonest!
I look good in a skirt...
...don't ya think?
Simply doesn't make sense!
NAJIMI! WASN'T THAT THING ON TV COOL LAST NIGHT?
YOU MEAN TETSUWAN WALKING?
I LOVE HOW THE LEADER WAS SO EASY-GOING!
NAJIMI! WANNA CHECK OUT A CLUB WITH ME?
SORRY, I'M BUSY! HOW ABOUT TOMOR-ROW?
OKAY!
HUFF
HUFF
WHEEZ
N-NAJIMI, HERE'S THE NOVEL I BOR-ROWED.
OH! DID YOU LIKE IT?
N-NAJIMI! DON'T SAY THE TITLE OUT LOUD!
SQUIRM
FIDGET

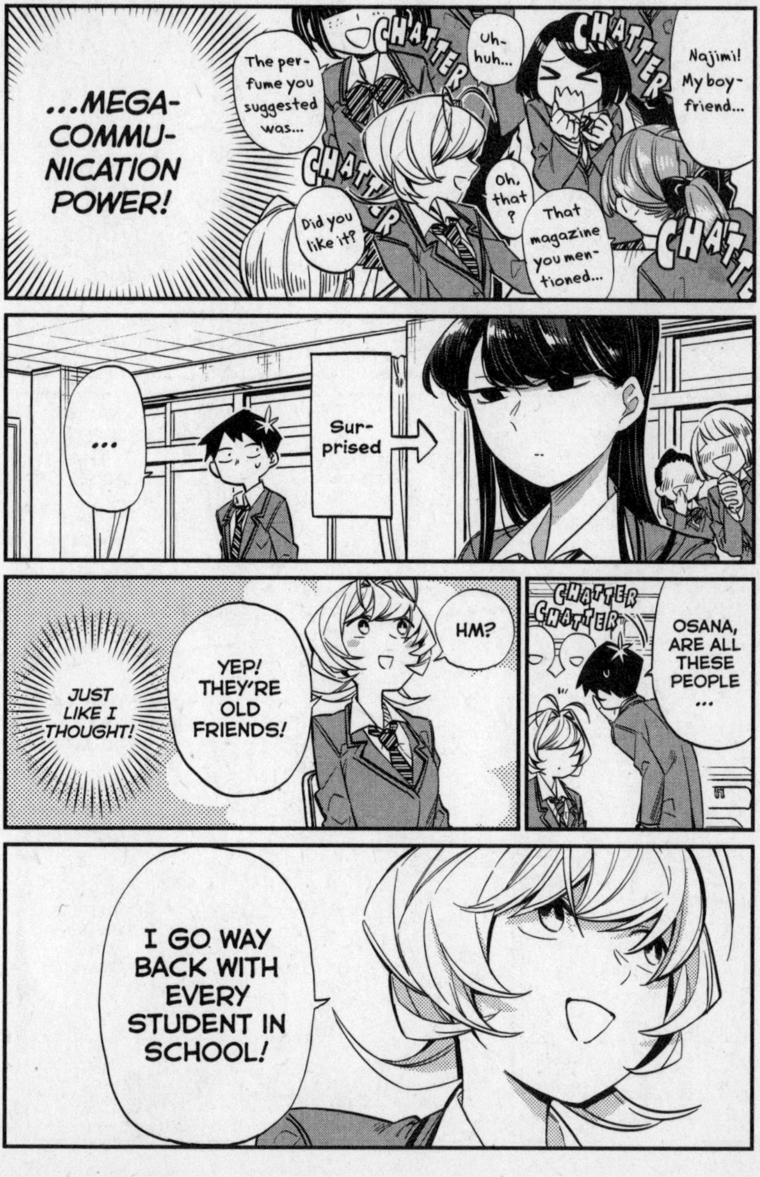
Najimi! My boyfriend...
CHATTER
Uh-huh...
CHATTER
The perfume you suggested was...
CHATTER
Oh, that?
That magazine you mentioned...
Did you like it?
CHATTER
...MEGA-COMMUNICATION POWER!
Surprised
...
CHATTER CHATTER
OSANA, ARE ALL THESE PEOPLE ...
HM?
YEP! THEY'RE OLD FRIENDS!
JUST LIKE I THOUGHT!
I GO WAY BACK WITH EVERY STUDENT IN SCHOOL!

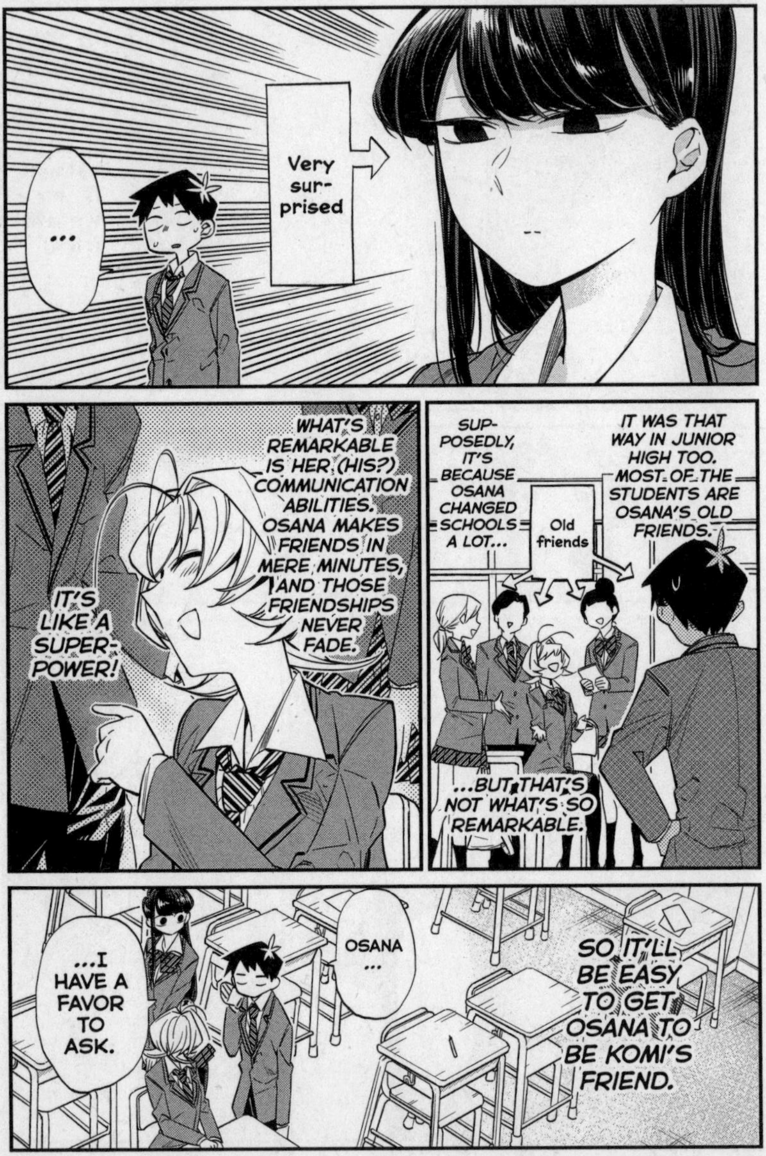
Very surprised
...
IT WAS THAT WAY IN JUNIOR HIGH TOO. MOST OF THE STUDENTS ARE OSANA'S OLD FRIENDS.
SUPPOSEDLY, IT'S BECAUSE OSANA CHANGED SCHOOLS A LOT...
Old friends
...BUT THAT'S NOT WHAT'S SO REMARKABLE.
WHAT'S REMARKABLE IS HER (HIS?) COMMUNICATION ABILITIES. OSANA MAKES FRIENDS IN MERE MINUTES, AND THOSE FRIENDSHIPS NEVER FADE.
IT'S LIKE A SUPERPOWER!
SO IT'LL BE EASY TO GET OSANA TO BE KOMI'S FRIEND.
OSANA...
...I HAVE A FAVOR TO ASK.

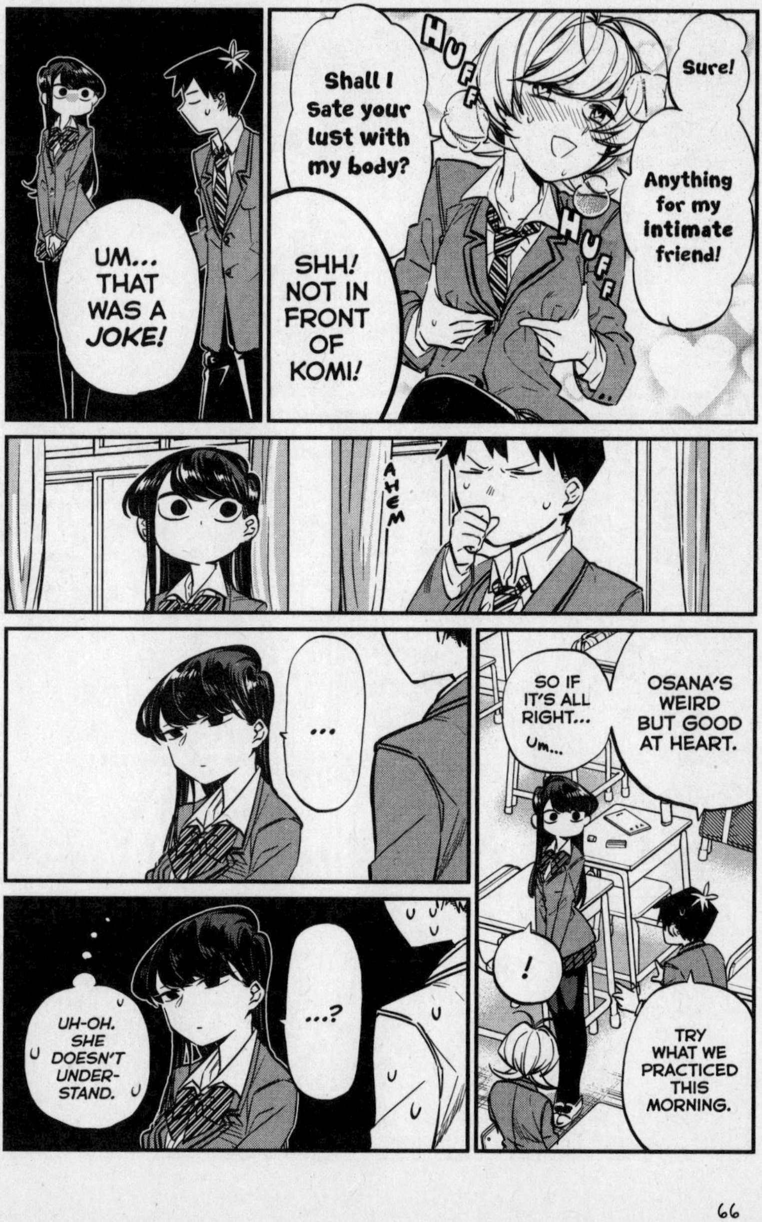
Sure!
Anything for my intimate friend!
HUFF
HUFF
Shall I sate your lust with my body?
SHH! NOT IN FRONT OF KOMI!
UM... THAT WAS A JOKE!
AHEM
OSANA'S WEIRD BUT GOOD AT HEART.
SO IF IT'S ALL RIGHT... Um...
!
TRY WHAT WE PRACTICED THIS MORNING.
...
...?
UH-OH. SHE DOESN'T UNDER-STAND.

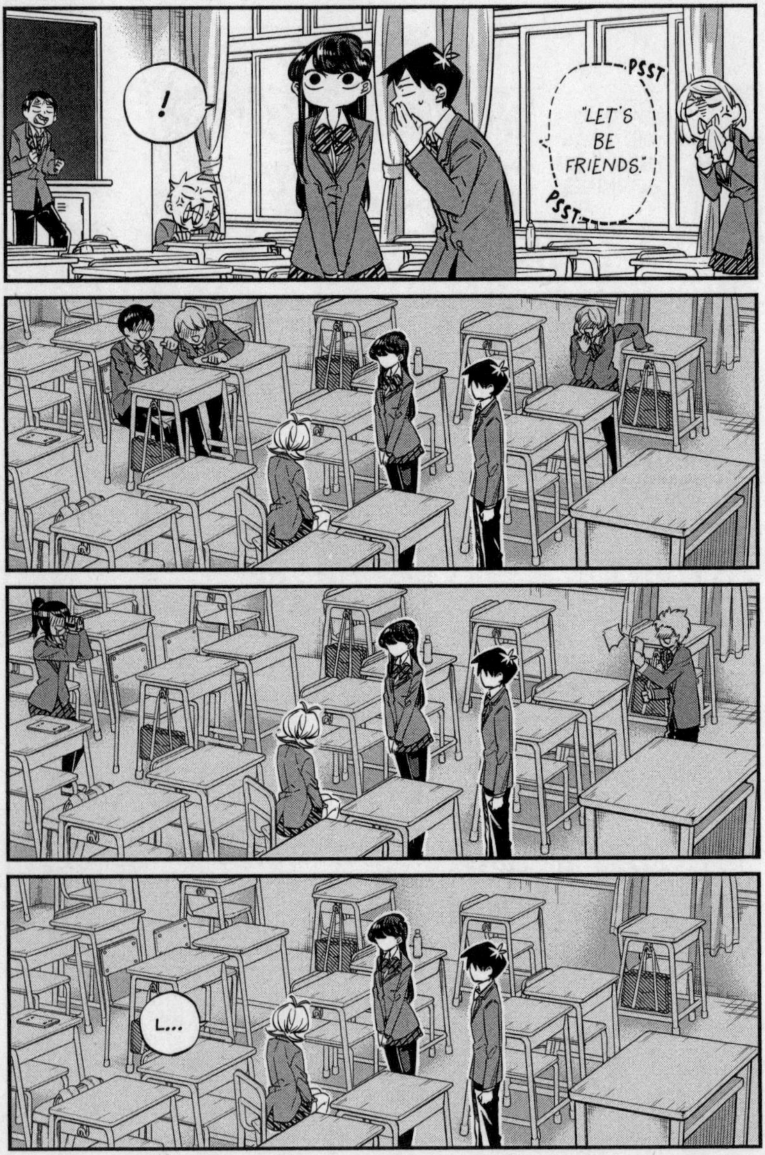
PSST
"LET'S BE FRIENDS."
PSST
!
L...

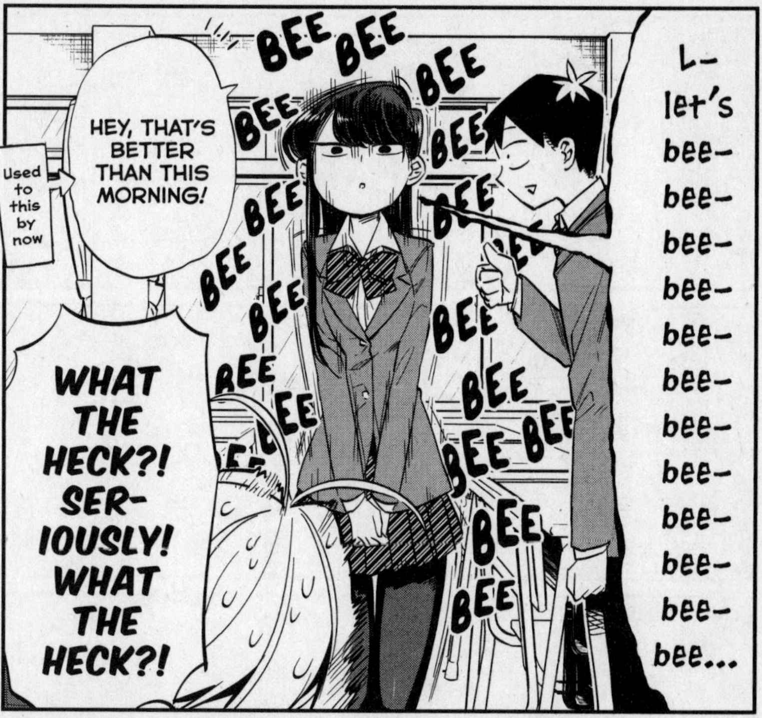
L-let's bee-bee-bee-bee-bee-bee-bee-bee-bee-bee-bee-bee...
BEE BEE BEE
HEY, THAT'S BETTER THAN THIS MORNING!
Used to this by now
WHAT THE HECK?! SER-IOUSLY! WHAT THE HECK?!
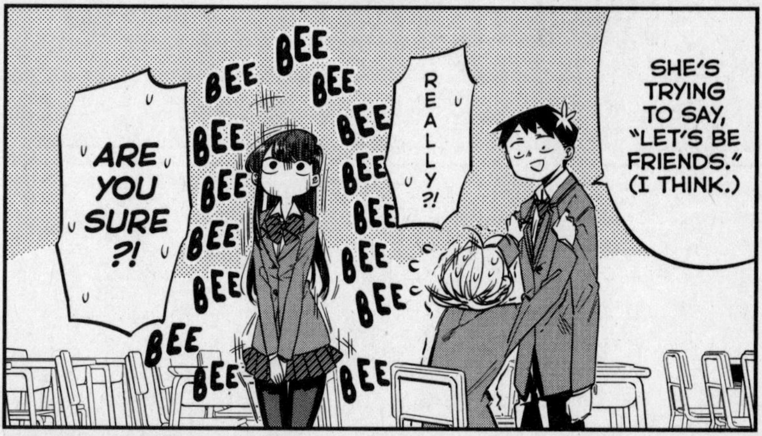
SHE'S TRYING TO SAY, "LET'S BE FRIENDS." (I THINK.)
REALLY?!
BEE BEE BEE
ARE YOU SURE?!

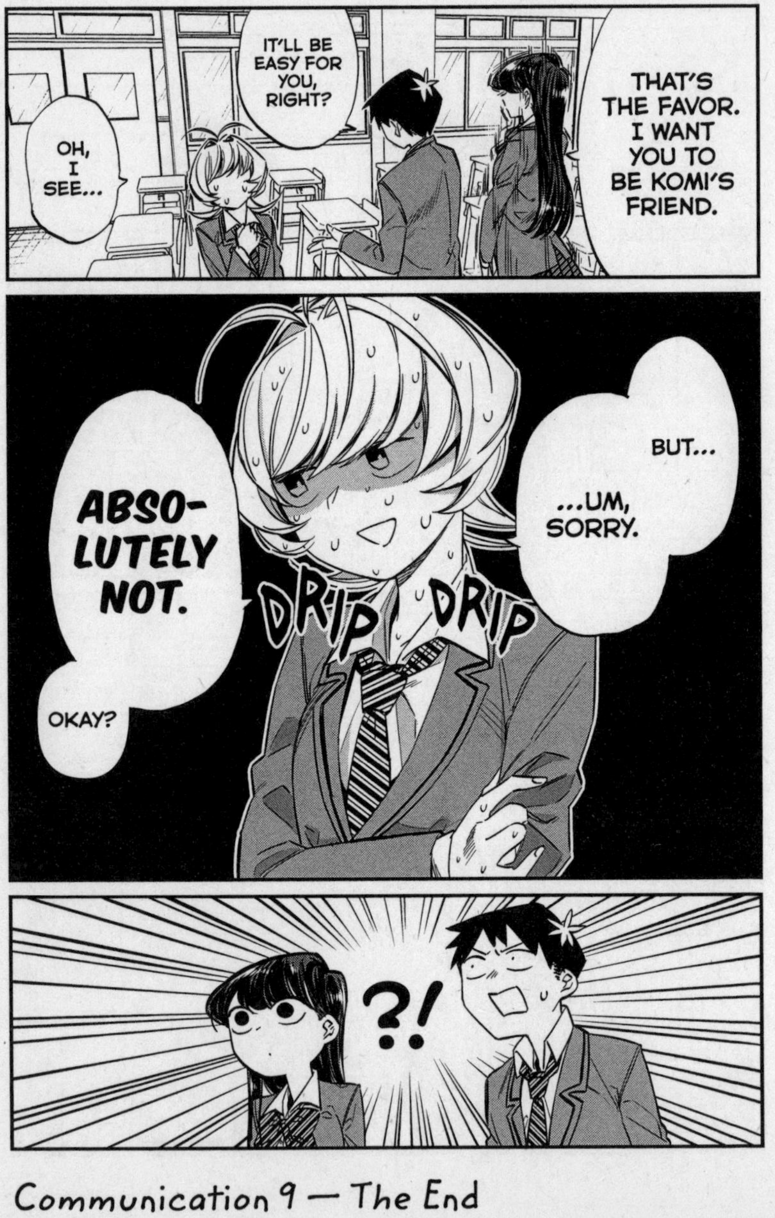
THAT'S THE FAVOR. I WANT YOU TO BE KOMI'S FRIEND.
IT'LL BE EASY FOR YOU, RIGHT?
OH, I SEE...
BUT...
...UM, SORRY.
DRIP DRIP
ABSO-LUTELY NOT.
OKAY?
?!

Communication 9 — The End

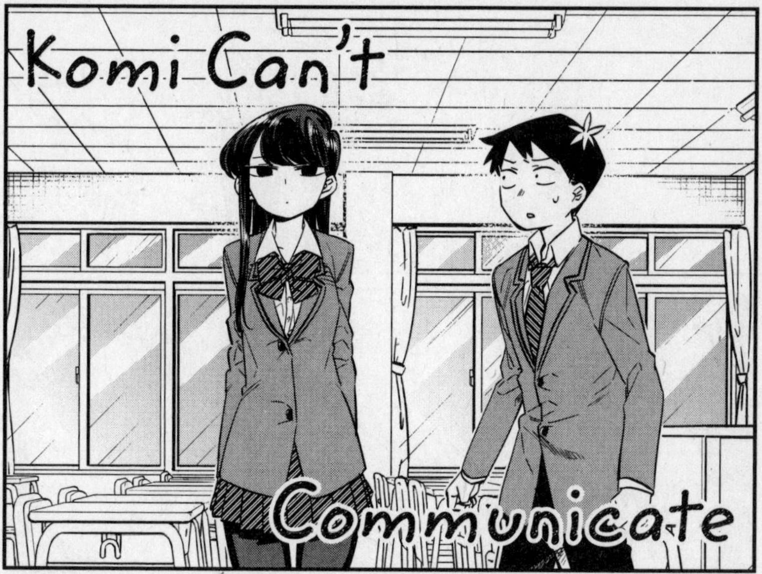
Komi Can't
Communicate

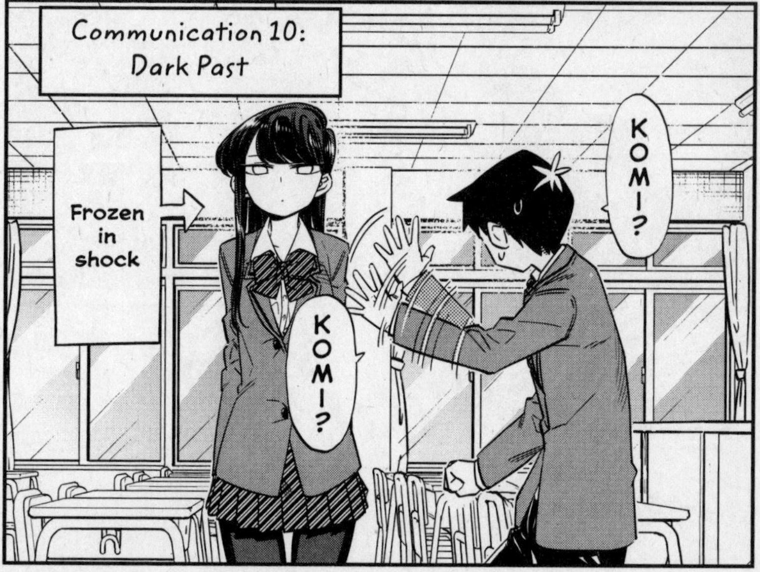
Communication 10: Dark Past
KOMI?
Frozen in shock
KOMI?

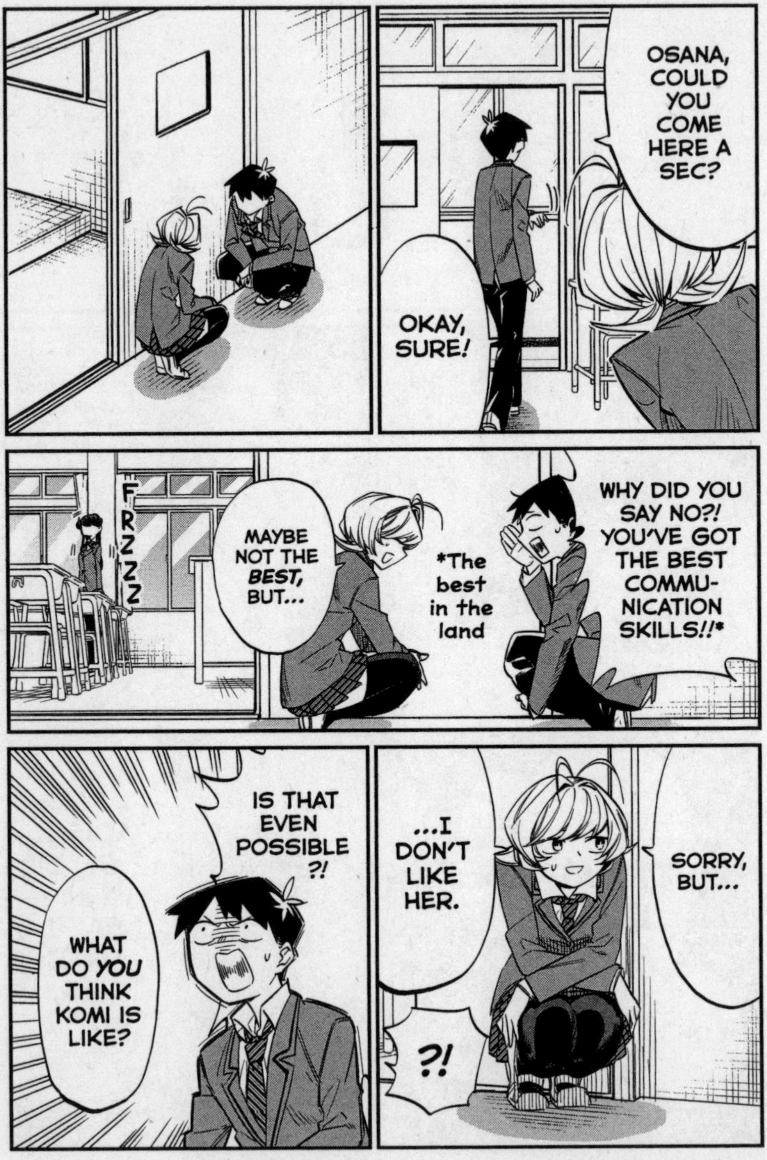
OSANA, COULD YOU COME HERE A SEC?
OKAY, SURE!
WHY DID YOU SAY NO?! YOU'VE GOT THE BEST COMMUNICATION SKILLS!!*
*The best in the land
MAYBE NOT THE *BEST,* BUT...
FRZZZ
SORRY, BUT...
...I DON'T LIKE HER.
?!
IS THAT EVEN POSSIBLE?!
WHAT DO *YOU* THINK KOMI IS LIKE?

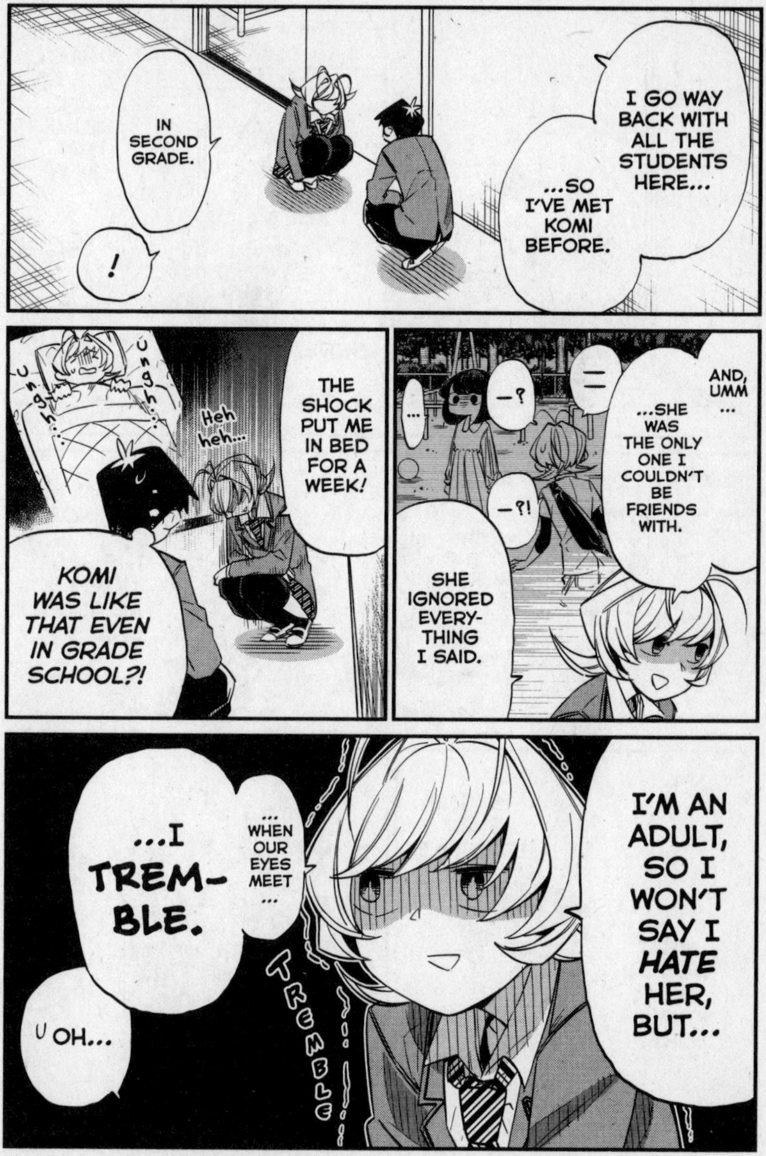
I GO WAY BACK WITH ALL THE STUDENTS HERE...
...SO I'VE MET KOMI BEFORE.
IN SECOND GRADE.
!
AND, UMM...
...SHE WAS THE ONLY ONE I COULDN'T BE FRIENDS WITH.
—
—?
...
—?!
SHE IGNORED EVERY-THING I SAID.
THE SHOCK PUT ME IN BED FOR A WEEK!
Heh heh...
Ungh...
Ungh...
KOMI WAS LIKE THAT EVEN IN GRADE SCHOOL?!
I'M AN ADULT, SO I WON'T SAY I *HATE* HER, BUT...
...WHEN OUR EYES MEET...
...I TREM-BLE.
TREMBLE
OH...

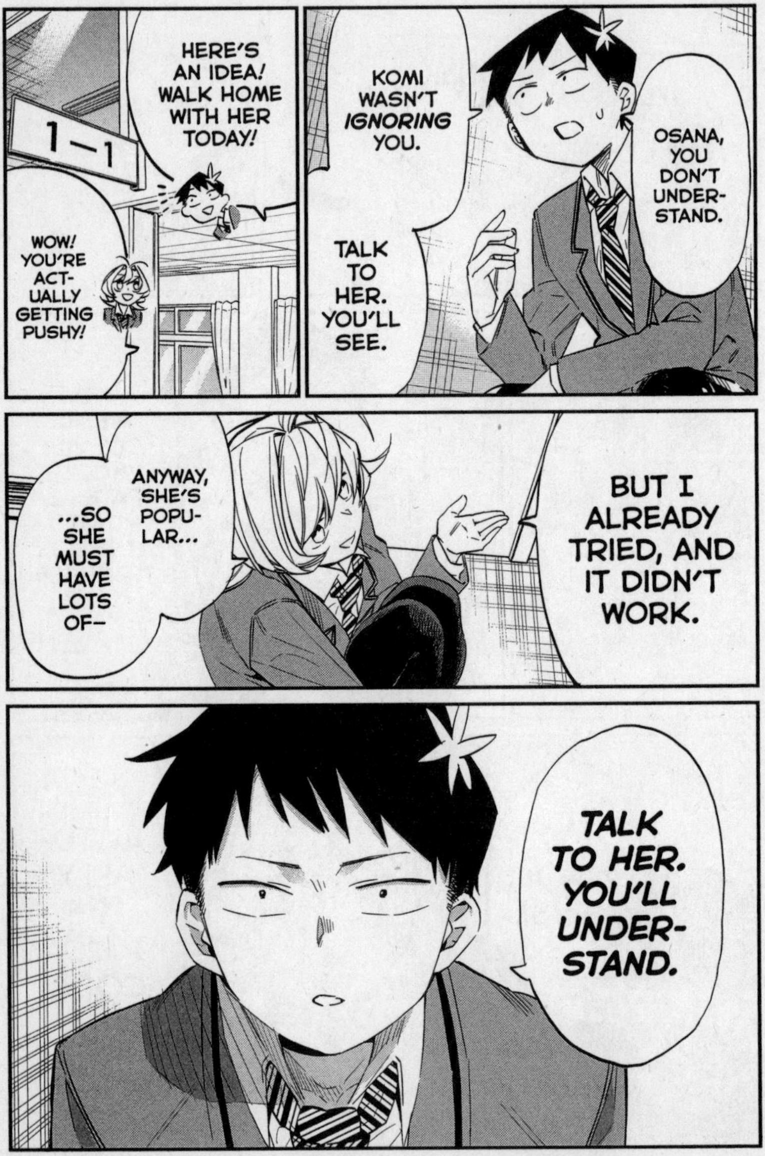
OSANA, YOU DON'T UNDER-STAND.
KOMI WASN'T *IGNORING* YOU.
TALK TO HER. YOU'LL SEE.
HERE'S AN IDEA! WALK HOME WITH HER TODAY!
1—1
WOW! YOU'RE ACT-UALLY GETTING PUSHY!
BUT I ALREADY TRIED, AND IT DIDN'T WORK.
ANYWAY, SHE'S POPU-LAR...
...SO SHE MUST HAVE LOTS OF–
TALK TO HER. YOU'LL UNDER-STAND.

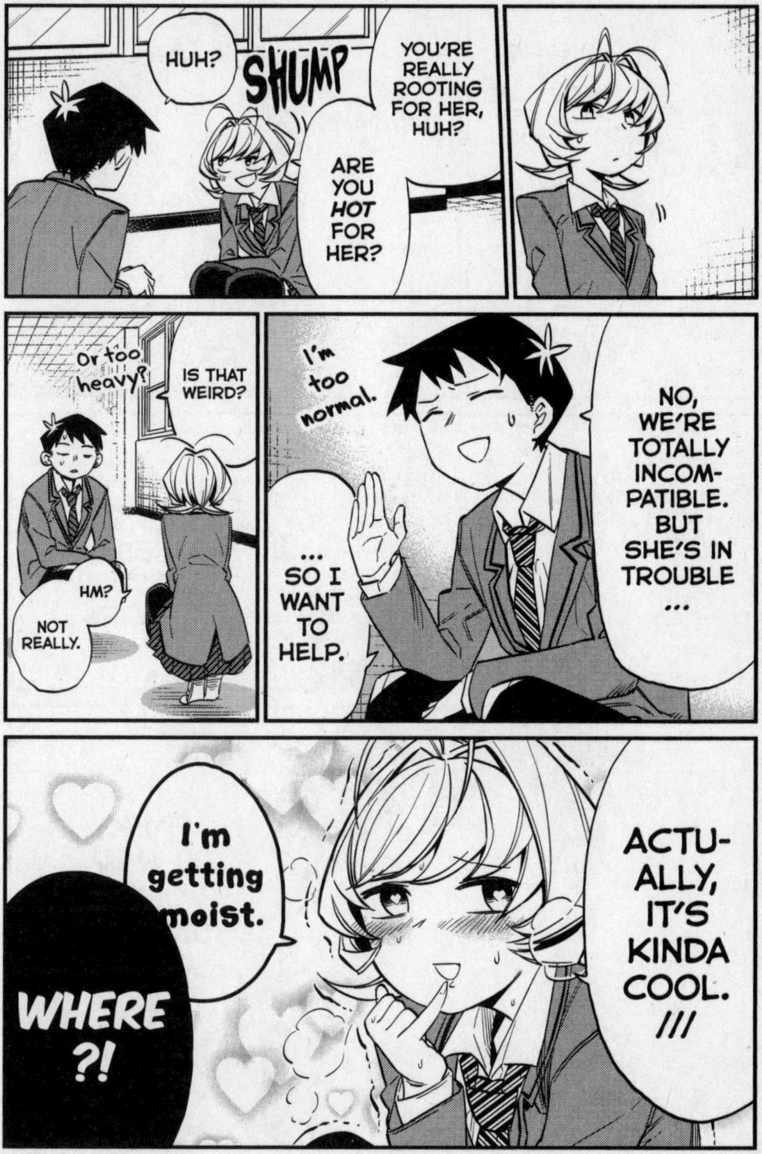
YOU'RE REALLY ROOTING FOR HER, HUH?
ARE YOU *HOT* FOR HER?
SHUMP
HUH?
NO, WE'RE TOTALLY INCOMPATIBLE. BUT SHE'S IN TROUBLE ...
I'm too normal.
... SO I WANT TO HELP.
IS THAT WEIRD?
Or too heavy?
HM?
NOT REALLY.
ACTUALLY, IT'S KINDA COOL. ///
I'm getting moist.
WHERE ?!

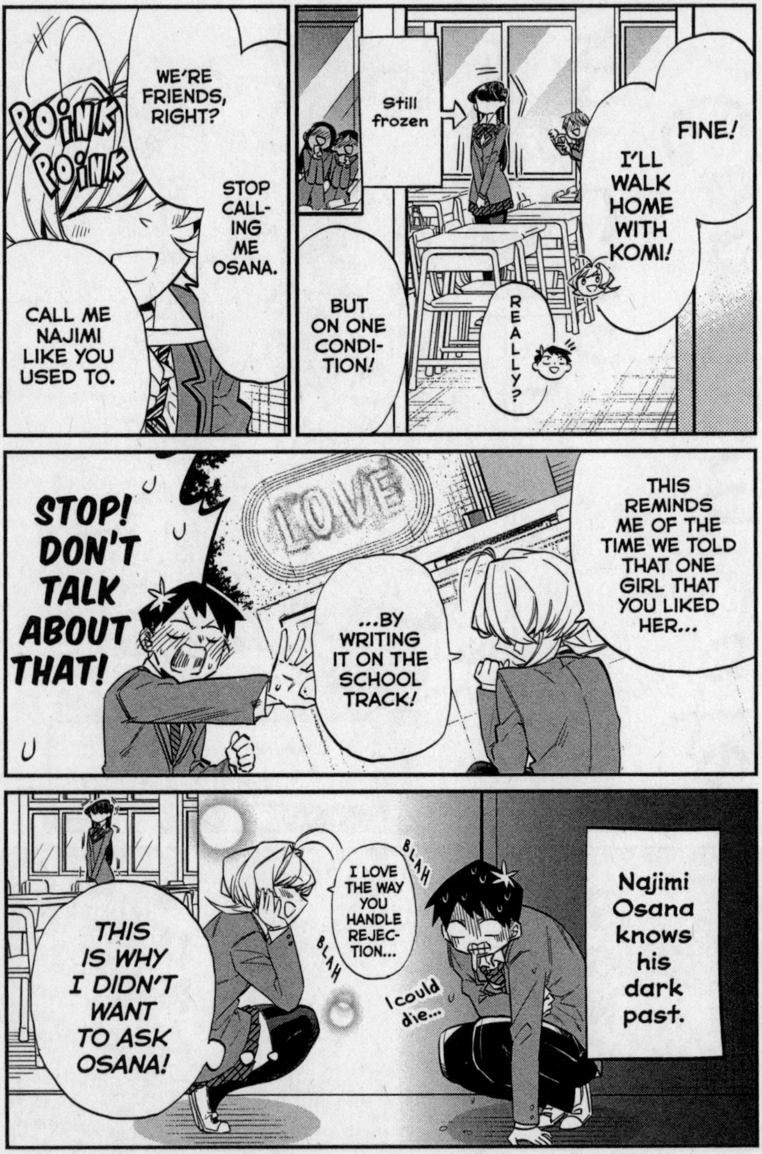
FINE! I'LL WALK HOME WITH KOMI!
REALLY?
BUT ON ONE CONDITION!
Still frozen
WE'RE FRIENDS, RIGHT?
STOP CALLING ME OSANA.
CALL ME NAJIMI LIKE YOU USED TO.
POINK POINK
THIS REMINDS ME OF THE TIME WE TOLD THAT ONE GIRL THAT YOU LIKED HER...
...BY WRITING IT ON THE SCHOOL TRACK!
LOVE
STOP! DON'T TALK ABOUT THAT!
Najimi Osana knows his dark past.
I could die...
I LOVE THE WAY YOU HANDLE REJECTION...
BLAH
BLAH
THIS IS WHY I DIDN'T WANT TO ASK OSANA!

Communication 10 — The End

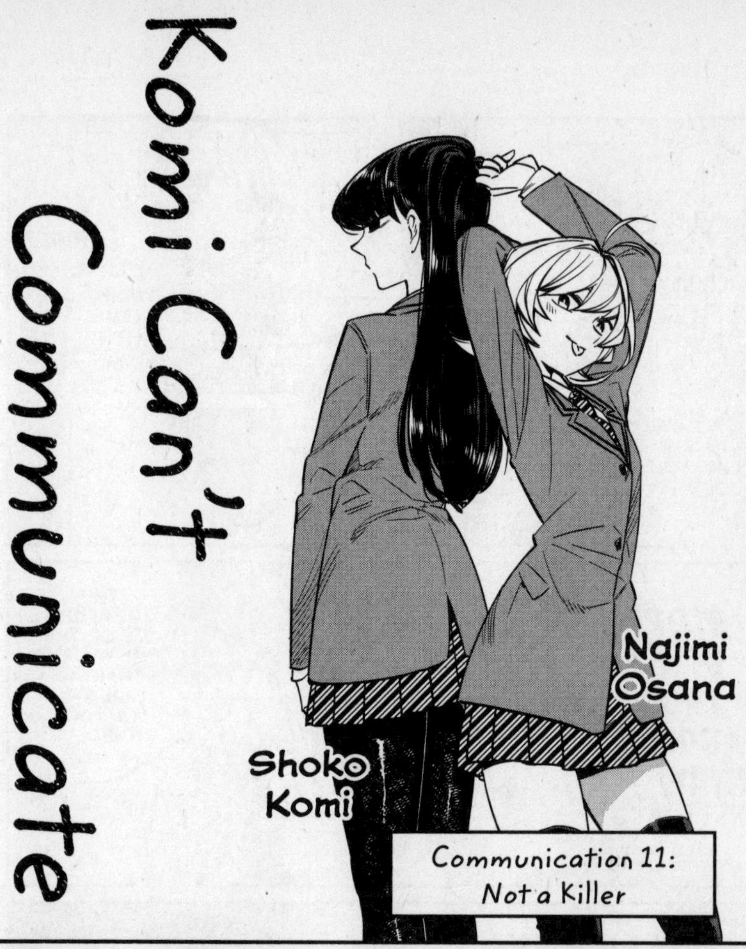
Komi Can't Communicate
Najimi Osana
Shoko Komi
Communication 11: Not a Killer

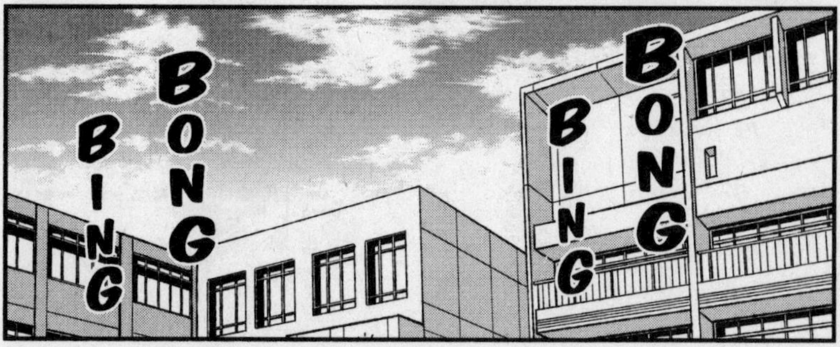
BONG
BING
BONG
BING

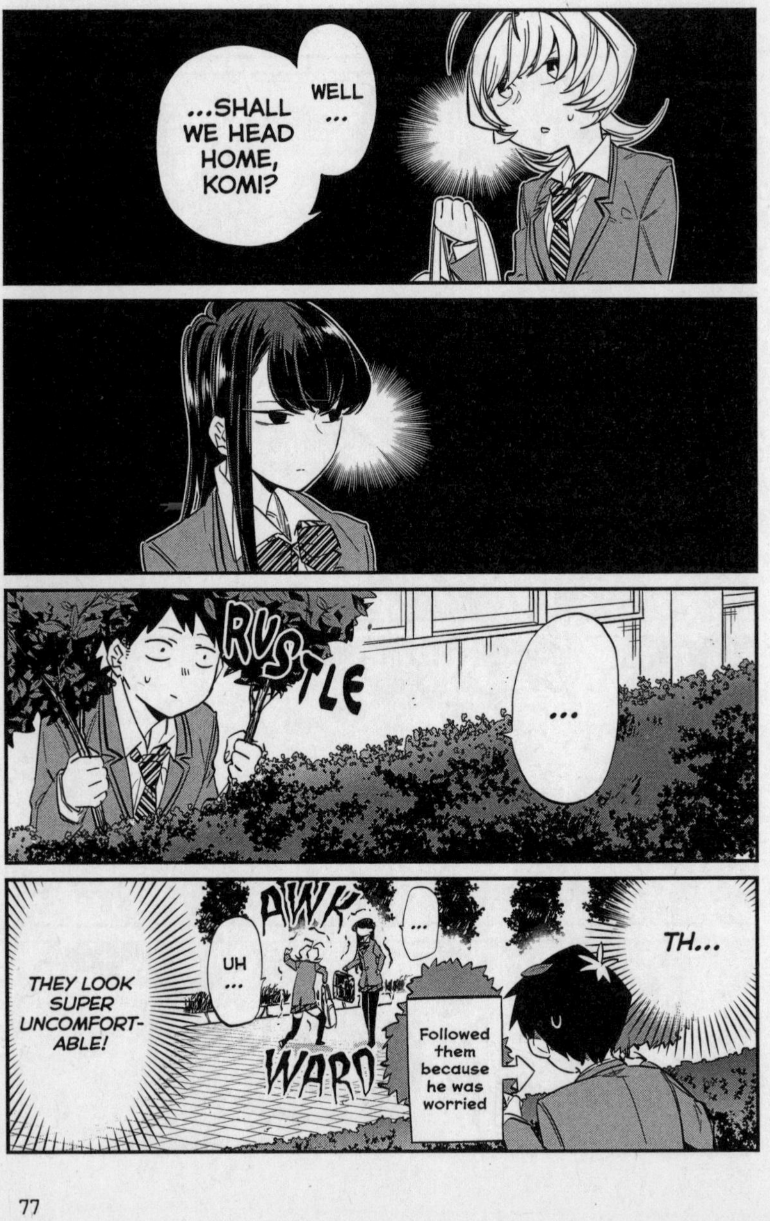
WELL ...
...SHALL WE HEAD HOME, KOMI?
RUSTLE
...
TH...
Followed them because he was worried
...
AWKWARD
UH ...
THEY LOOK SUPER UNCOMFORT-ABLE!

From Najimi's Perspective

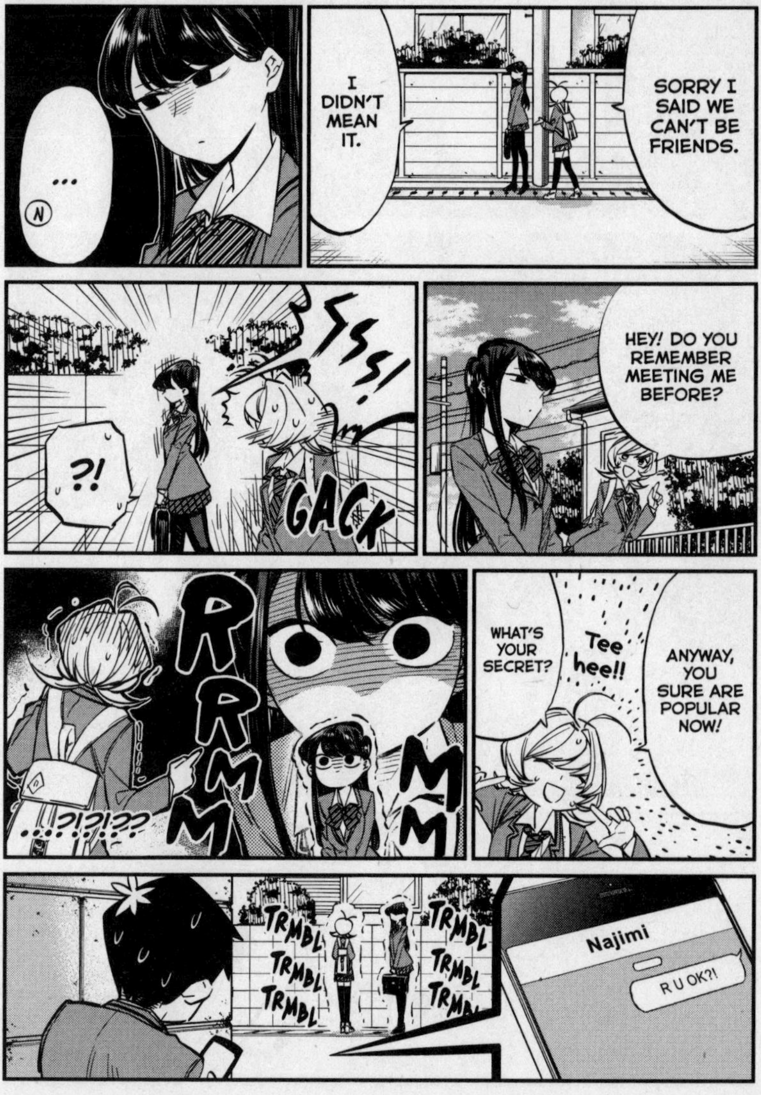

SORRY I SAID WE CAN'T BE FRIENDS.
I DIDN'T MEAN IT.
...
N
HEY! DO YOU REMEMBER MEETING ME BEFORE?
SSS!
GACK
?!
ANYWAY, YOU SURE ARE POPULAR NOW!
Tee hee!!
WHAT'S YOUR SECRET?
RRRM
MMM
...?!?!?!??
Najimi
R U OK?!
TRMBL
TRMBL
TRMBL
TRMBL
TRMBL
TRMBL

From Tadano's Perspective

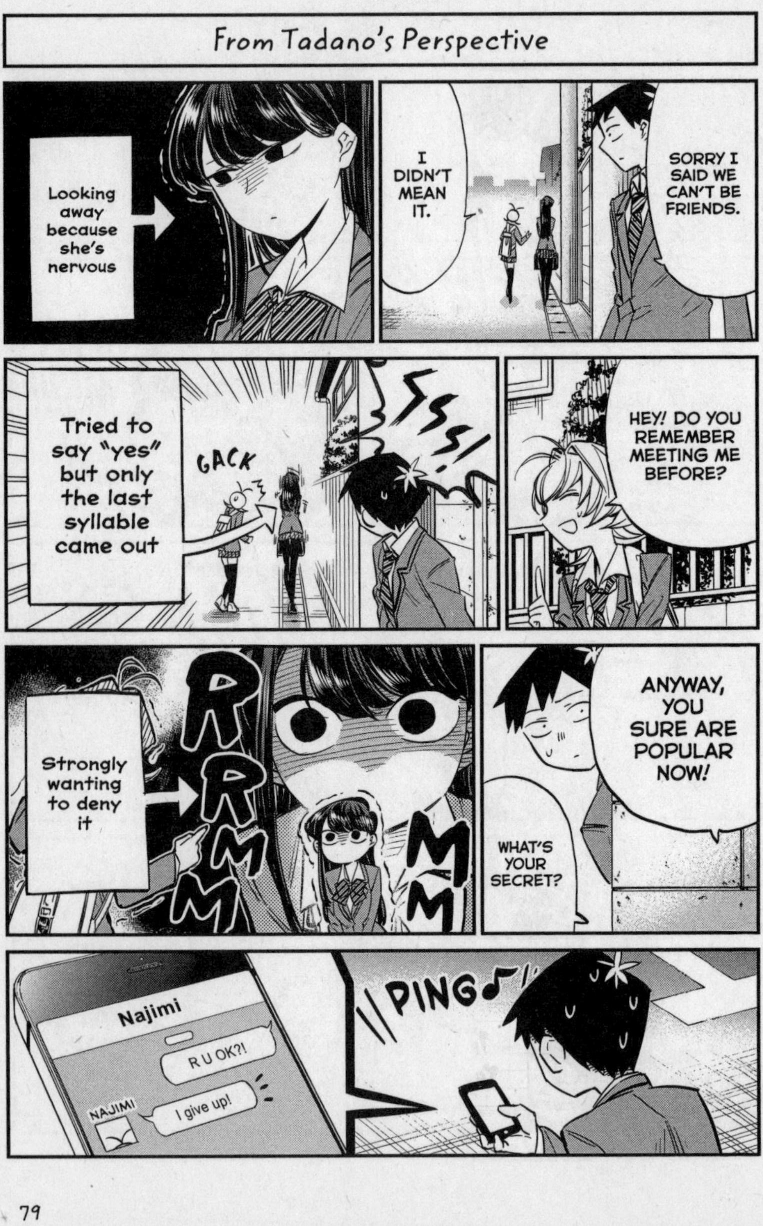
SORRY I SAID WE CAN'T BE FRIENDS.
I DIDN'T MEAN IT.
Looking away because she's nervous
HEY! DO YOU REMEMBER MEETING ME BEFORE?
SSS!
GACK
Tried to say "yes" but only the last syllable came out
ANYWAY, YOU SURE ARE POPULAR NOW!
WHAT'S YOUR SECRET?
RRMMMM
Strongly wanting to deny it
PING♪
Najimi
R U OK?!
NAJIMI
I give up!

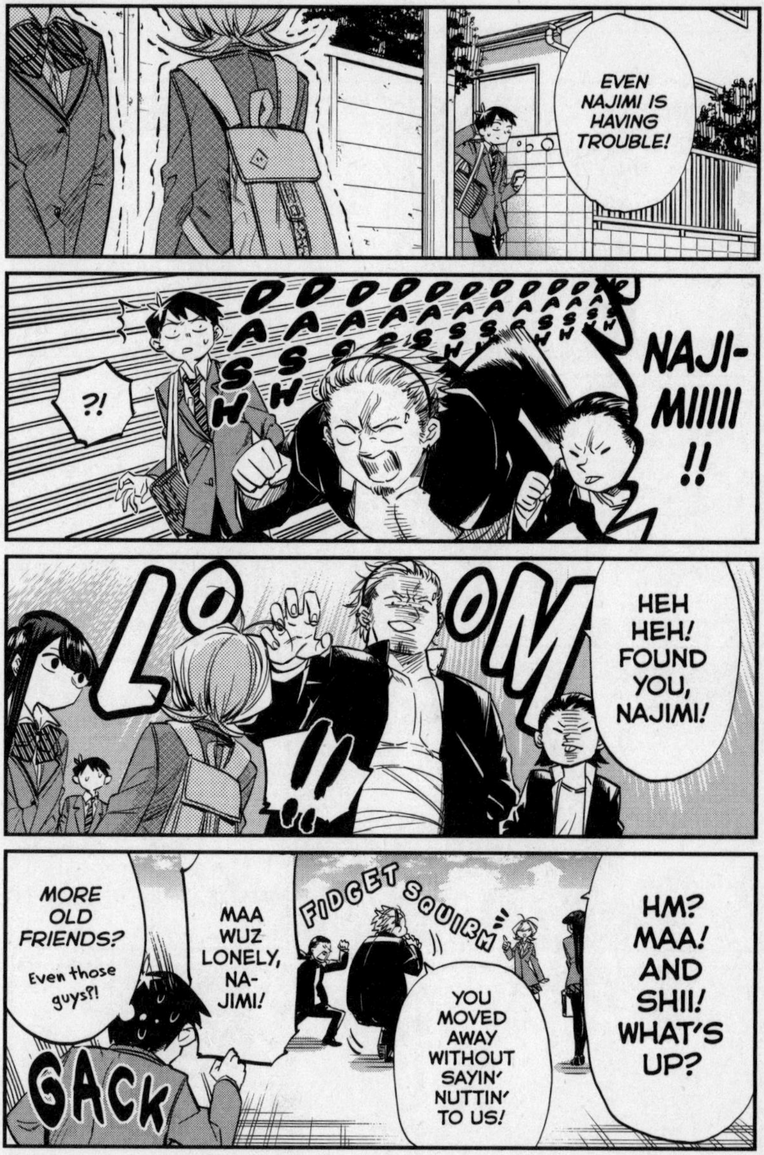
EVEN NAJIMI IS HAVING TROUBLE!
NAJI-MIIIIII !!
DASH
?!
HEH HEH! FOUND YOU, NAJIMI!
LOOM
!!
HM? MAA! AND SHII! WHAT'S UP?
YOU MOVED AWAY WITHOUT SAYIN' NUTTIN' TO US!
FIDGET SQUIRM
MAA WUZ LONELY, NA-JIMI!
MORE OLD FRIENDS?
Even those guys?!
GACK

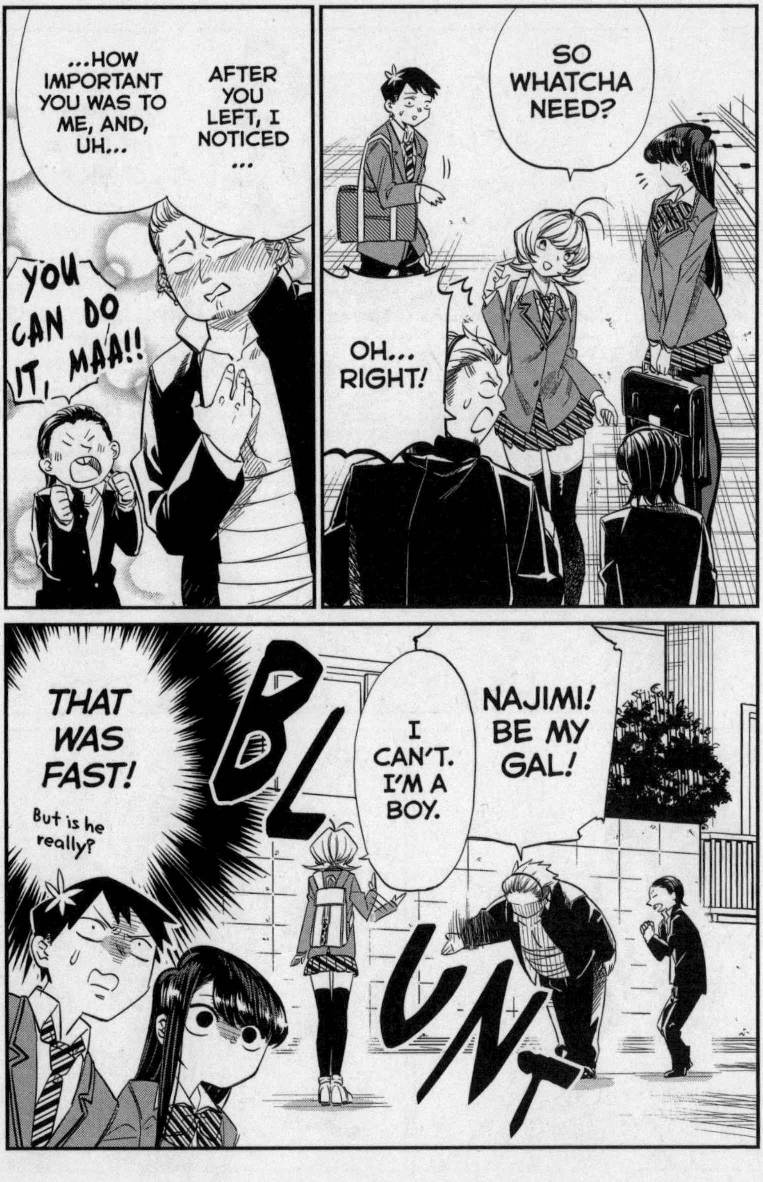
SO WHATCHA NEED?
OH... RIGHT!
AFTER YOU LEFT, I NOTICED ...
...HOW IMPORTANT YOU WAS TO ME, AND, UH...
YOU CAN DO IT, MAA!!
NAJIMI! BE MY GAL!
I CAN'T. I'M A BOY.
BLUNT
THAT WAS FAST!
But is he really?

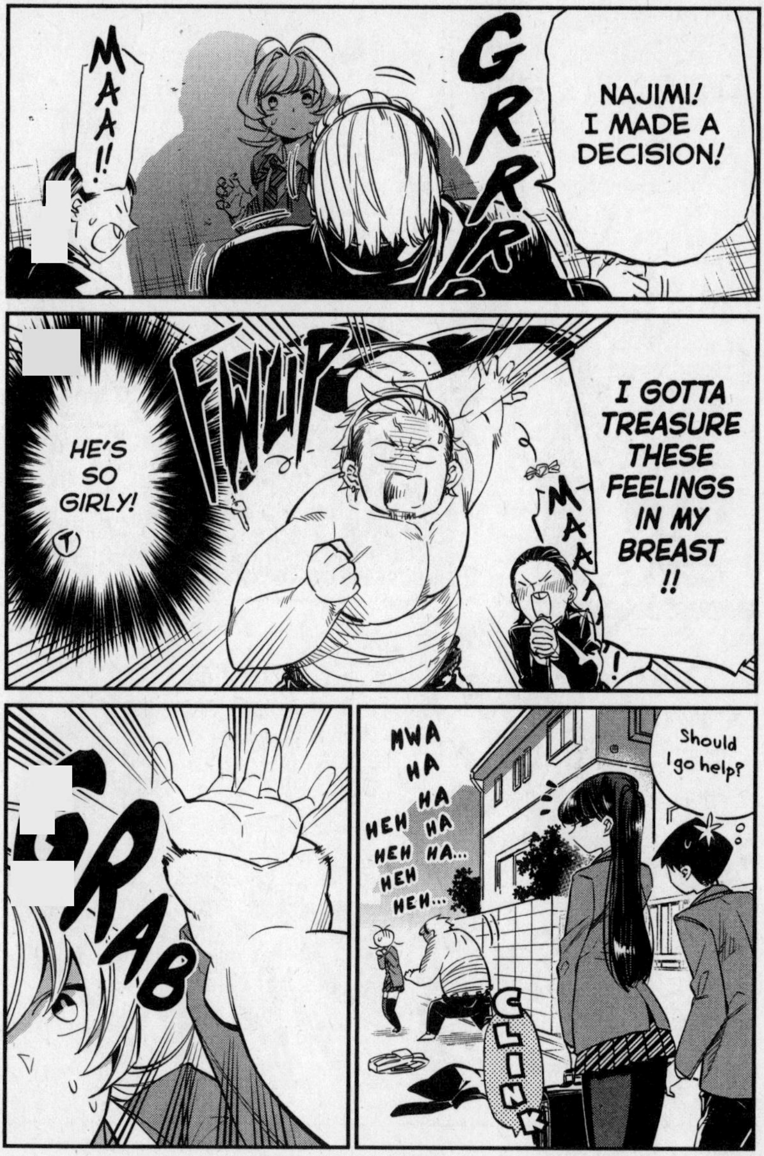
NAJIMI! I MADE A DECISION!
GRRR
MAA!!
I GOTTA TREASURE THESE FEELINGS IN MY BREAST!!
MAAA!
FWUP
HE'S SO GIRLY!
Should I go help?
MWA HA HA HA HA...
HEH HEH HEH HEH...
CLINK
GRAB

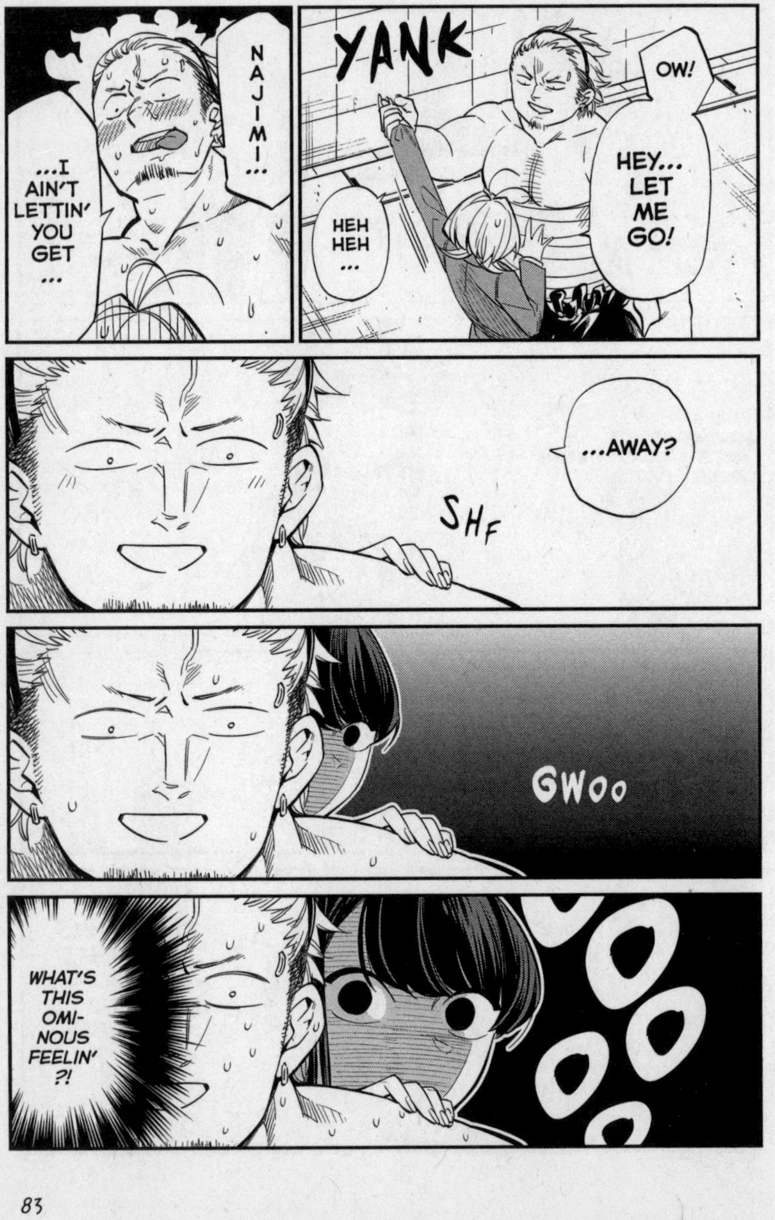
YANK
OW!
HEY... LET ME GO!
HEH HEH ...
NAJIMI...
...I AIN'T LETTIN' YOU GET ...
...AWAY?
SHF
GWOO
WHAT'S THIS OMI-NOUS FEELIN' ?!

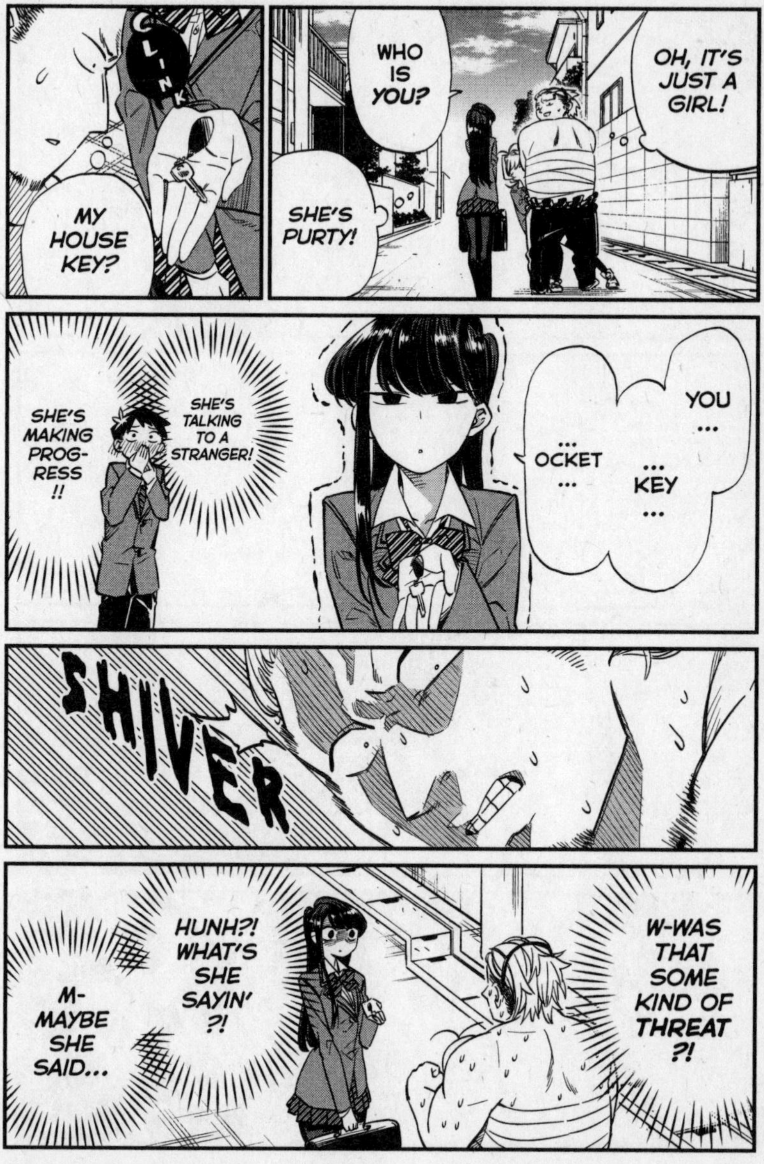
OH, IT'S JUST A GIRL!
WHO IS YOU?
SHE'S PURTY!
CLINK
MY HOUSE KEY?
YOU ...
... KEY ...
... OCKET ...
SHE'S TALKING TO A STRANGER!
SHE'S MAKING PROG-RESS !!
SHIVER
W-WAS THAT SOME KIND OF THREAT ?!
HUNH?! WHAT'S SHE SAYIN' ?!
M-MAYBE SHE SAID...

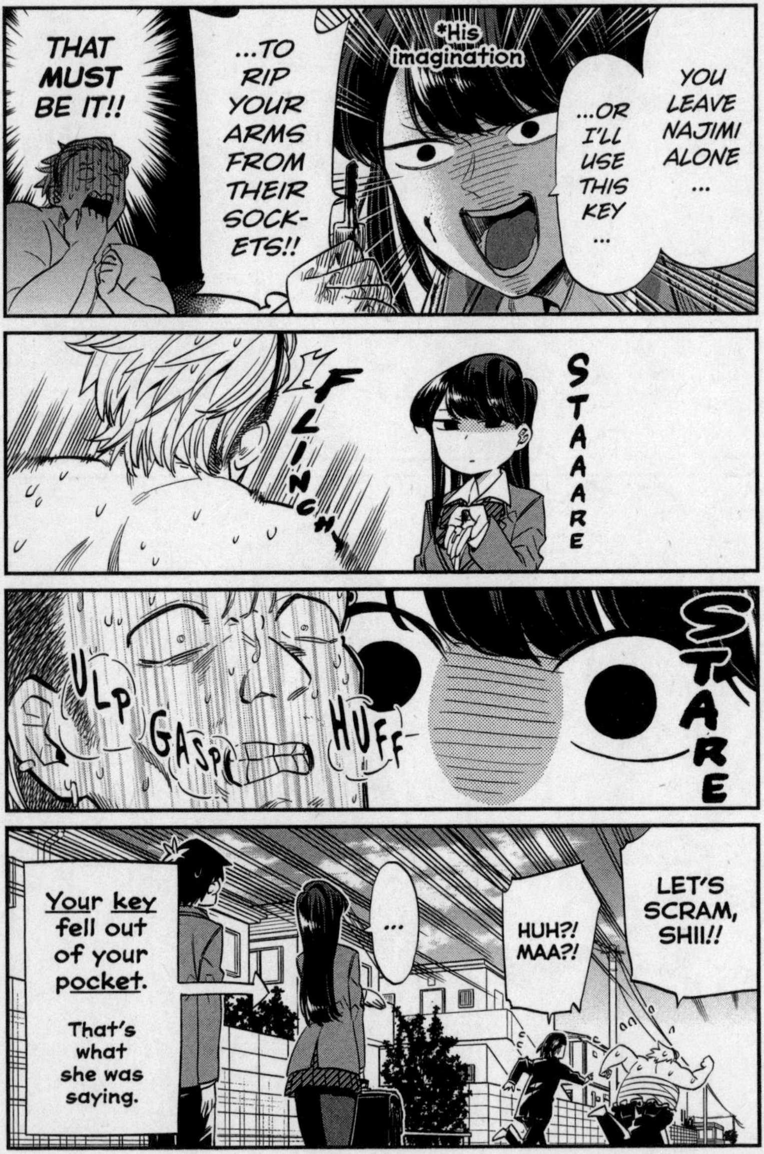
YOU LEAVE NAJIMI ALONE ...
...OR I'LL USE THIS KEY ...
*His imagination
...TO RIP YOUR ARMS FROM THEIR SOCK-ETS!!
THAT MUST BE IT!!
STAAAARE
FLINCH
STARE
HUFF
GASP
ULP
LET'S SCRAM, SHII!!
HUH?! MAA?!
...
Your key fell out of your pocket.
That's what she was saying.

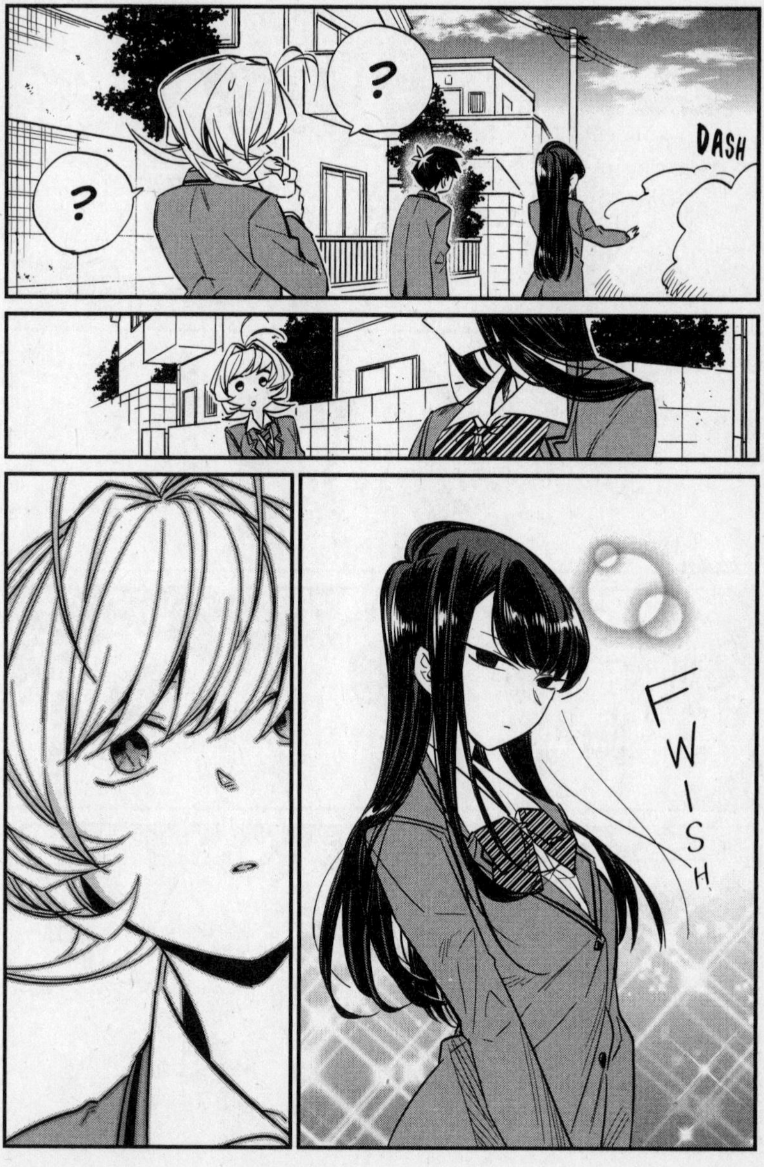
DASH
?
?
FWISH

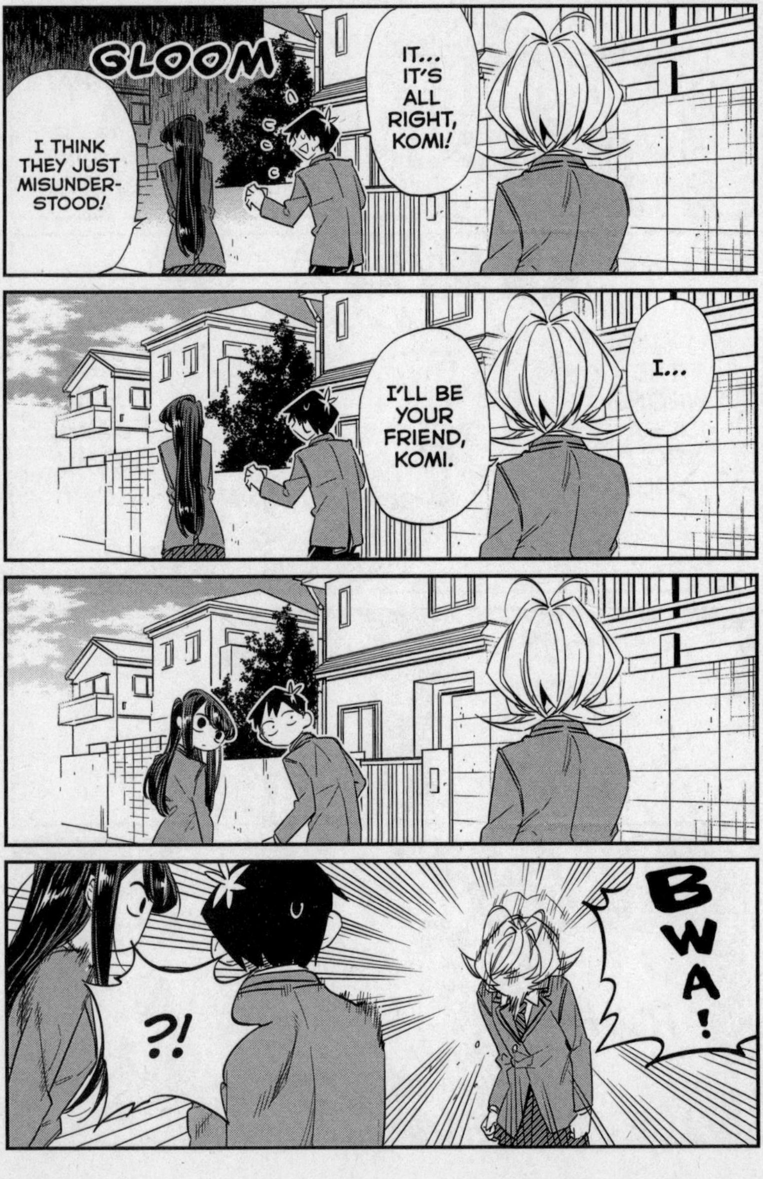
IT... IT'S ALL RIGHT, KOMI!
GLOOM
I THINK THEY JUST MISUNDER-STOOD!
I...
I'LL BE YOUR FRIEND, KOMI.
BWA!
?!

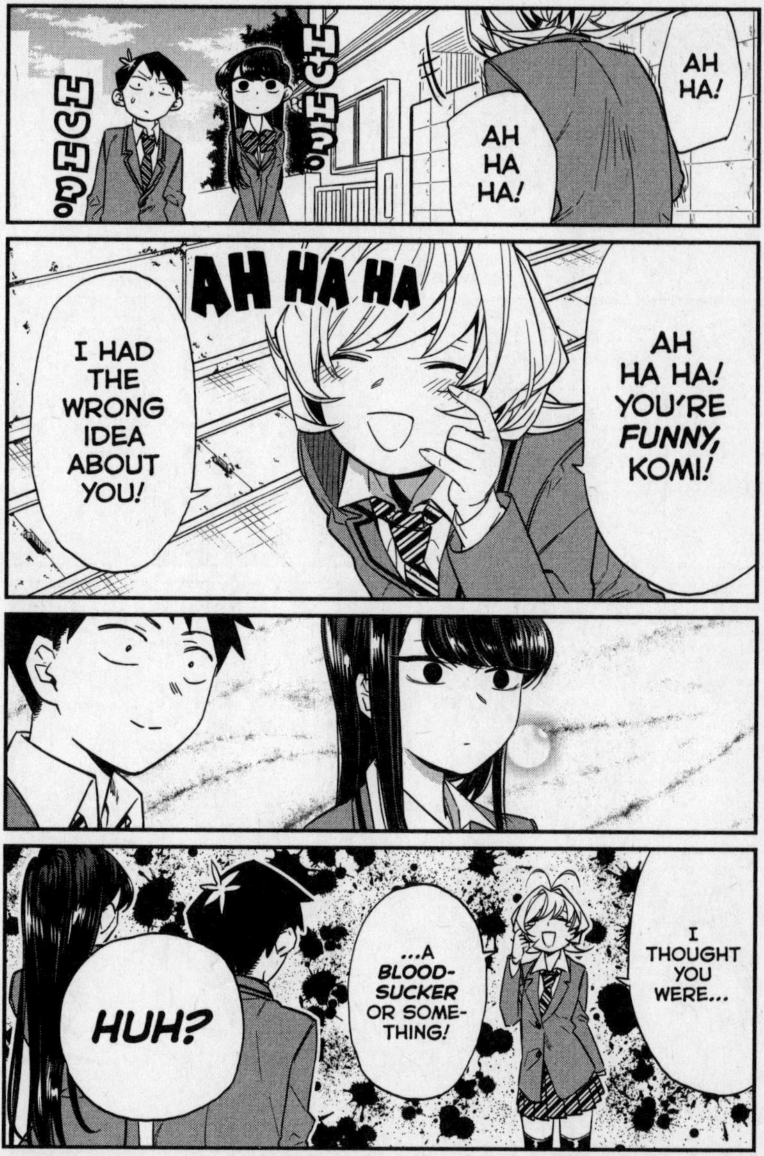
AH HA!
AH HA HA!
HUH?!
HUH?!
AH HA HA
AH HA HA! YOU'RE *FUNNY*, KOMI!
I HAD THE WRONG IDEA ABOUT YOU!
I THOUGHT YOU WERE...
...A *BLOOD-SUCKER* OR SOME-THING!
HUH?

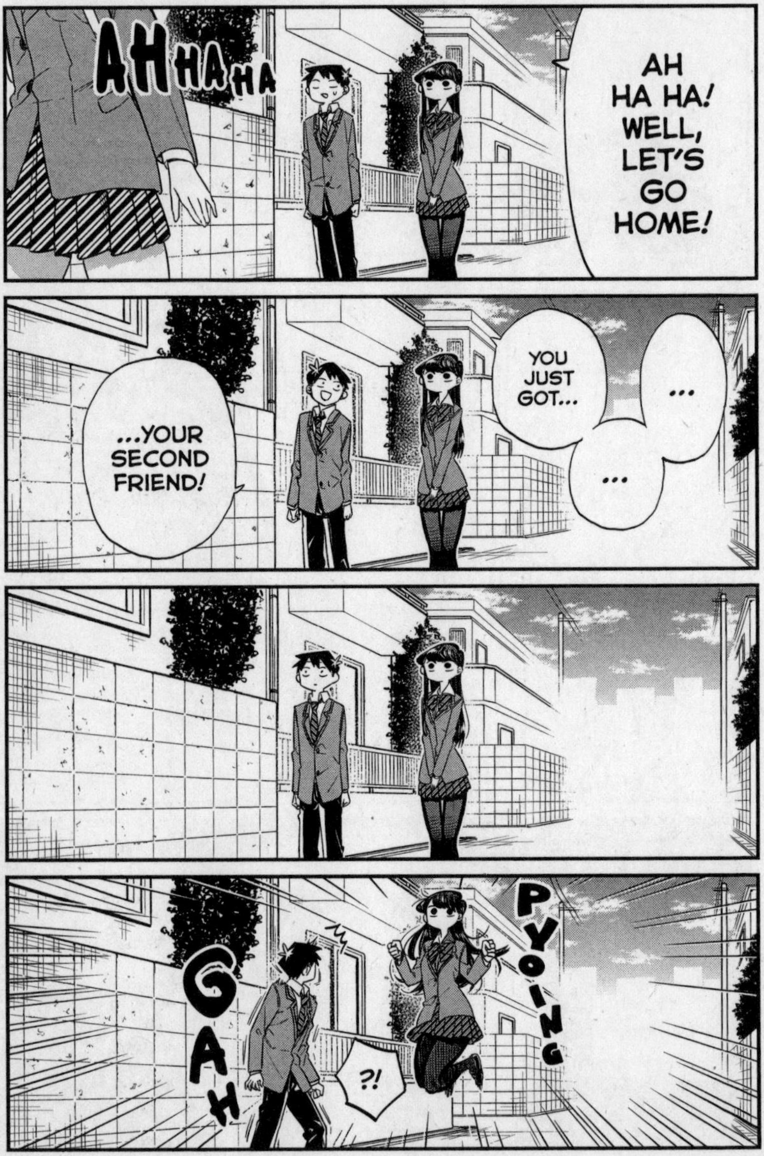
AH HA HA! WELL, LET'S GO HOME!
AH HA HA
YOU JUST GOT...
...
...
...YOUR SECOND FRIEND!
PYOING
GAH
?!

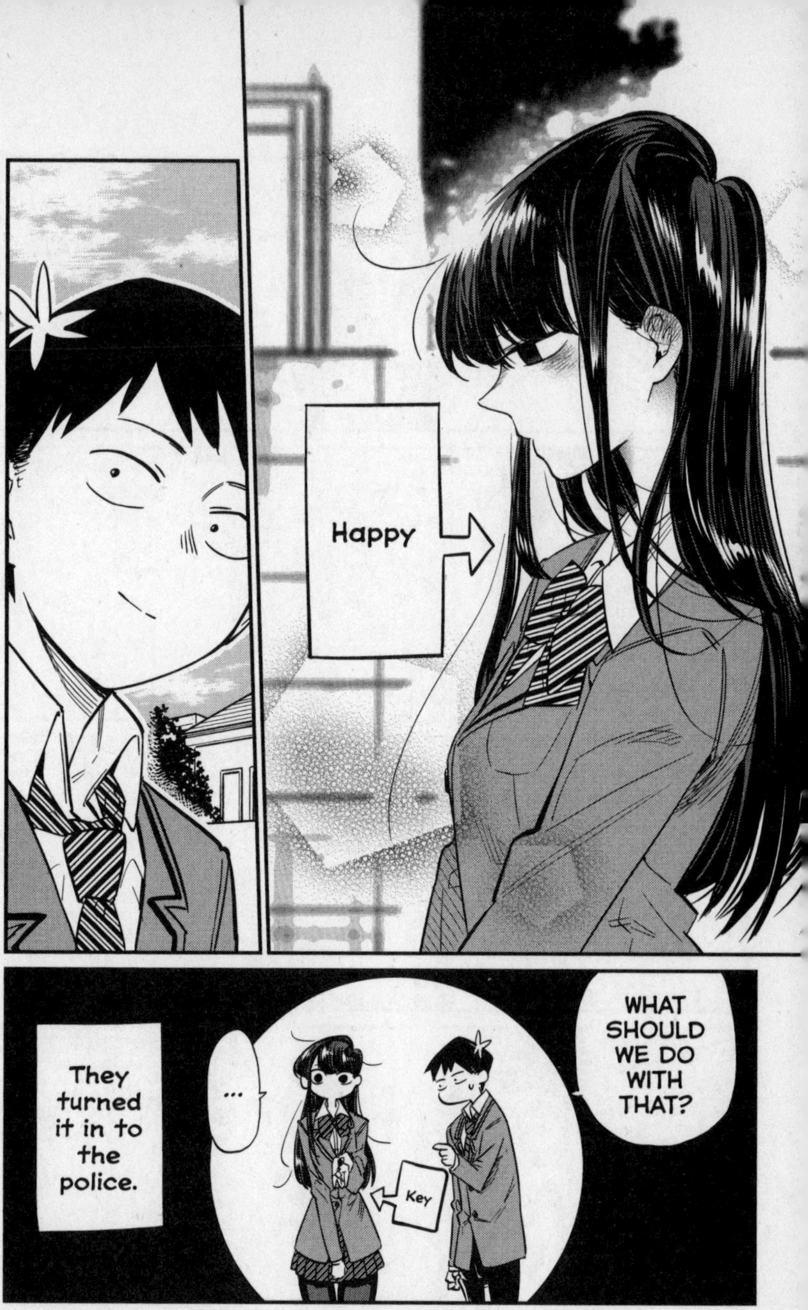
Happy
WHAT SHOULD WE DO WITH THAT?
...
Key
They turned it in to the police.

Communication 11 — The End

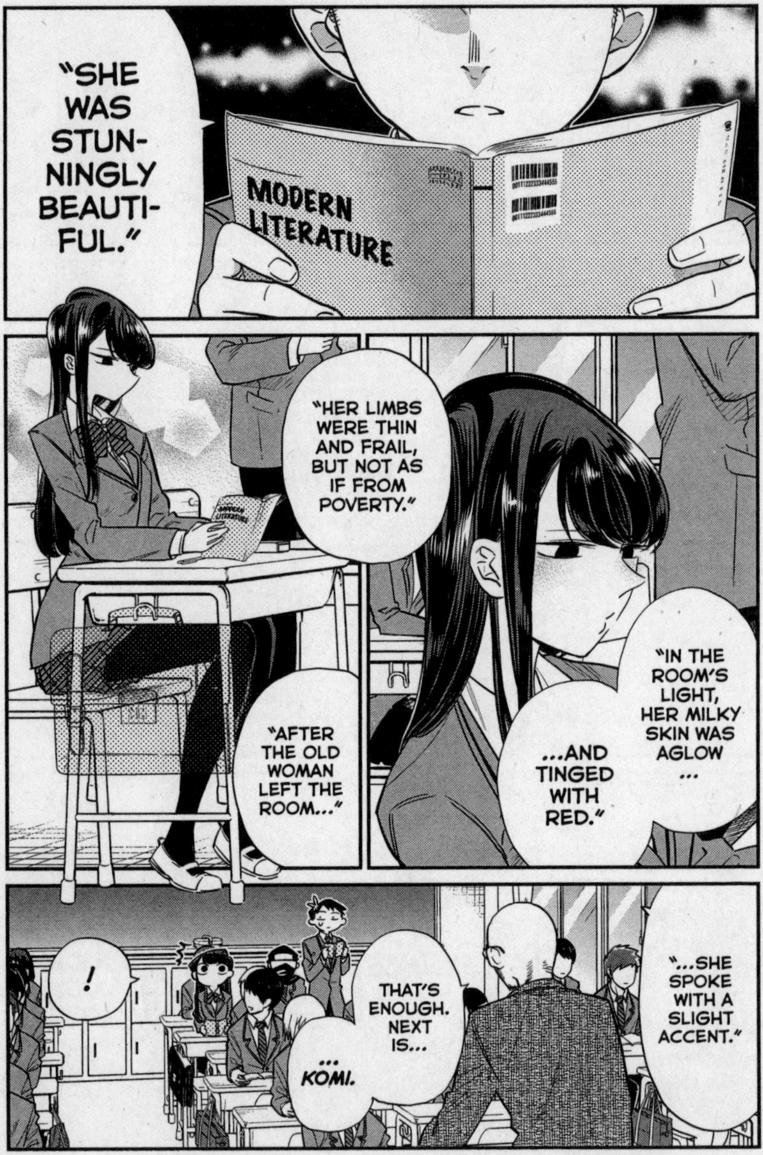
"SHE WAS STUNNINGLY BEAUTIFUL."
MODERN LITERATURE
"HER LIMBS WERE THIN AND FRAIL, BUT NOT AS IF FROM POVERTY."
"IN THE ROOM'S LIGHT, HER MILKY SKIN WAS AGLOW ...
...AND TINGED WITH RED."
"AFTER THE OLD WOMAN LEFT THE ROOM..."
"...SHE SPOKE WITH A SLIGHT ACCENT."
THAT'S ENOUGH. NEXT IS...
... KOMI.
!

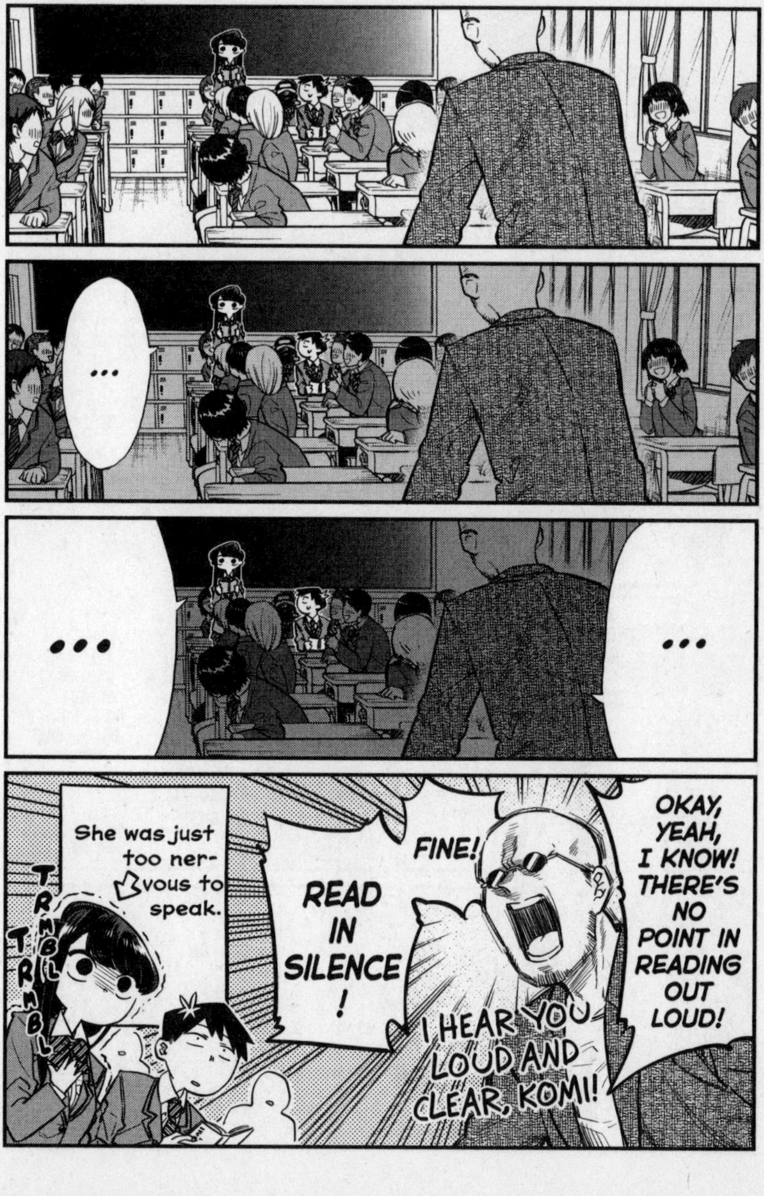
...
...
...
OKAY, YEAH, I KNOW! THERE'S NO POINT IN READING OUT LOUD!
I HEAR YOU LOUD AND CLEAR, KOMI!
FINE!
READ IN SILENCE!
She was just too ner-vous to speak.
TRMBL
TRMBL

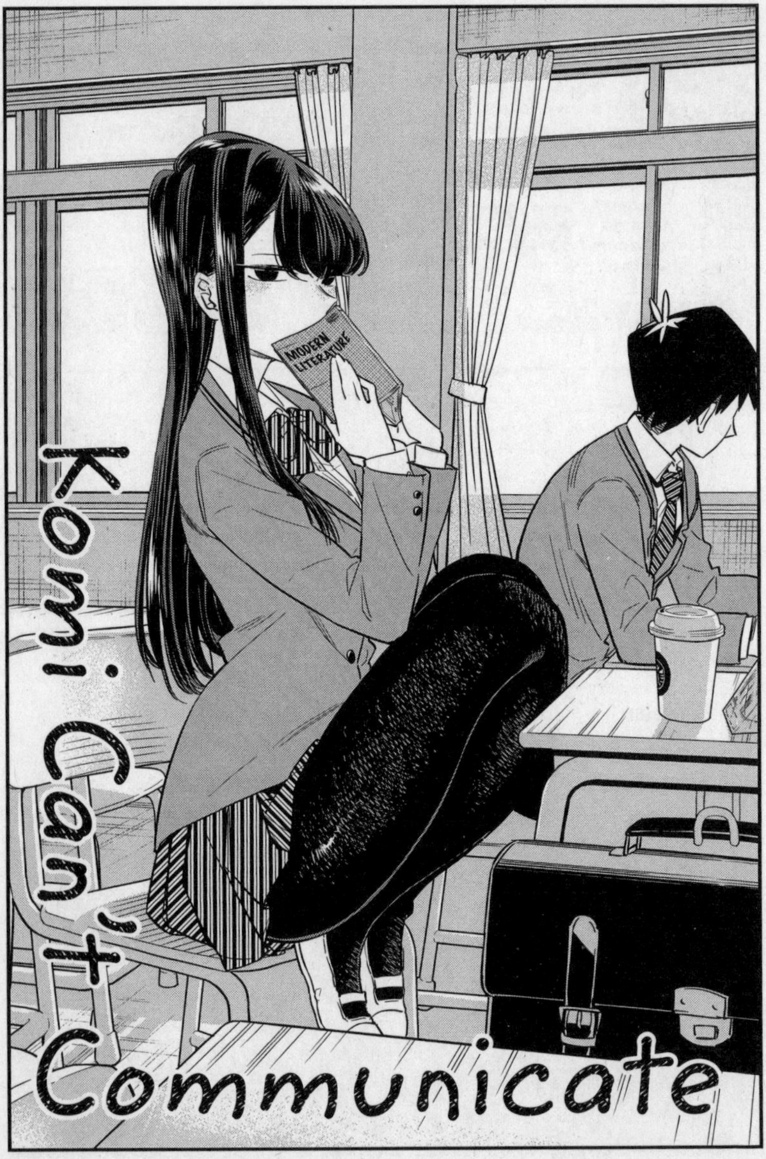
Komi Can't
Communicate
MODERN LITERATURE

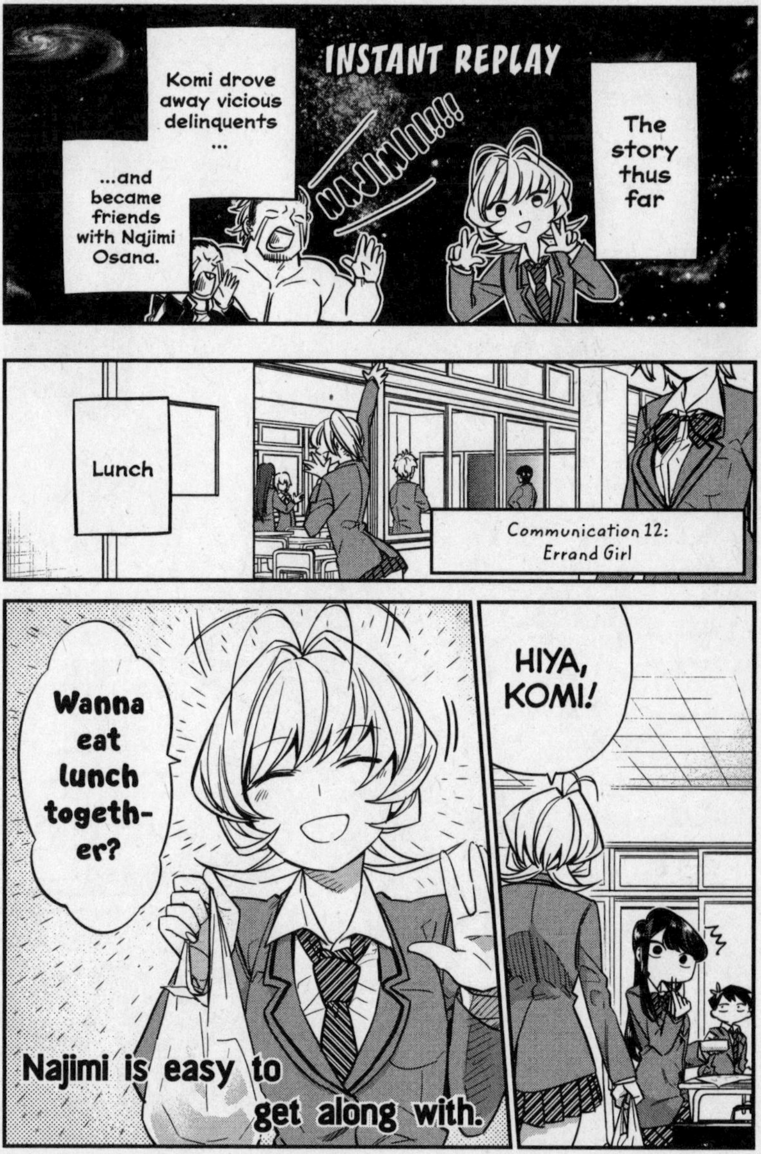
INSTANT REPLAY
The story thus far
NAJIMIIII!!!
Komi drove away vicious delinquents ...
...and became friends with Najimi Osana.
Communication 12: Errand Girl
Lunch
HIYA, KOMI!
Wanna eat lunch togeth-er?
Najimi is easy to get along with.

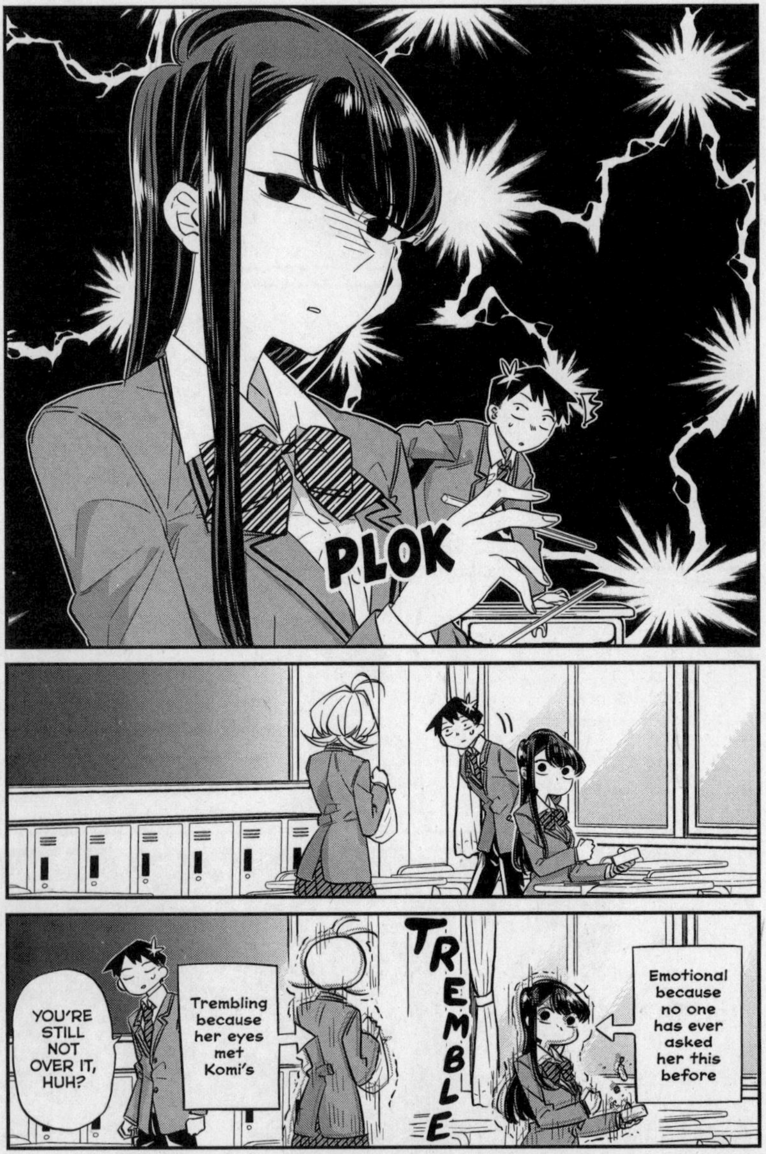
PLOK
Emotional because no one has ever asked her this before
TREMBLE
Trembling because her eyes met Komi's
YOU'RE STILL NOT OVER IT, HUH?

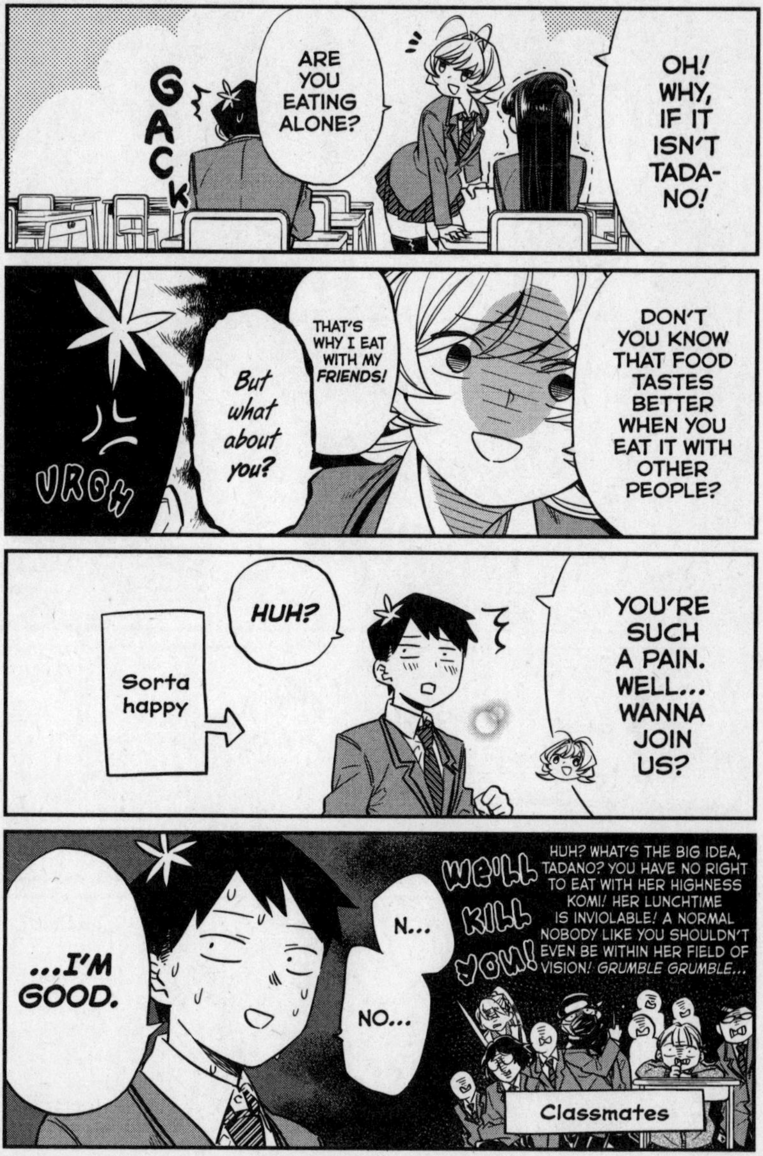
OH! WHY, IF IT ISN'T TADANO!
ARE YOU EATING ALONE?
GACK
DON'T YOU KNOW THAT FOOD TASTES BETTER WHEN YOU EAT IT WITH OTHER PEOPLE?
THAT'S WHY I EAT WITH MY FRIENDS!
But what about you?
URGH
YOU'RE SUCH A PAIN. WELL... WANNA JOIN US?
HUH?
Sorta happy
HUH? WHAT'S THE BIG IDEA, TADANO? YOU HAVE NO RIGHT TO EAT WITH HER HIGHNESS KOMI! HER LUNCHTIME IS INVIOLABLE! A NORMAL NOBODY LIKE YOU SHOULDN'T EVEN BE WITHIN HER FIELD OF VISION! GRUMBLE GRUMBLE...
WE'LL KILL YOU!
Classmates
N...
NO...
...I'M GOOD.

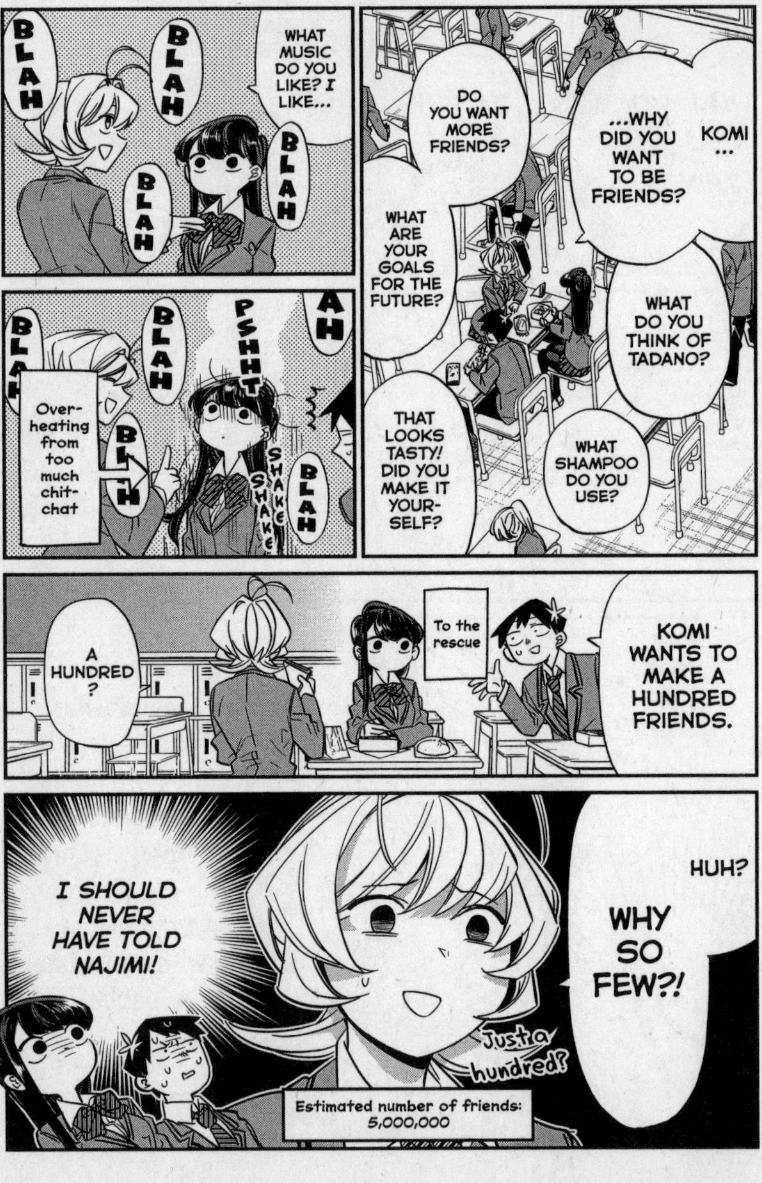
KOMI ...
...WHY DID YOU WANT TO BE FRIENDS?
DO YOU WANT MORE FRIENDS?
WHAT ARE YOUR GOALS FOR THE FUTURE?
WHAT DO YOU THINK OF TADANO?
WHAT SHAMPOO DO YOU USE?
THAT LOOKS TASTY! DID YOU MAKE IT YOURSELF?
WHAT MUSIC DO YOU LIKE? I LIKE...
BLAH
BLAH
BLAH
BLAH
AH
PSHHT
BLAH
BLAH
SHAKE SHAKE
BLAH
BLAH
Over-heating from too much chit-chat
KOMI WANTS TO MAKE A HUNDRED FRIENDS.
To the rescue
A HUNDRED ?
HUH?
WHY SO FEW?!
Just a hundred?
I SHOULD NEVER HAVE TOLD NAJIMI!
Estimated number of friends: 5,000,000

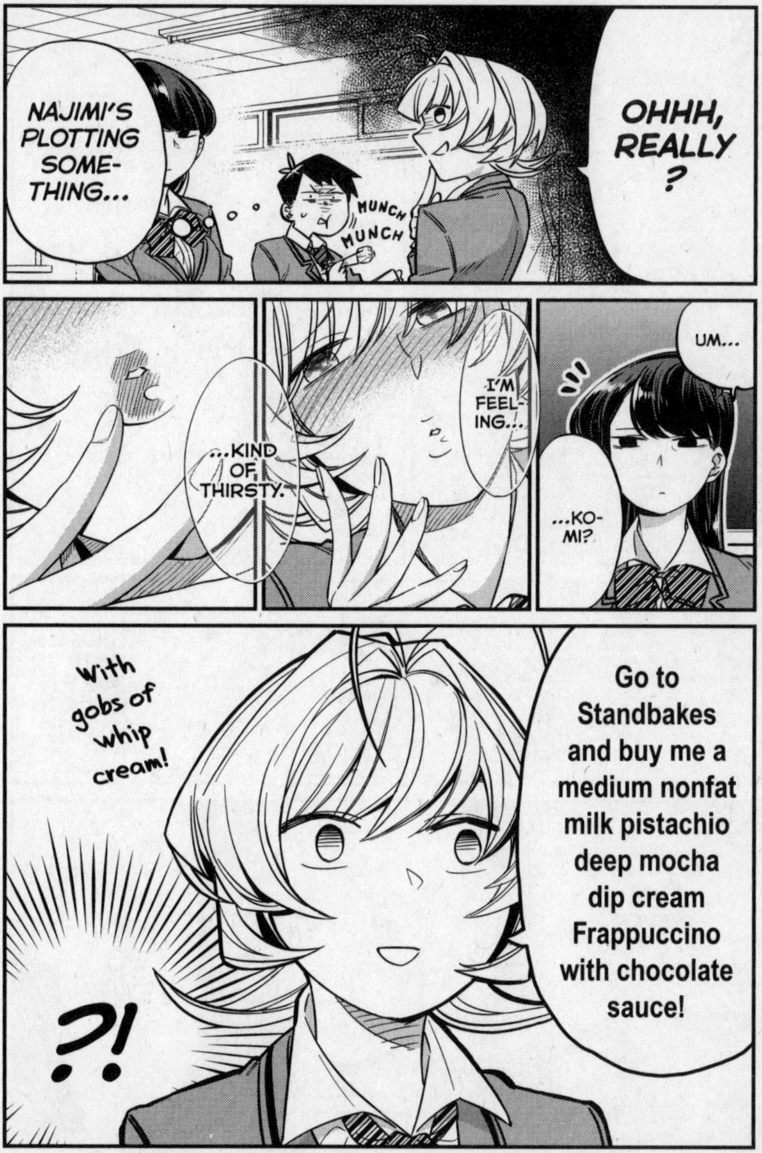
OHHH, REALLY?
NAJIMI'S PLOTTING SOME- THING...
MUNCH
MUNCH
UM...
...KO- MI?
I'M FEEL- ING...
...KIND OF THIRSTY.
Go to Standbakes and buy me a medium nonfat milk pistachio deep mocha dip cream Frappuccino with chocolate sauce!
With gobs of whip cream!
?!

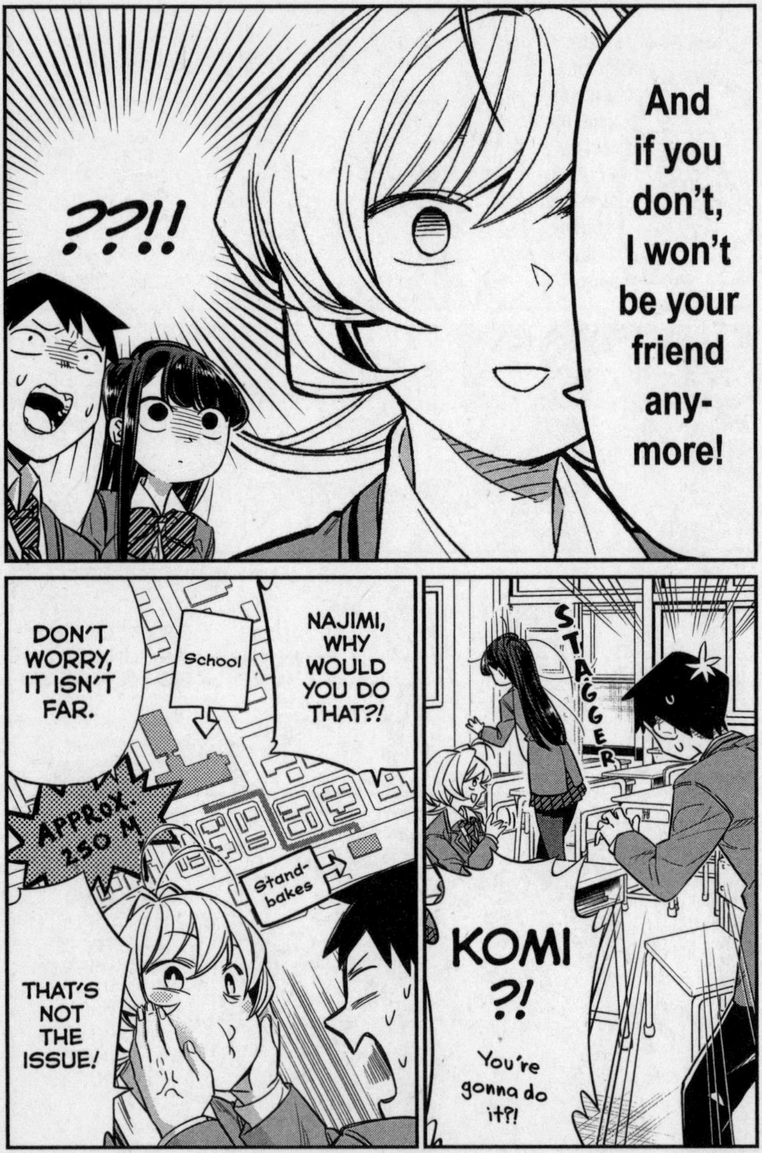
And if you don't, I won't be your friend any-more!
??!!
STAGGER
KOMI ?!
You're gonna do it?!
NAJIMI, WHY WOULD YOU DO THAT?!
DON'T WORRY, IT ISN'T FAR.
School
Stand-bakes
APPROX. 250 M
THAT'S NOT THE ISSUE!

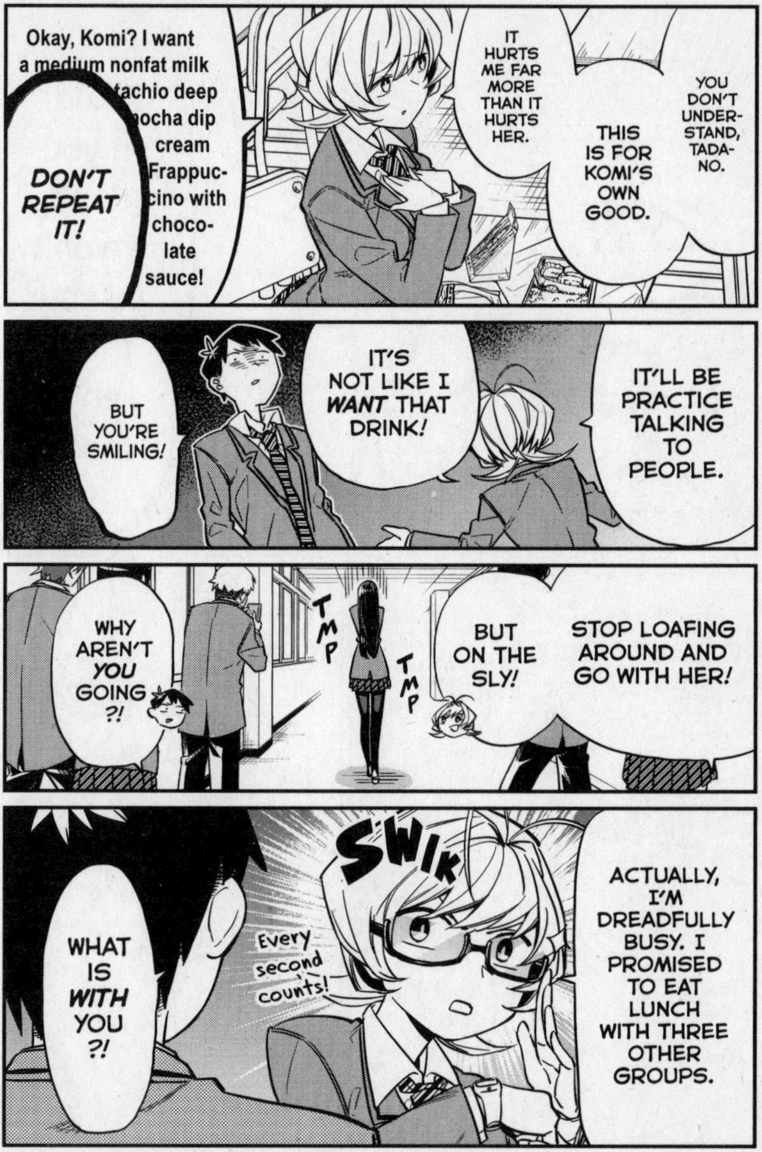
YOU DON'T UNDERSTAND, TADANO.
THIS IS FOR KOMI'S OWN GOOD.
IT HURTS ME FAR MORE THAN IT HURTS HER.
Okay, Komi? I want a medium nonfat milk ...tachio deep ...ocha dip cream Frappuccino with chocolate sauce!
DON'T REPEAT IT!
IT'LL BE PRACTICE TALKING TO PEOPLE.
IT'S NOT LIKE I WANT THAT DRINK!
BUT YOU'RE SMILING!
STOP LOAFING AROUND AND GO WITH HER!
BUT ON THE SLY!
TMP
TMP
WHY AREN'T YOU GOING?!
ACTUALLY, I'M DREADFULLY BUSY. I PROMISED TO EAT LUNCH WITH THREE OTHER GROUPS.
SWIK
Every second counts!
WHAT IS WITH YOU?!

Communication 12 — The End

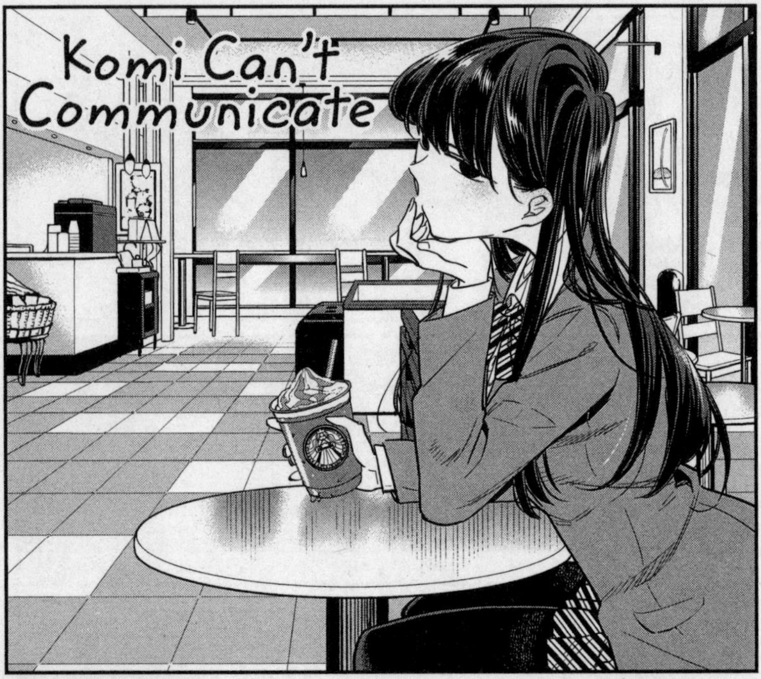

Komi Can't Communicate

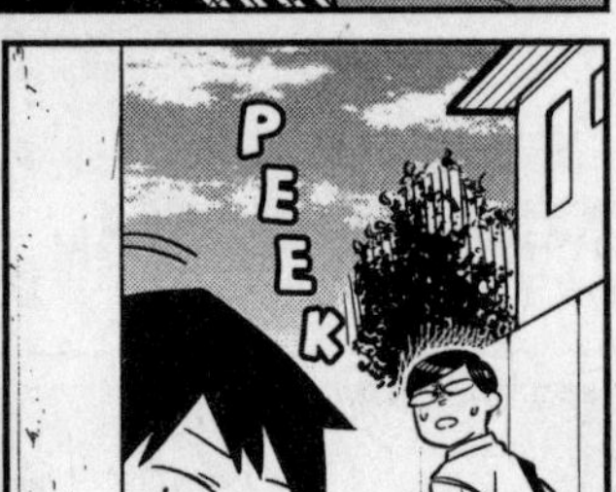

PEEK

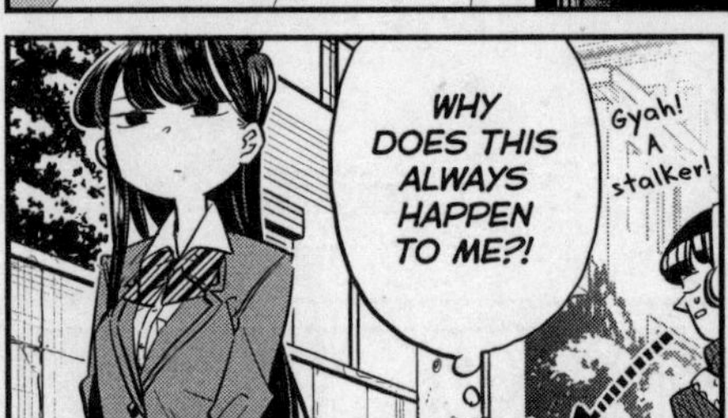

WHY DOES THIS ALWAYS HAPPEN TO ME?!
Gyah! A stalker!
A stalker?
Mama! A stalker!

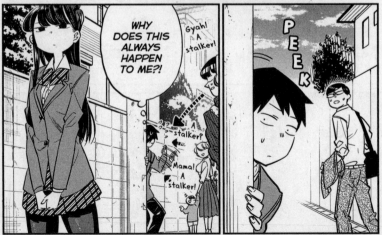

Communication 13: First Errand

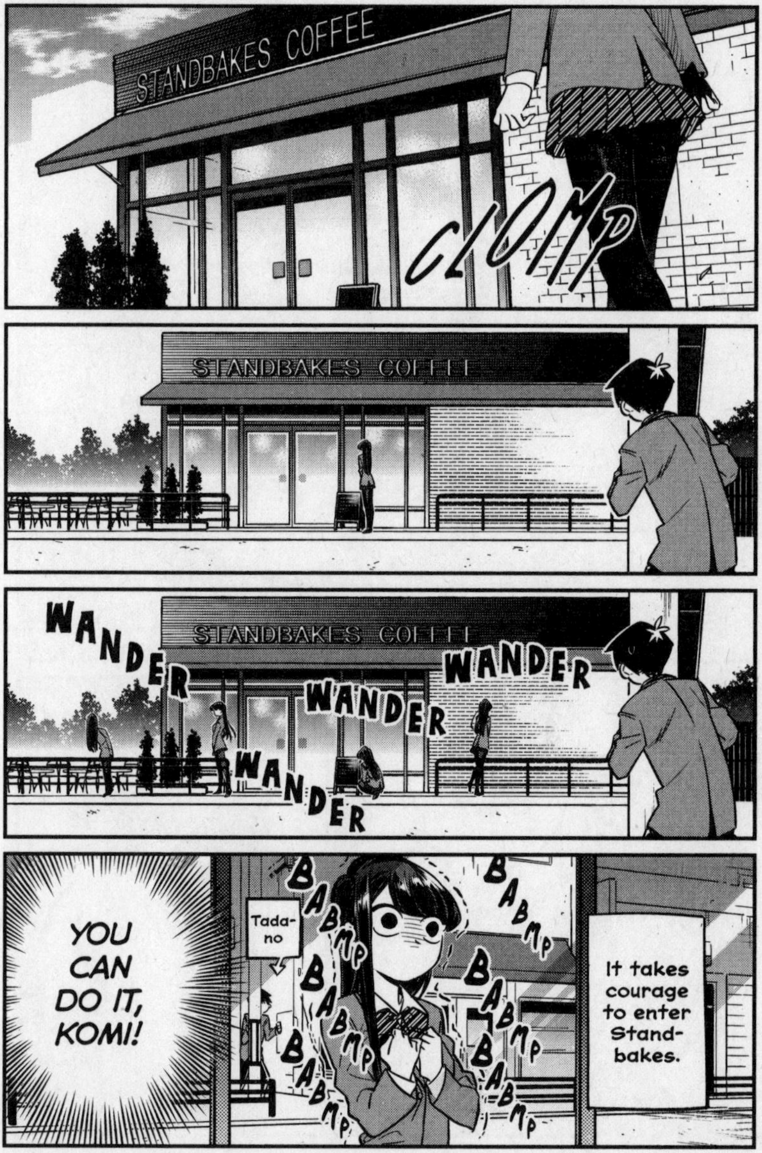
STANDBAKES COFFEE
CLOMP
STANDBAKES COFFEE
STANDBAKES COFFEE
WANDER
WANDER
WANDER
WANDER
It takes courage to enter Standbakes.
BABMP
BABMP
BABMP
BABMP
BABMP
BABMP
BABMP
BABMP
Tadano
YOU CAN DO IT, KOMI!

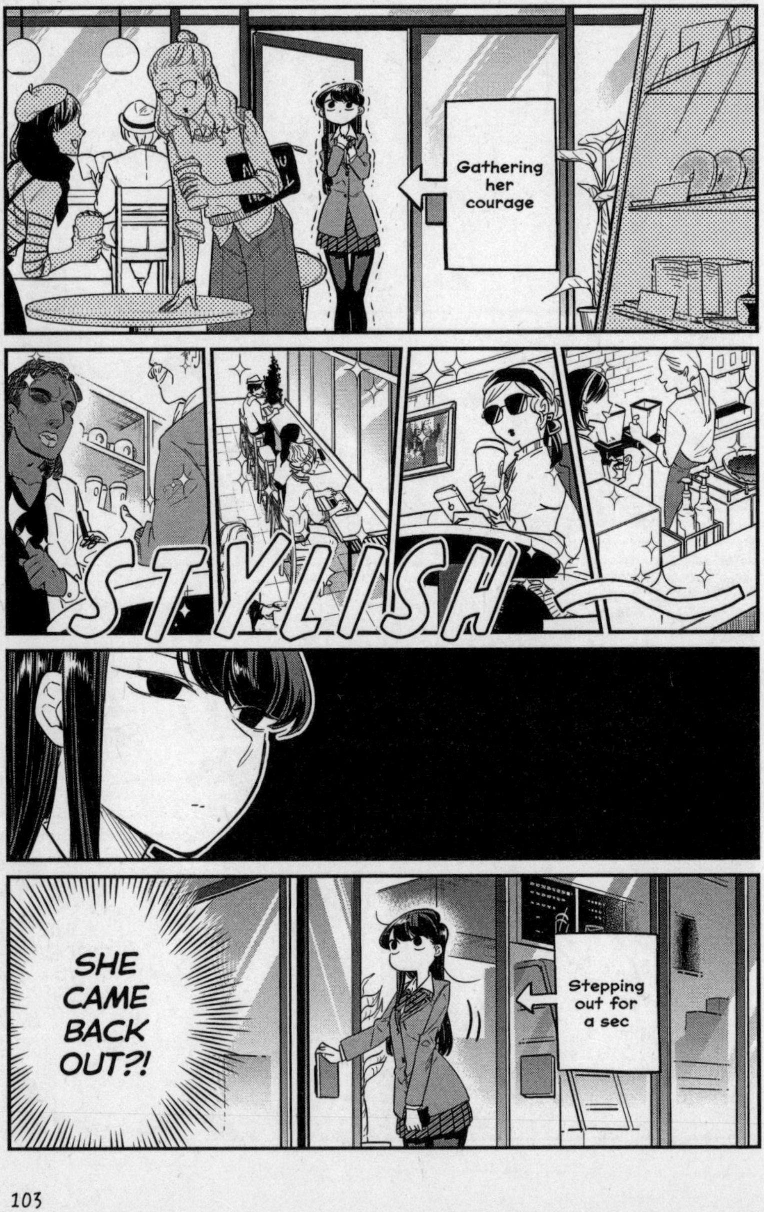
Gathering her courage
STYLISH~
Stepping out for a sec
SHE CAME BACK OUT?!

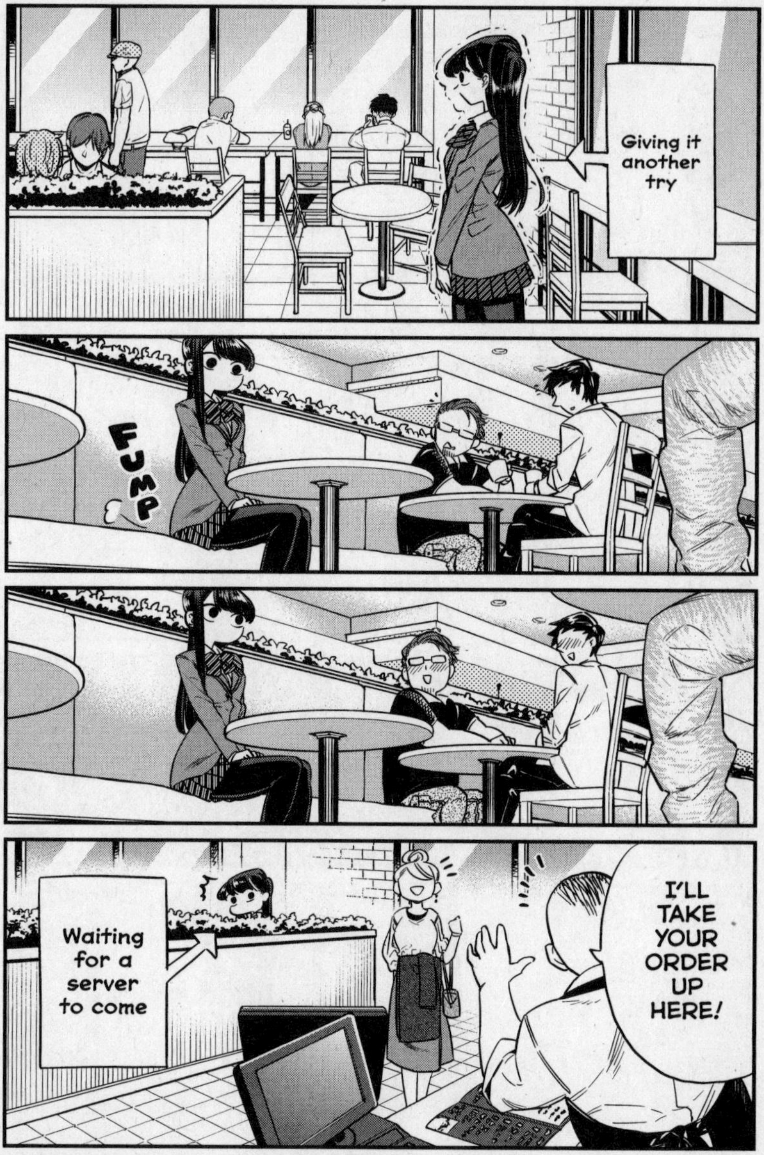
Giving it another try
FUMP
I'LL TAKE YOUR ORDER UP HERE!
Waiting for a server to come

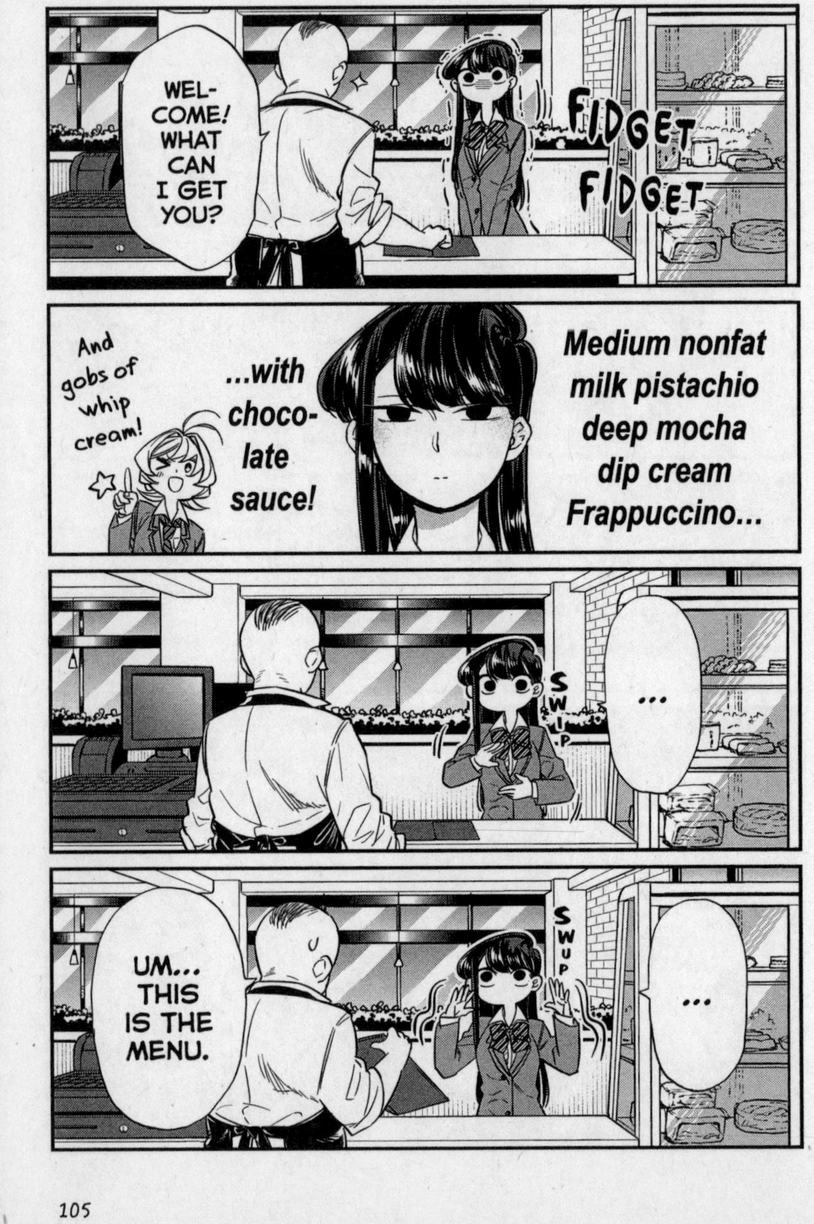
FIDGET FIDGET
WEL-COME! WHAT CAN I GET YOU?
Medium nonfat milk pistachio deep mocha dip cream Frappuccino...
...with choco-late sauce!
And gobs of whip cream!
...
SWIP
...
SWUP
UM... THIS IS THE MENU.

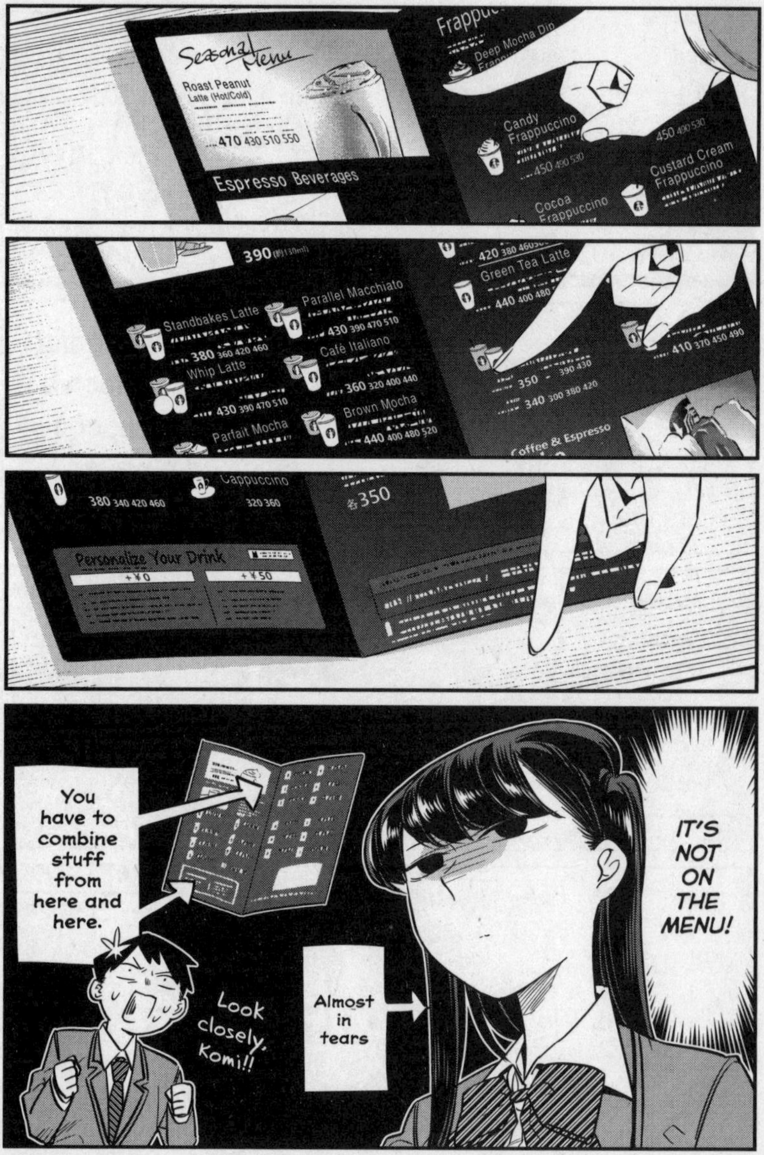
Seasonal Menu
Roast Peanut
Latte (Hot/Cold)
470 430 510 550
Espresso Beverages
Frappu
Deep Mocha Dip
Candy
Frappuccino
450 490 530
450 490 530
Custard Cream
Frappuccino
Cocoa
Frappuccino
390
Standbakes Latte
380 360 420 460
Parallel Macchiato
430 390 470 510
Whip Latte
430 390 470 510
Café Italiano
360 320 400 440
Parfait Mocha
Brown Mocha
440 400 480 520
420 380 460
Green Tea Latte
440 400 480
410 370 450 490
350 390 430
340 300 380 420
Coffee & Espresso
380 340 420 460
Cappuccino
320 360
各350
Personalize Your Drink
+¥0
+¥50
You have to combine stuff from here and here.
Look closely, Komi!!
Almost in tears
IT'S NOT ON THE MENU!

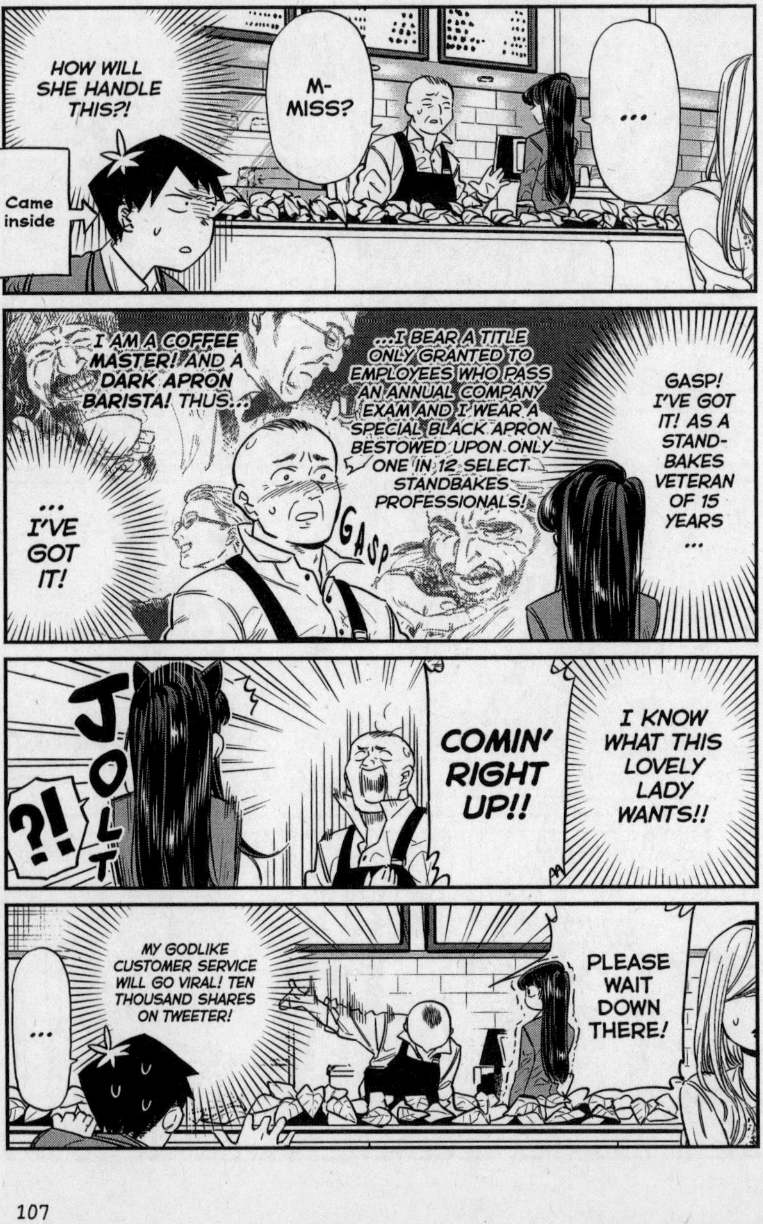
...
M-MISS?
HOW WILL SHE HANDLE THIS?!
Came inside
GASP! I'VE GOT IT! AS A STAND-BAKES VETERAN OF 15 YEARS ...
...I BEAR A TITLE ONLY GRANTED TO EMPLOYEES WHO PASS AN ANNUAL COMPANY EXAM AND I WEAR A SPECIAL BLACK APRON BESTOWED UPON ONLY ONE IN 12 SELECT STANDBAKES PROFESSIONALS!
I AM A COFFEE MASTER! AND A DARK APRON BARISTA! THUS...
GASP
... I'VE GOT IT!
I KNOW WHAT THIS LOVELY LADY WANTS!!
COMIN' RIGHT UP!!
JOLT
?!
PLEASE WAIT DOWN THERE!
MY GODLIKE CUSTOMER SERVICE WILL GO VIRAL! TEN THOUSAND SHARES ON TWEETER!
...

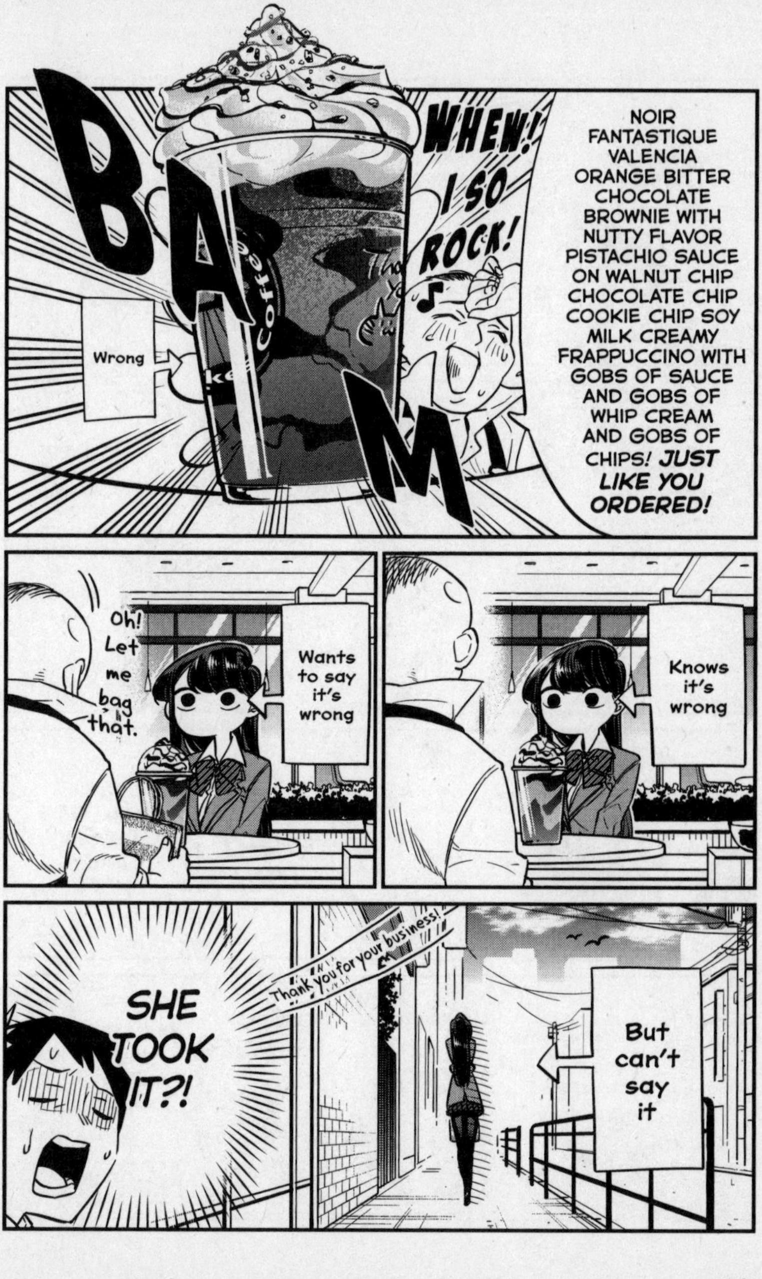
NOIR FANTASTIQUE VALENCIA ORANGE BITTER CHOCOLATE BROWNIE WITH NUTTY FLAVOR PISTACHIO SAUCE ON WALNUT CHIP CHOCOLATE CHIP COOKIE CHIP SOY MILK CREAMY FRAPPUCCINO WITH GOBS OF SAUCE AND GOBS OF WHIP CREAM AND GOBS OF CHIPS! JUST LIKE YOU ORDERED!
WHEW! I SO ROCK!
BAM
Wrong
Knows it's wrong
Oh! Let me bag that.
Wants to say it's wrong
But can't say it
Thank you for your business!
SHE TOOK IT?!

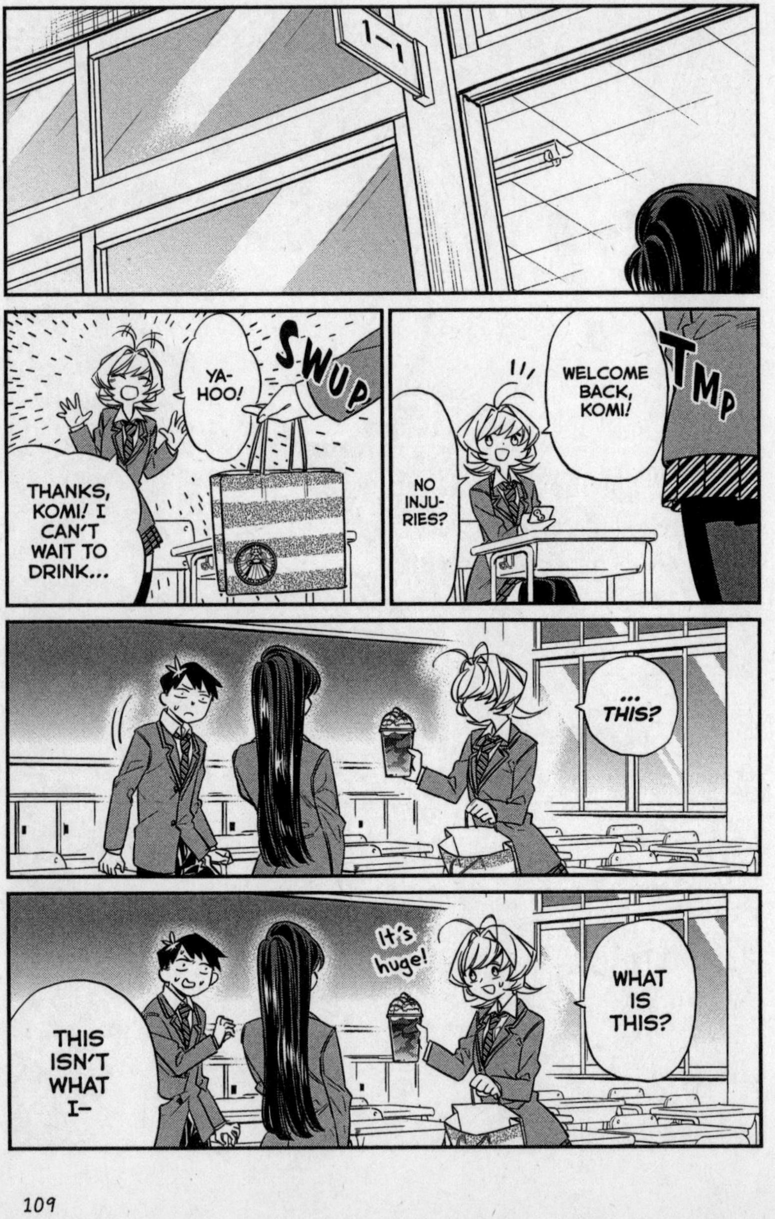
1-1
TMP
WELCOME BACK, KOMI!
NO INJURIES?
SWUP
YA-HOO!
THANKS, KOMI! I CAN'T WAIT TO DRINK...
... THIS?
WHAT IS THIS?
It's huge!
THIS ISN'T WHAT I–

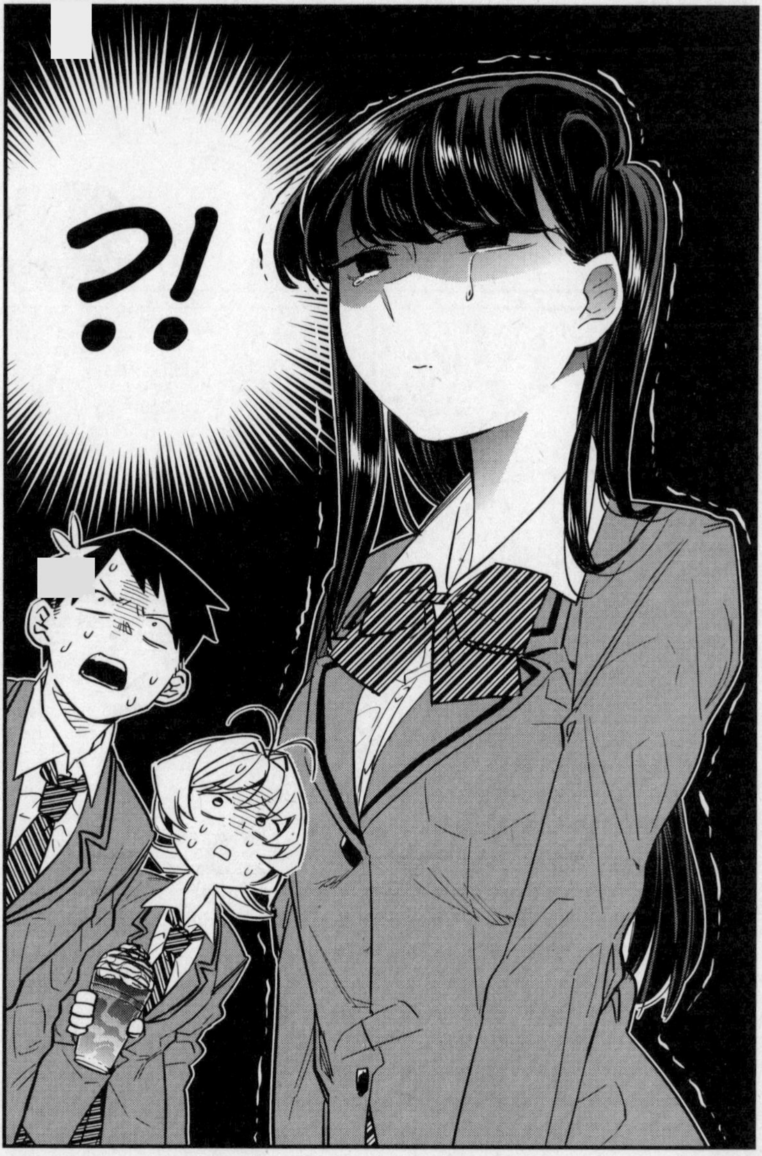
?!

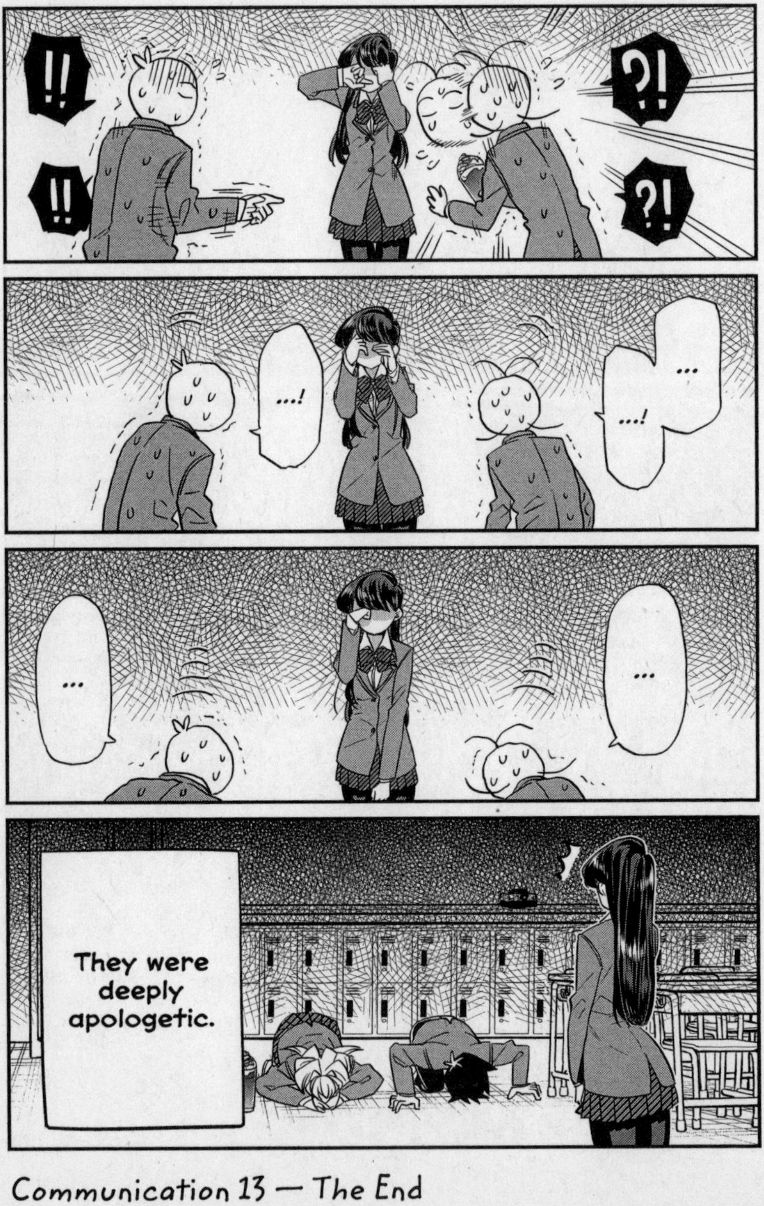
?!
?!
!!
!!
...
...!
...!
...
...
They were deeply apologetic.

Communication 13 — The End

Bonus

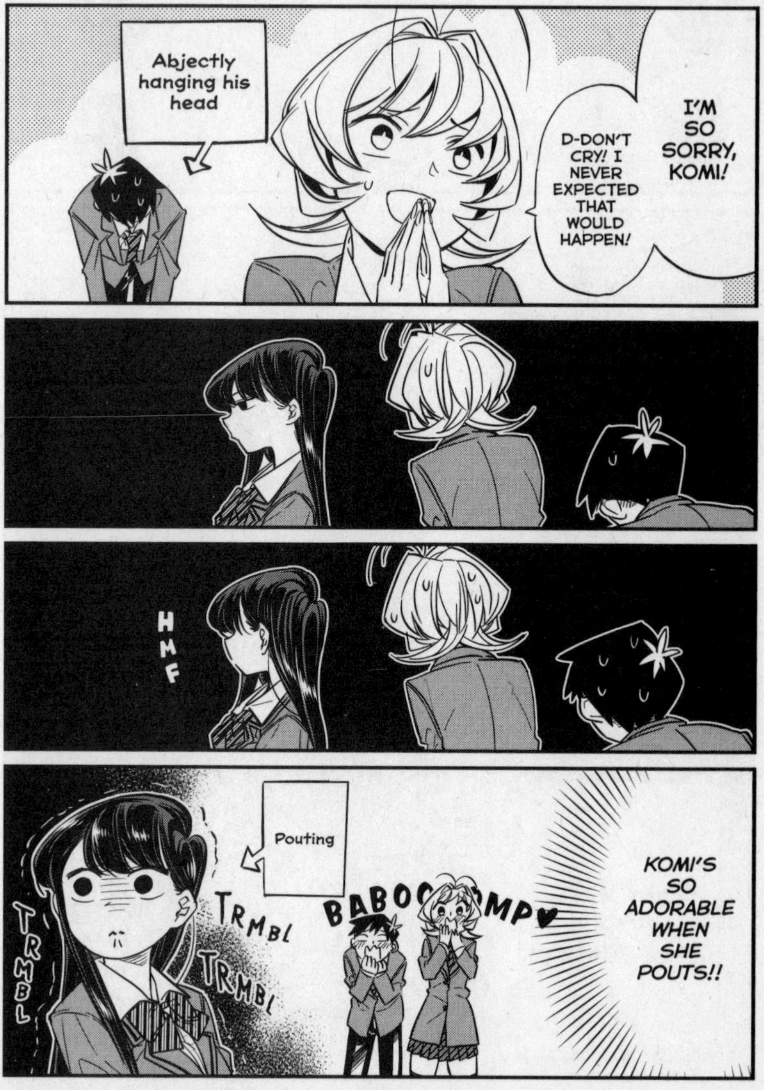
I'M SO SORRY, KOMI!
D-DON'T CRY! I NEVER EXPECTED THAT WOULD HAPPEN!
Abjectly hanging his head
HMF
KOMI'S SO ADORABLE WHEN SHE POUTS!!
TRMBL
Pouting
TRMBL
TRMBL

Bonus — The End

Komi Can't Communicate

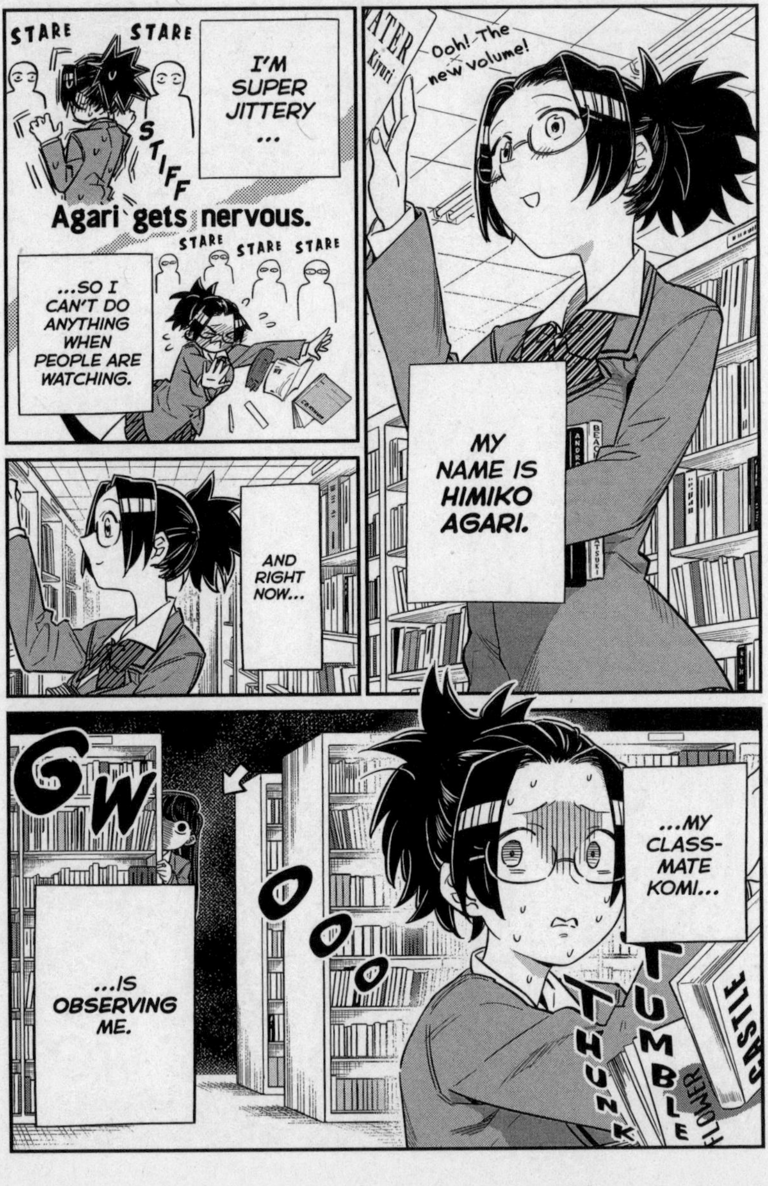

Ooh! The new volume!
MY NAME IS HIMIKO AGARI.
STARE STARE
I'M SUPER JITTERY...
STIFF
Agari gets nervous.
STARE STARE STARE
...SO I CAN'T DO ANYTHING WHEN PEOPLE ARE WATCHING.
AND RIGHT NOW...
...MY CLASSMATE KOMI...
TUMBLE
THUNK
CASTLE
FLOWER
OOO
GW
...IS OBSERVING ME.

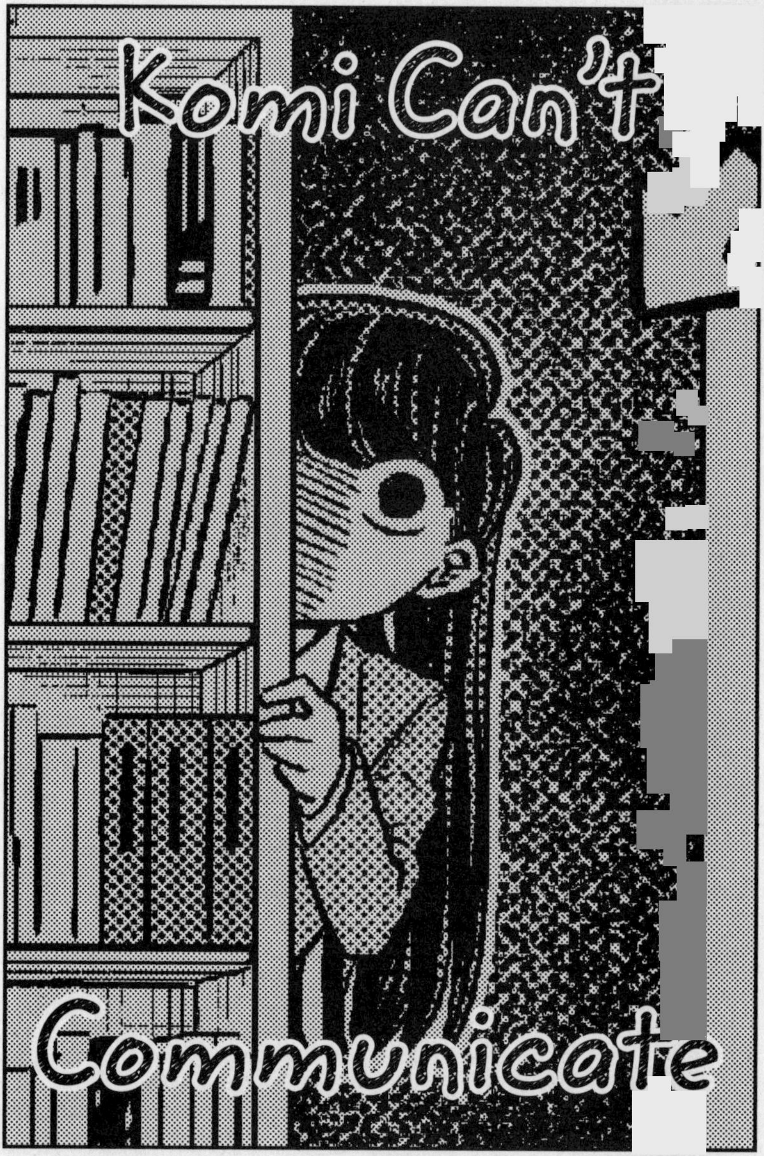
Komi Can't
Communicate

Communication 14-A: Nervous

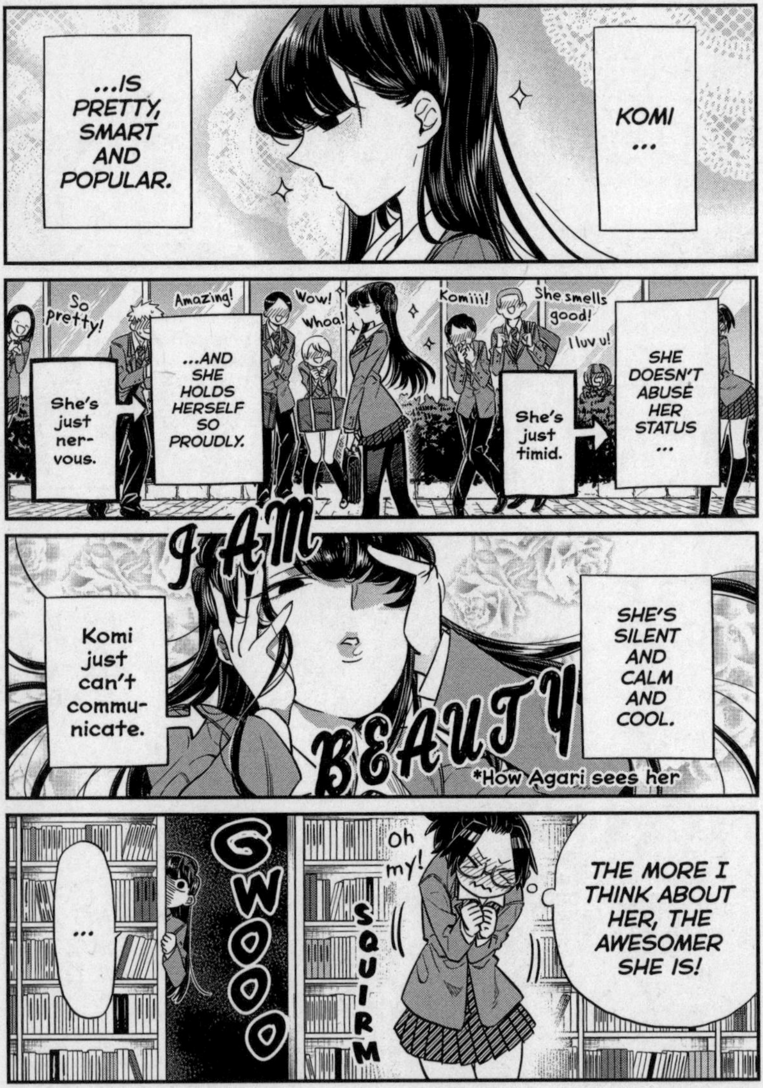
KOMI...
...IS PRETTY, SMART AND POPULAR.
SHE DOESN'T ABUSE HER STATUS...
She's just timid.
She smells good!
Iluv u!
Komiii!
Wow!
Whoa!
...AND SHE HOLDS HERSELF SO PROUDLY.
Amazing!
She's just nervous.
So pretty!
SHE'S SILENT AND CALM AND COOL.
I AM BEAUTY
*How Agari sees her
Komi just can't communicate.
THE MORE I THINK ABOUT HER, THE AWESOMER SHE IS!
Oh my!
SQUIRM
GWOOO
...

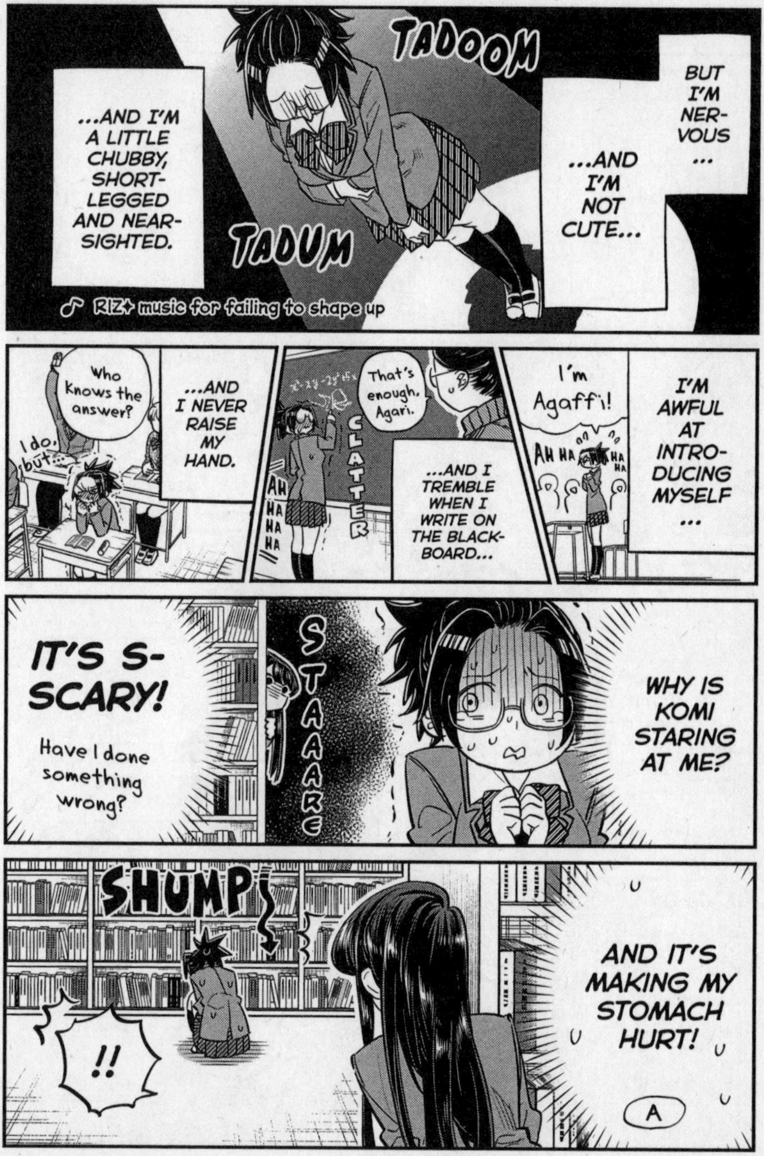
BUT I'M NERVOUS...
...AND I'M NOT CUTE...
TADOOM
...AND I'M A LITTLE CHUBBY, SHORT-LEGGED AND NEAR-SIGHTED.
TADUM
♪ RIZ♪ music for failing to shape up
I'M AWFUL AT INTRODUCING MYSELF...
I'm Agaffi!
AH HA HA HA
That's enough, Agari.
CLATTER
...AND I TREMBLE WHEN I WRITE ON THE BLACKBOARD...
AH HA HA HA HA
...AND I NEVER RAISE MY HAND.
Who knows the answer?
I do, but...
WHY IS KOMI STARING AT ME?
STAAAARE
IT'S S-SCARY!
Have I done something wrong?
AND IT'S MAKING MY STOMACH HURT!
SHUMP
!!
A

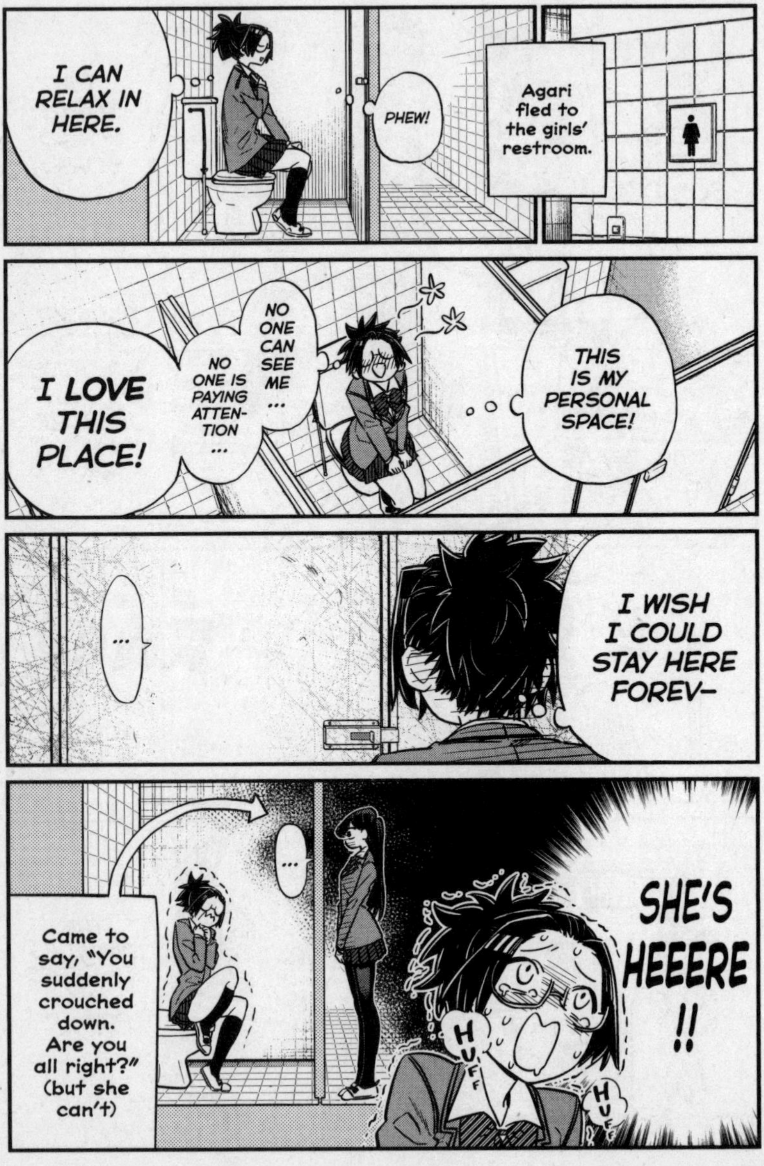
Agari fled to the girls' restroom.
PHEW!
I CAN RELAX IN HERE.
THIS IS MY PERSONAL SPACE!
NO ONE CAN SEE ME ...
NO ONE IS PAYING ATTENTION ...
I LOVE THIS PLACE!
I WISH I COULD STAY HERE FOREV–
...
SHE'S HEEERE !!
HUFF
HUFF
...
Came to say, "You suddenly crouched down. Are you all right?" (but she can't)

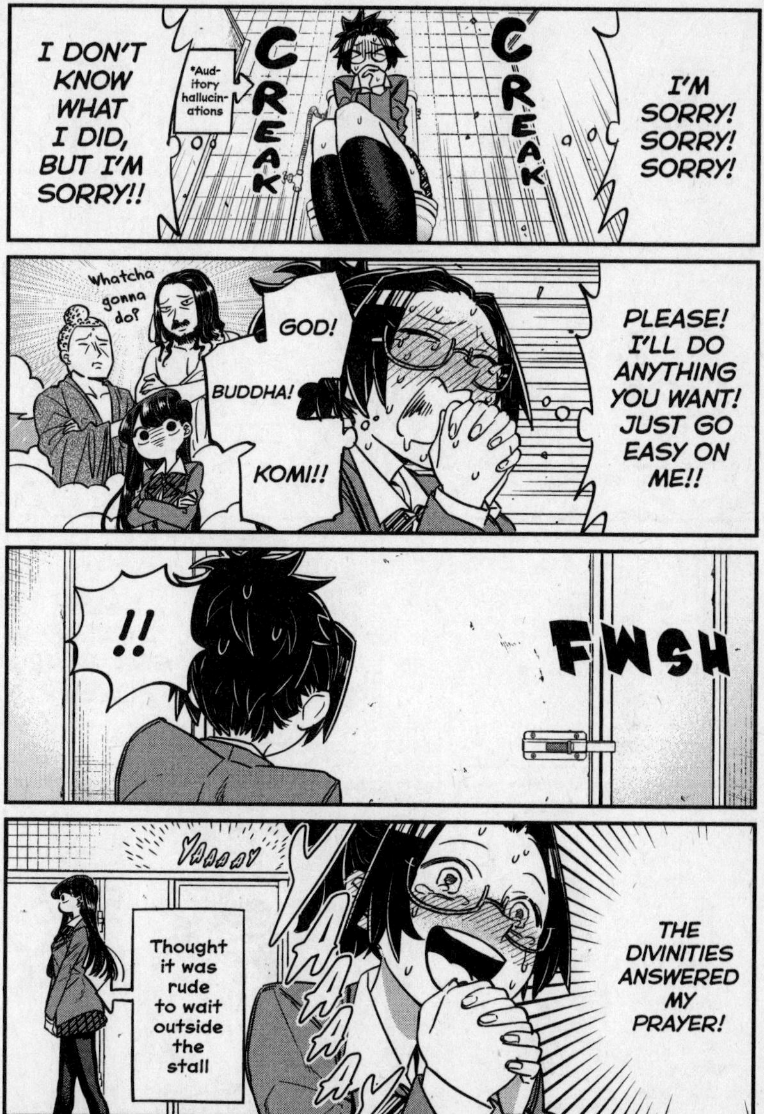
I'M SORRY! SORRY! SORRY!
CREAK
CREAK
*Auditory hallucinations
I DON'T KNOW WHAT I DID, BUT I'M SORRY!!
PLEASE! I'LL DO ANYTHING YOU WANT! JUST GO EASY ON ME!!
GOD!
BUDDHA!
KOMI!!
Whatcha gonna do?
FWSH
!!
THE DIVINITIES ANSWERED MY PRAYER!
YAAAAY
Thought it was rude to wait outside the stall

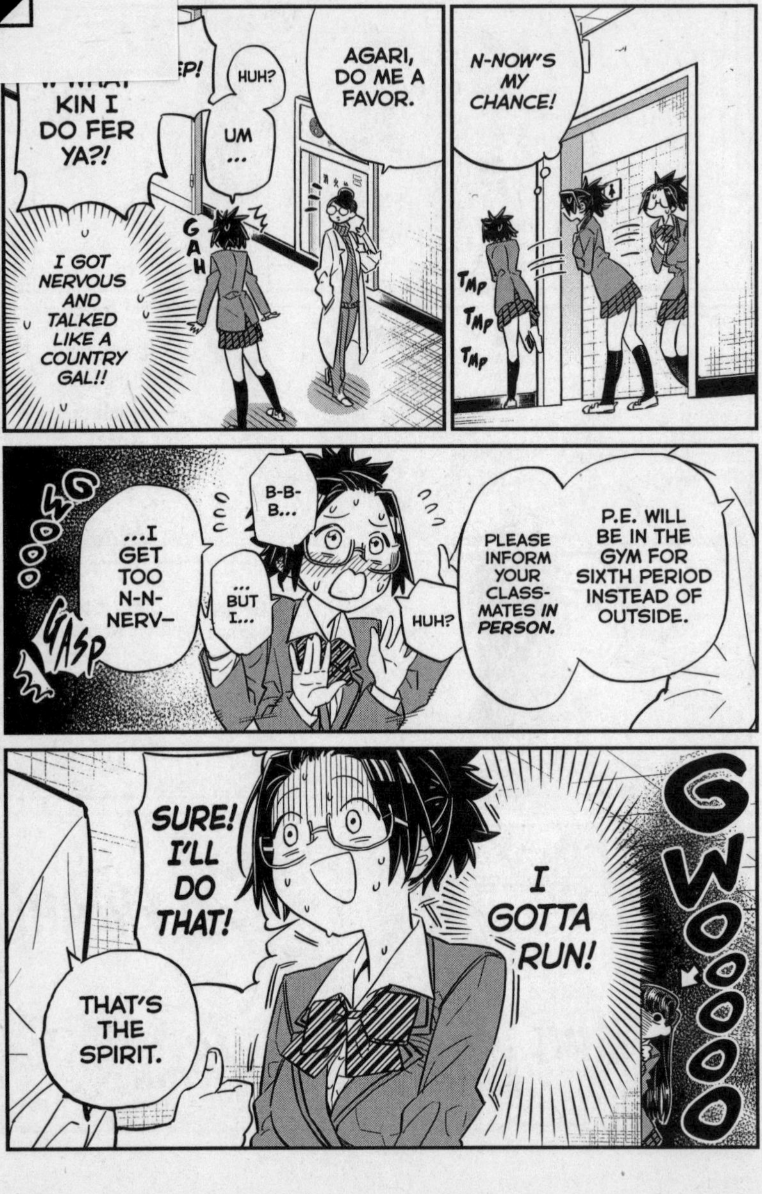
N-NOW'S MY CHANCE!
TMP
TMP
TMP
AGARI, DO ME A FAVOR.
HUH?
UM ...
EP!
KIN I DO FER YA?!
GAH
I GOT NERVOUS AND TALKED LIKE A COUNTRY GAL!!
P.E. WILL BE IN THE GYM FOR SIXTH PERIOD INSTEAD OF OUTSIDE.
PLEASE INFORM YOUR CLASSMATES IN PERSON.
HUH?
B-B-B...
... BUT I...
...I GET TOO N-N-NERV—
GWOOOO
GASP
GWOOOOO
I GOTTA RUN!
SURE! I'LL DO THAT!
THAT'S THE SPIRIT.

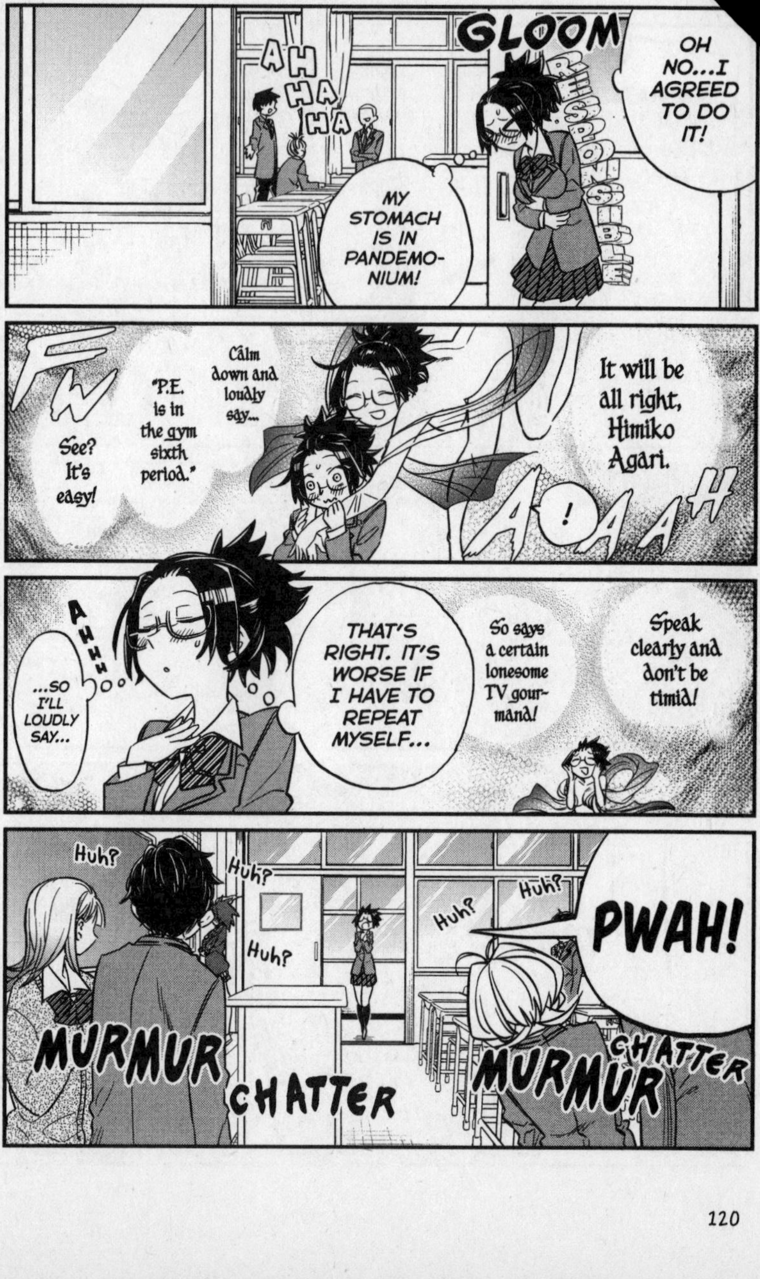
OH NO...I AGREED TO DO IT!
GLOOM
RESPONSIBLE
MY STOMACH IS IN PANDEMONIUM!
AH HA HA HA
It will be all right, Himiko Agari.
AAAAH
!
Calm down and loudly say...
"P.E. is in the gym sixth period."
See? It's easy!
FW
Speak clearly and don't be timid!
So says a certain lonesome TV gour-mand!
THAT'S RIGHT. IT'S WORSE IF I HAVE TO REPEAT MYSELF...
AHHH
...SO I'LL LOUDLY SAY...
PWAH!
Huh?
Huh?
Huh?
Huh?
Huh?
CHATTER
MURMUR
CHATTER
MURMUR

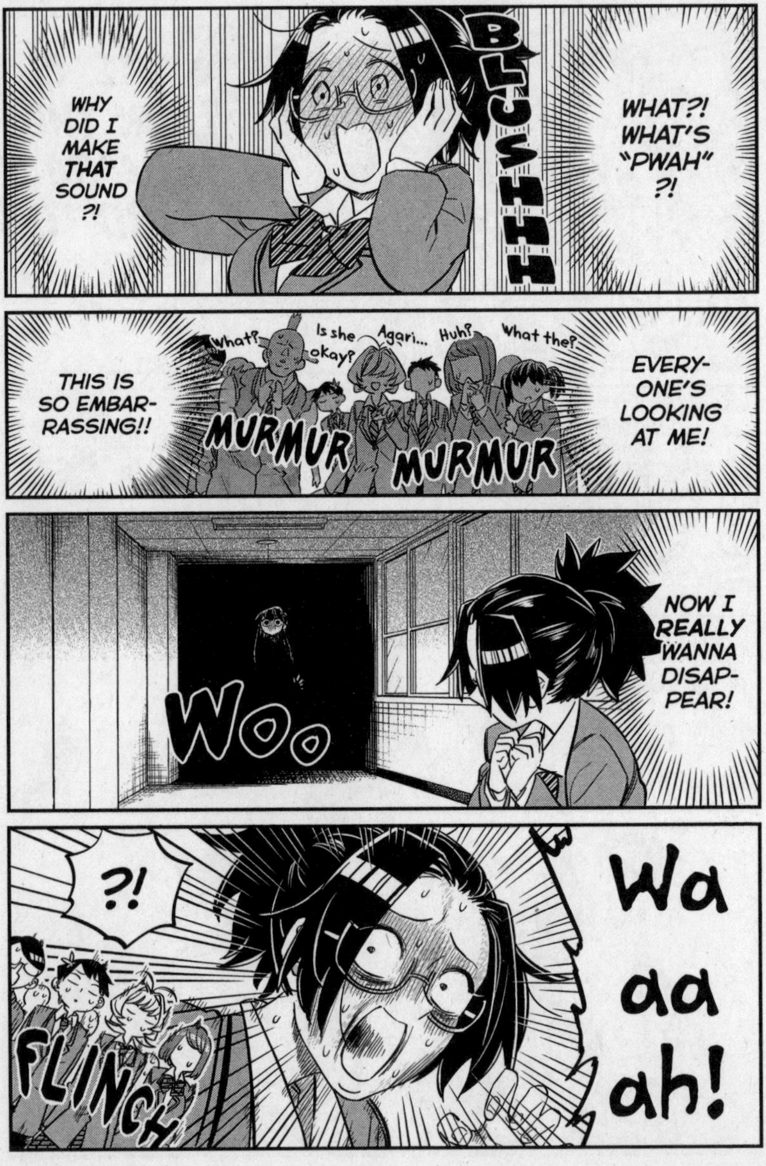

WHAT?! WHAT'S "PWAH" ?!
BLUSHHH
WHY DID I MAKE THAT SOUND ?!
EVERY-ONE'S LOOKING AT ME!
What the?
Huh?
Agari...
Is she okay?
What?
MURMUR MURMUR
THIS IS SO EMBAR-RASSING!!
NOW I REALLY WANNA DISAP-PEAR!
WOO
Wa aa ah!
?!
FLINCH

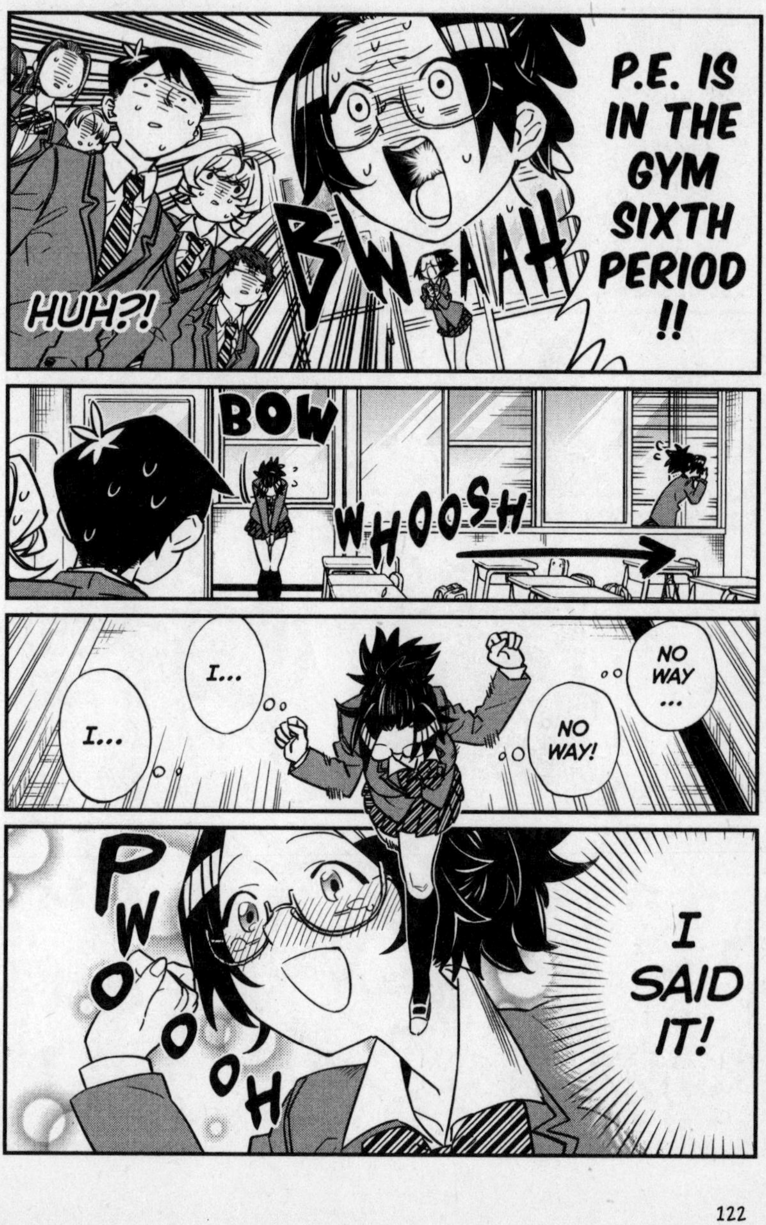
P.E. IS IN THE GYM SIXTH PERIOD!!
BWAAH
HUH?!
BOW
WHOOSH
NO WAY...
NO WAY!
I...
I...
I SAID IT!
PWOOOOH

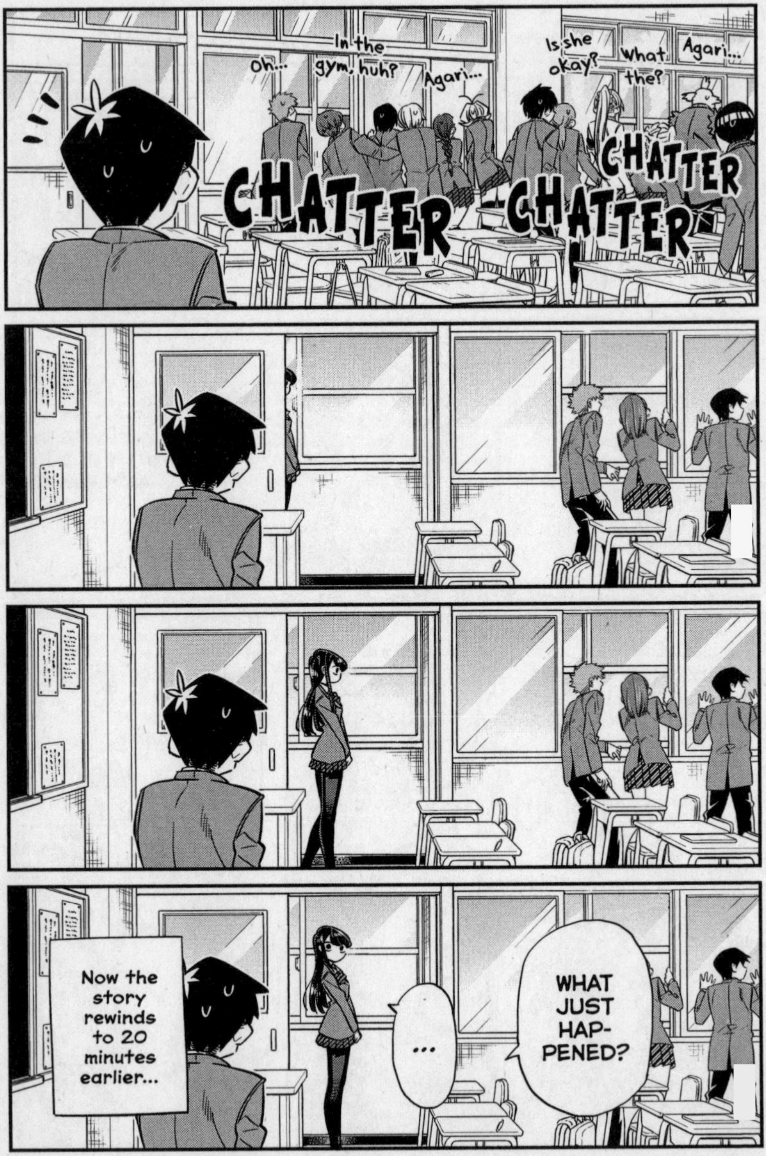
Agari...
What the?
Is she okay?
Agari...
In the gym, huh?
Oh...
CHATTER
CHATTER
CHATTER
WHAT JUST HAP-PENED?
...
Now the story rewinds to 20 minutes earlier...

Communication 14-A — The End

Communication 14-B: Nervous

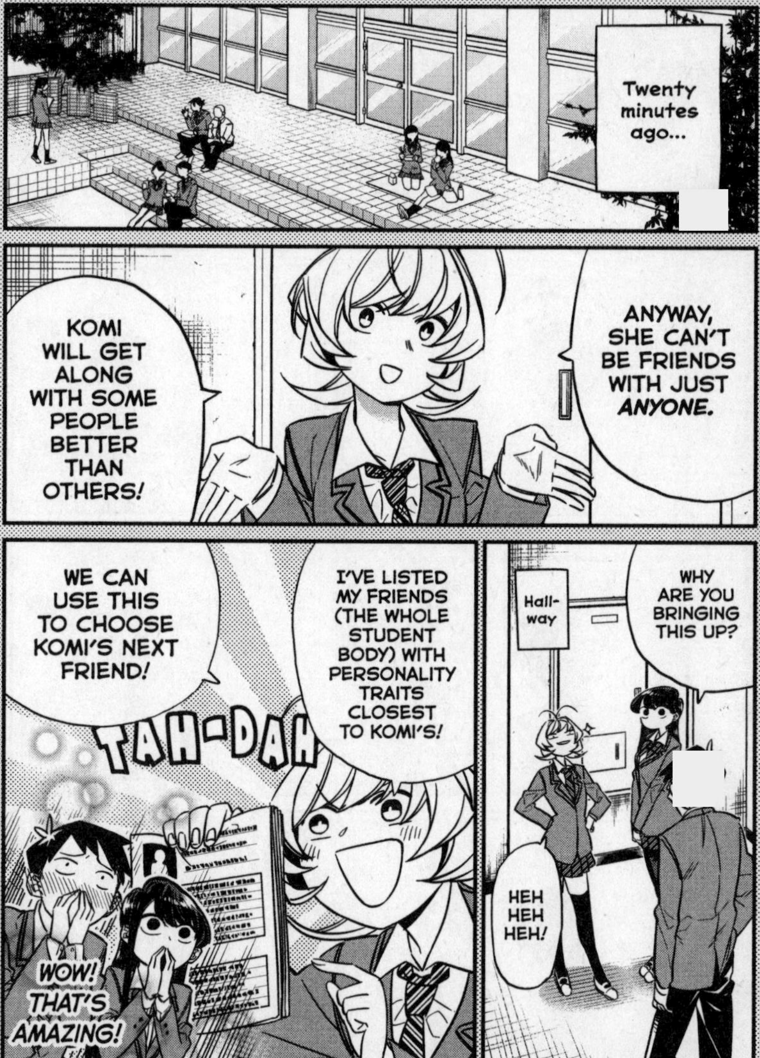
Twenty minutes ago...
ANYWAY, SHE CAN'T BE FRIENDS WITH JUST ANYONE.
KOMI WILL GET ALONG WITH SOME PEOPLE BETTER THAN OTHERS!
Hall-way
WHY ARE YOU BRINGING THIS UP?
HEH HEH HEH!
I'VE LISTED MY FRIENDS (THE WHOLE STUDENT BODY) WITH PERSONALITY TRAITS CLOSEST TO KOMI'S!
WE CAN USE THIS TO CHOOSE KOMI'S NEXT FRIEND!
TAH-DAH
WOW! THAT'S AMAZING!

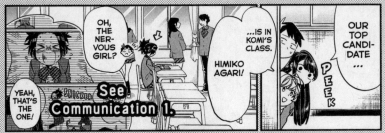

OUR TOP CANDIDATE ...
PEEK
...IS IN KOMI'S CLASS.
HIMIKO AGARI!
OH, THE NERVOUS GIRL?
YEAH, THAT'S THE ONE!
SNICKER
See Communication 1.
Is someone looking at me?
JITTER
JITTER
SHE'S GREAT, BUT SHE SUCKS AT INTERPERSONAL RELATIONS.
TO BE PRECISE ...
...IF A SINGLE PERSON EVEN LOOKS AT HER, SHE BLUSHES, GOES INTO CONVULSIONS, CAN'T BREATHE, STAMMERS, SWEATS BULLETS, GETS STOMACH CRAMPS, ETC., ETC.
TH-THAT SOUNDS SEVERE!
PHEW
Feels an intense affinity
K...
KOMI...!
HEIGHT: 5'6". SIGN: PISCES. BLOOD TYPE: B. FAVORITE FOODS: TOMATOES, AVOCADOS, WHITE RICE. MEASUREMENTS: 34-27...

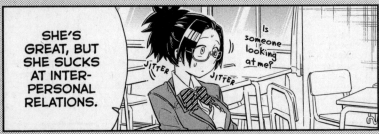

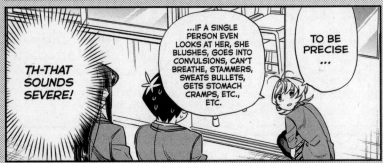

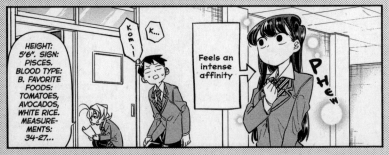

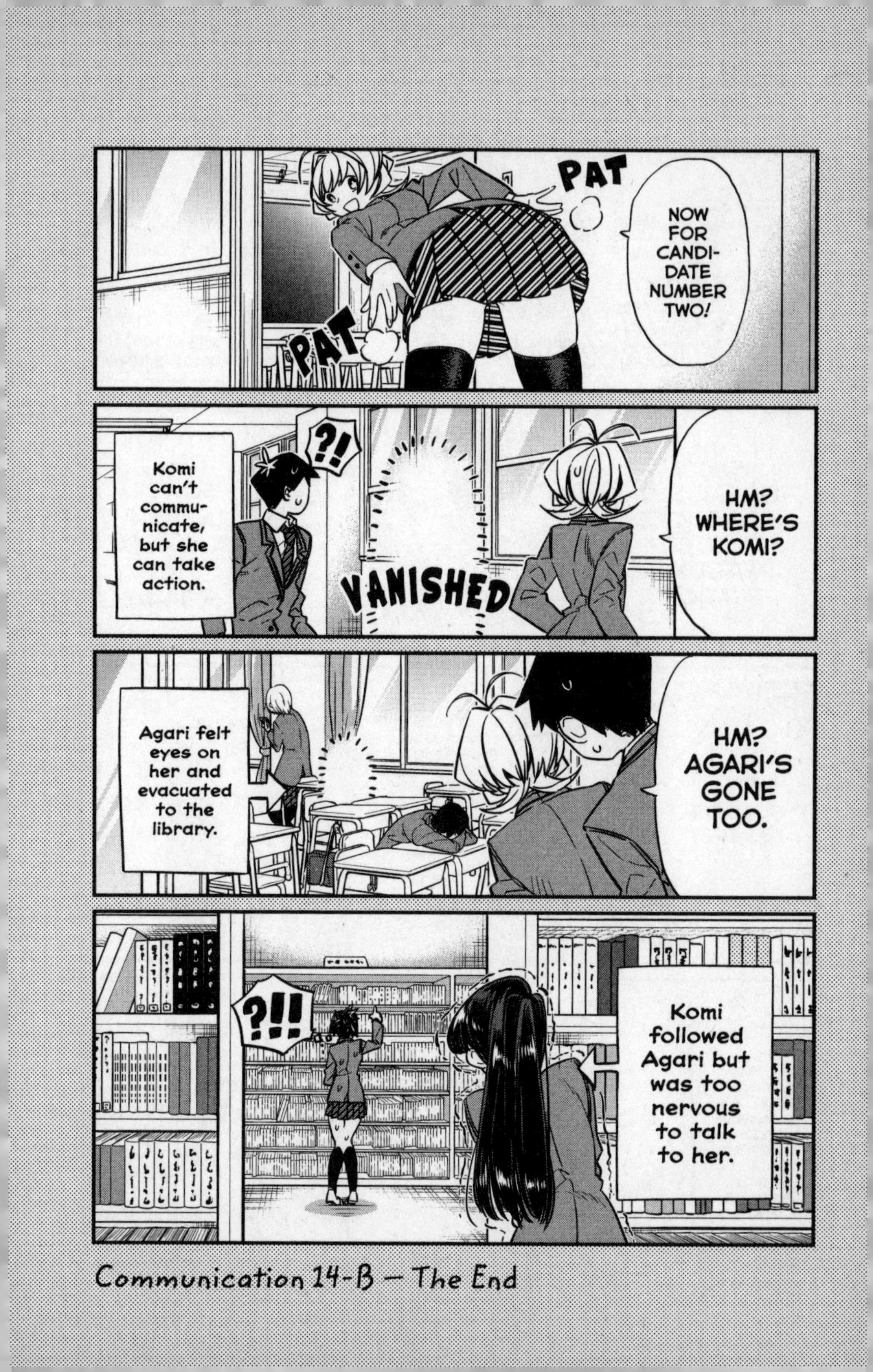
PAT
NOW FOR CANDIDATE NUMBER TWO!
PAT
HM? WHERE'S KOMI?
?!
VANISHED
Komi can't communicate, but she can take action.
HM? AGARI'S GONE TOO.
Agari felt eyes on her and evacuated to the library.
Komi followed Agari but was too nervous to talk to her.
?!!

Communication 14-B — The End

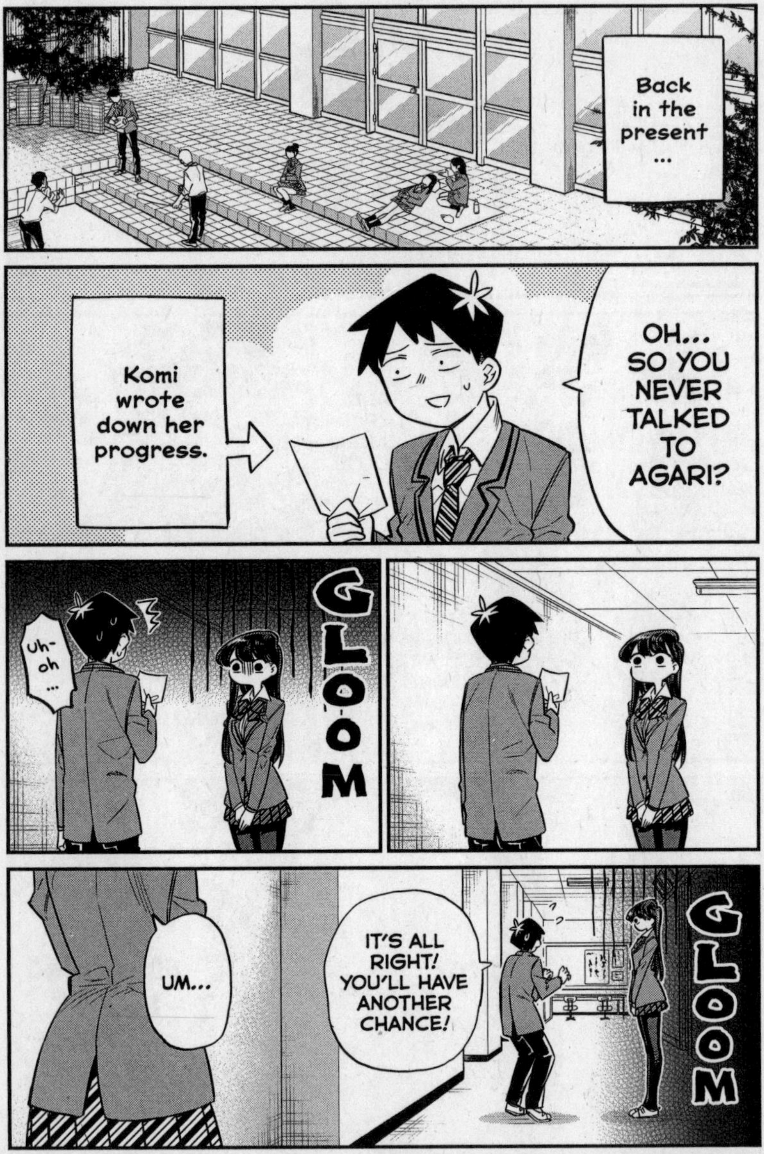
Back in the present ...
OH... SO YOU NEVER TALKED TO AGARI?
Komi wrote down her progress.
GLOOM
Uh-oh ...
GLOOM
IT'S ALL RIGHT! YOU'LL HAVE ANOTHER CHANCE!
UM...

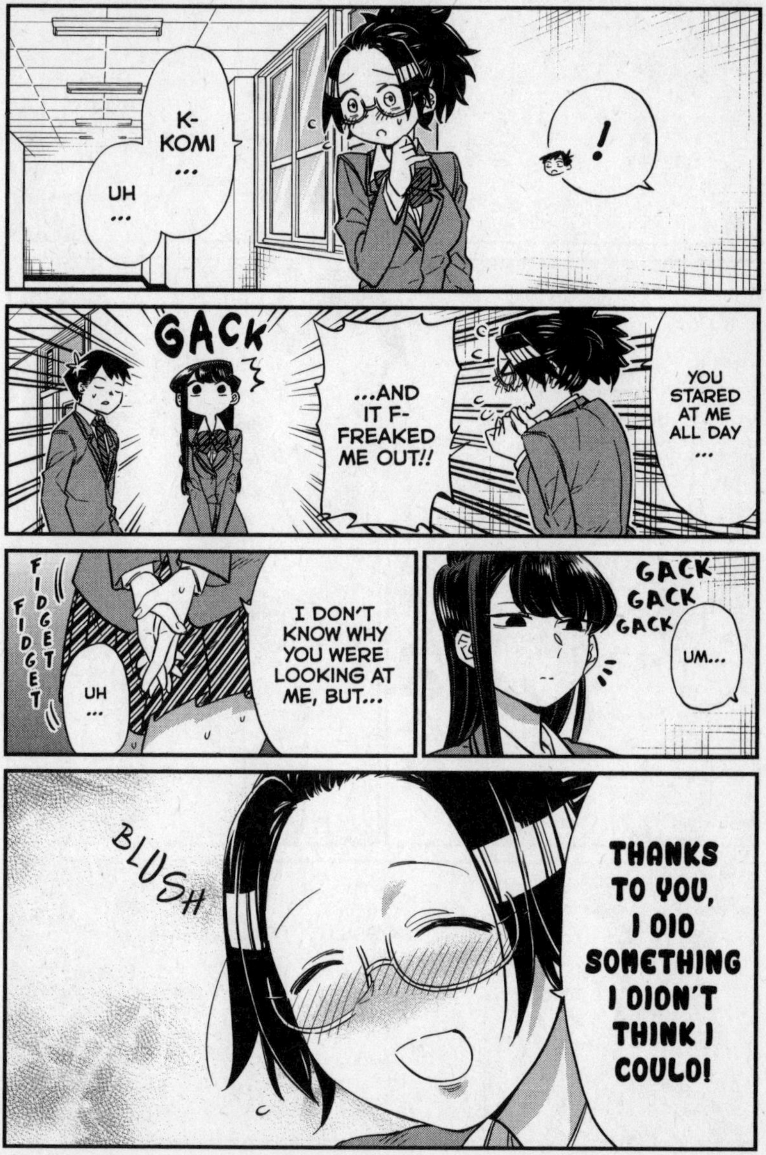
!
K-KOMI...
UH...
YOU STARED AT ME ALL DAY...
...AND IT F-FREAKED ME OUT!!
GACK
GACK GACK GACK
UM...
I DON'T KNOW WHY YOU WERE LOOKING AT ME, BUT...
FIDGET FIDGET
UH...
THANKS TO YOU, I DID SOMETHING I DIDN'T THINK I COULD!
BLUSH

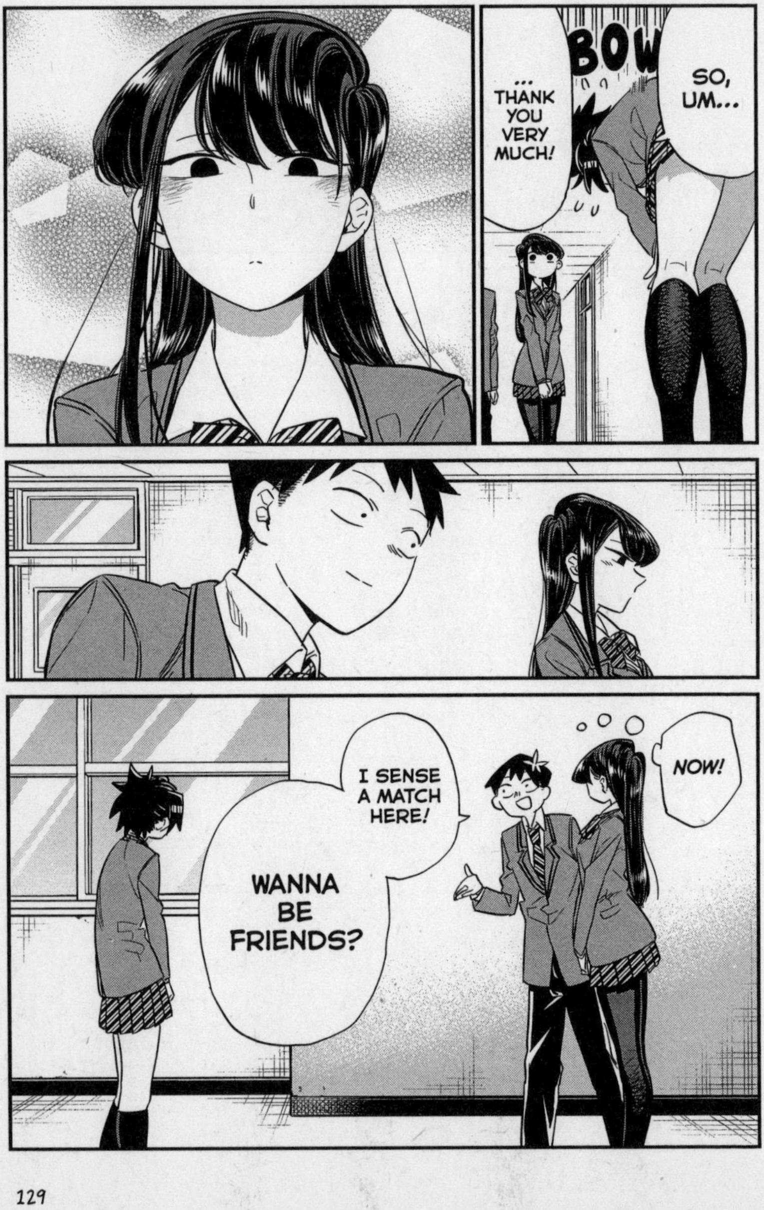
SO, UM...
BOW
...THANK YOU VERY MUCH!
NOW!
I SENSE A MATCH HERE!
WANNA BE FRIENDS?

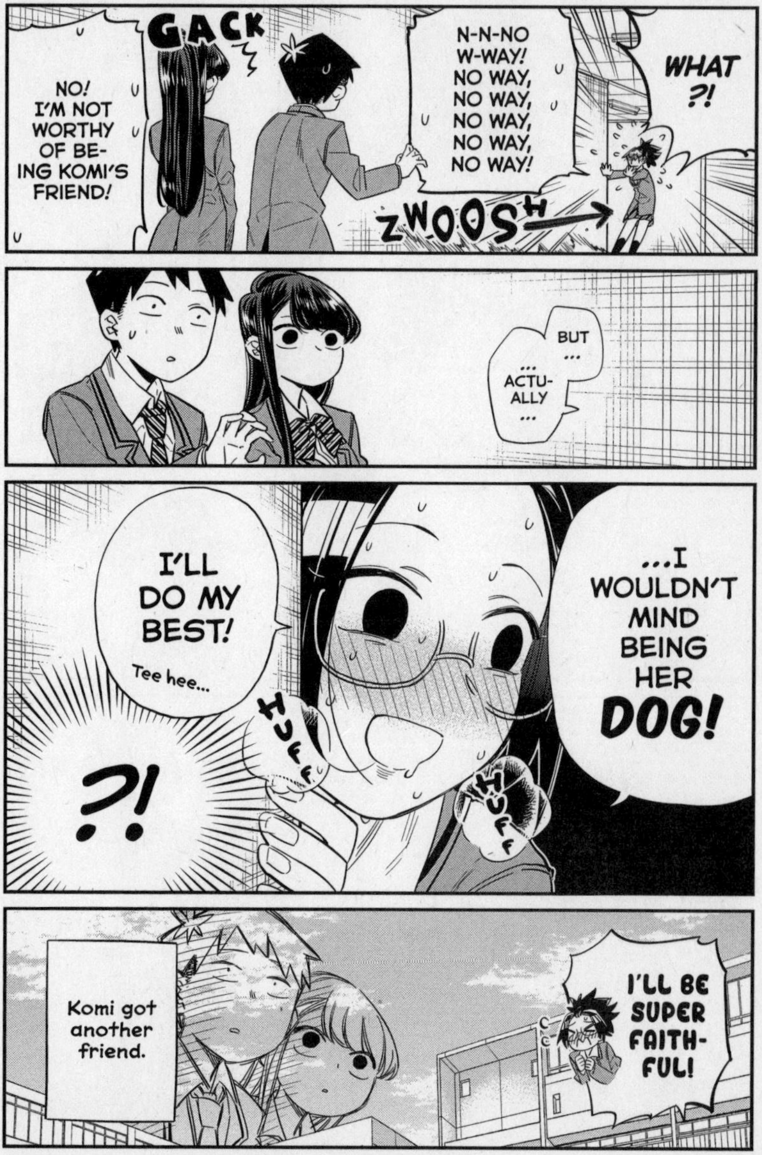
WHAT ?!
ZWOOSH
N-N-NO W-WAY! NO WAY, NO WAY, NO WAY, NO WAY, NO WAY!
GACK
NO! I'M NOT WORTHY OF BE-ING KOMI'S FRIEND!
BUT ... ... ACTU-ALLY ...
...I WOULDN'T MIND BEING HER DOG!
HUFF
HUFF
I'LL DO MY BEST!
Tee hee...
?!
I'LL BE SUPER FAITH-FUL!
Komi got another friend.

Communication 14 — The End

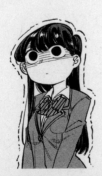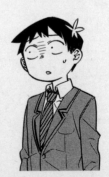

Komi Can't Communicate

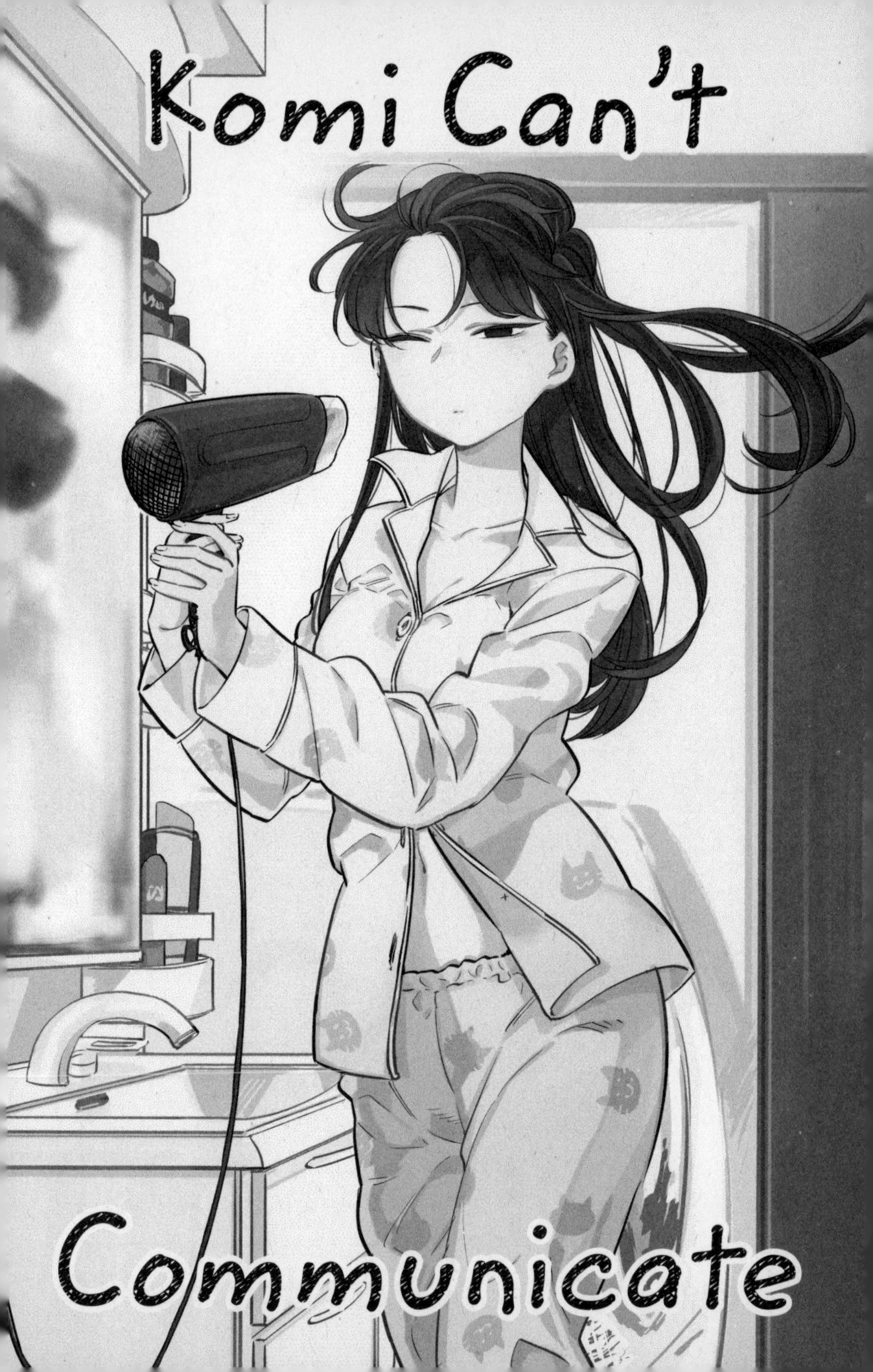
Komi Can't
Communicate

Communication 15: Going to School

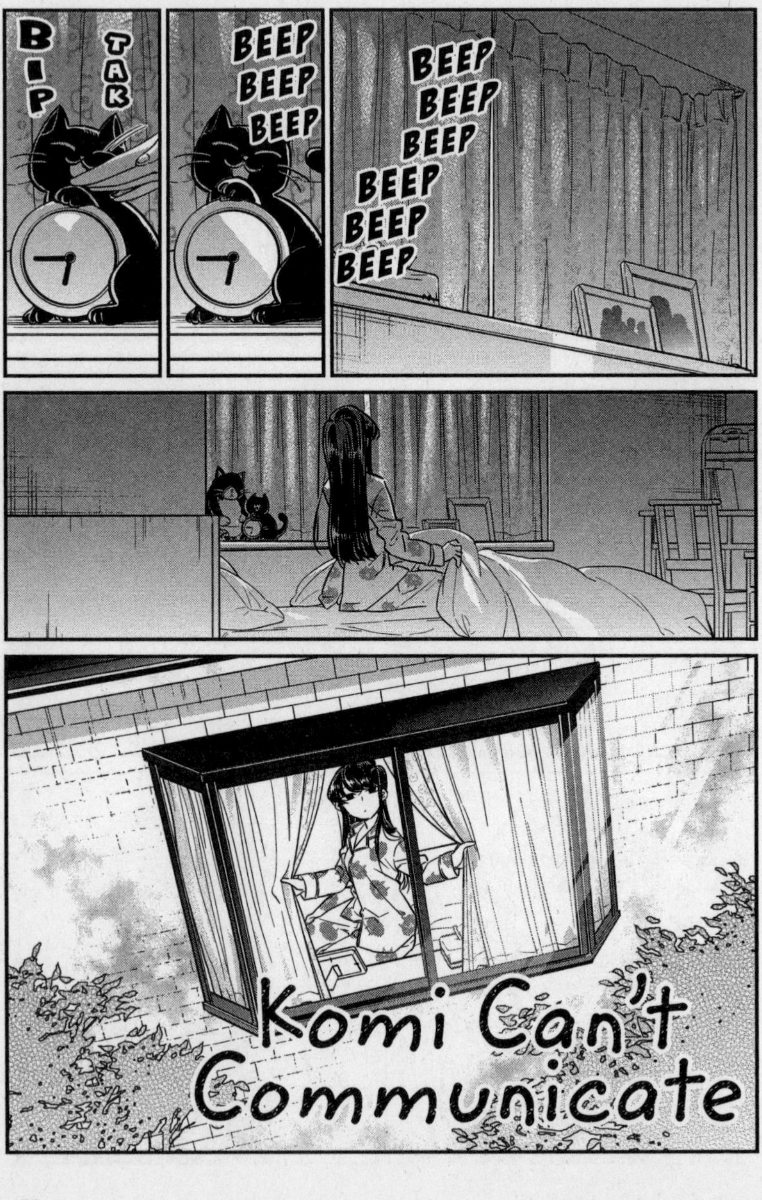
BEEP
BEEP
BEEP
BEEP
BEEP
BEEP
BEEP
BEEP
BEEP
BIP
TAK
Komi Can't Communicate

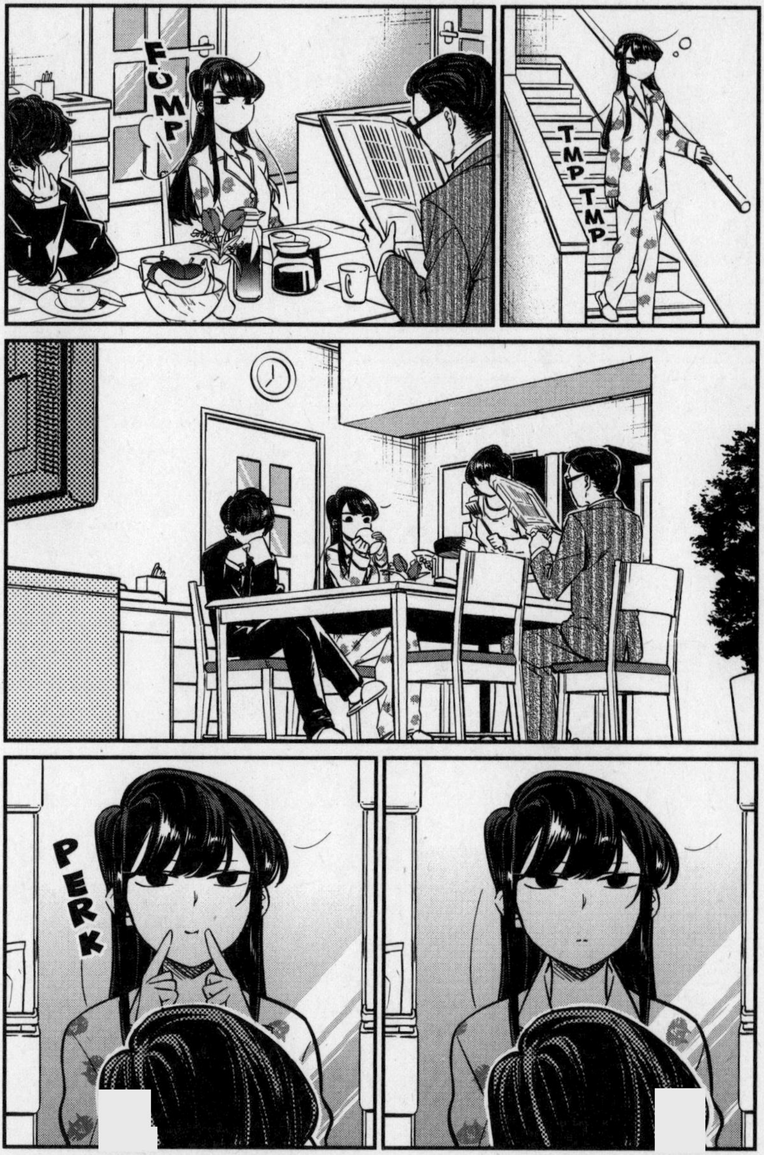
TMP TMP TMP
FUMP
PERK

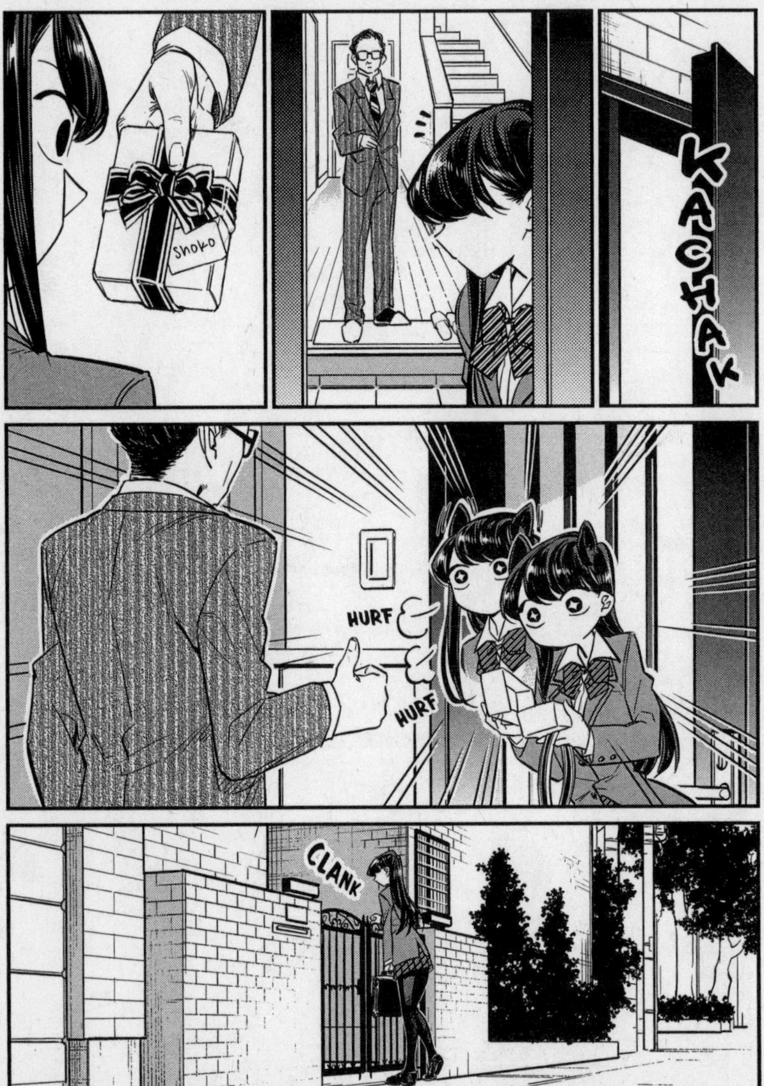
KACHAK
SHOKO
HURF
HURF
CLANK

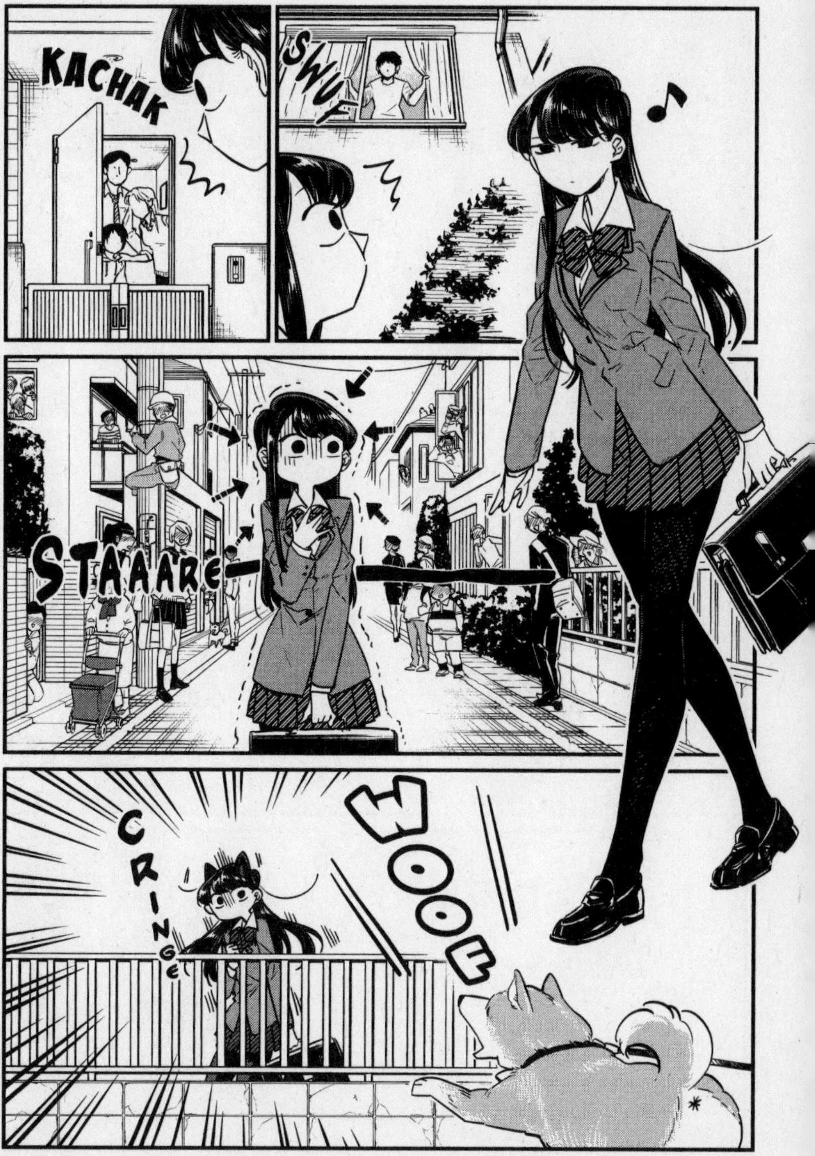
SWUF
KACHAK
STAAARE
WOOF
CRINGE

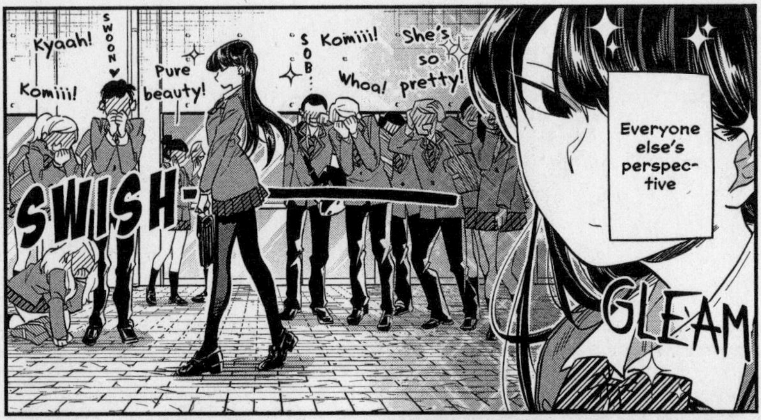
Everyone else's perspective
GLEAM
She's so pretty!
Whoa!
Komiii!
SOB...
Pure beauty!
SWOON ♥
Kyaah!
Komiii!
SWISH

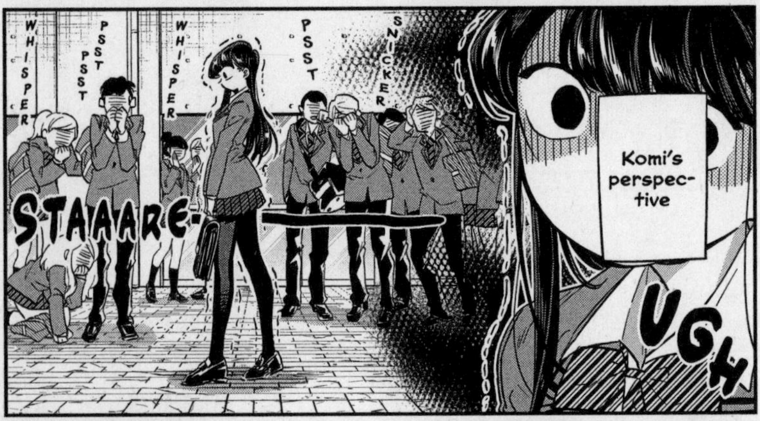
Komi's perspective
UGH
SNICKER
PSST
WHISPER
PSST PSST
WHISPER
STAAARE

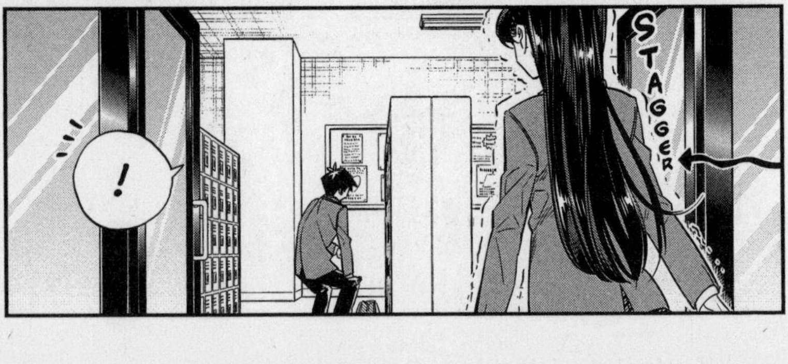
STAGGER
!

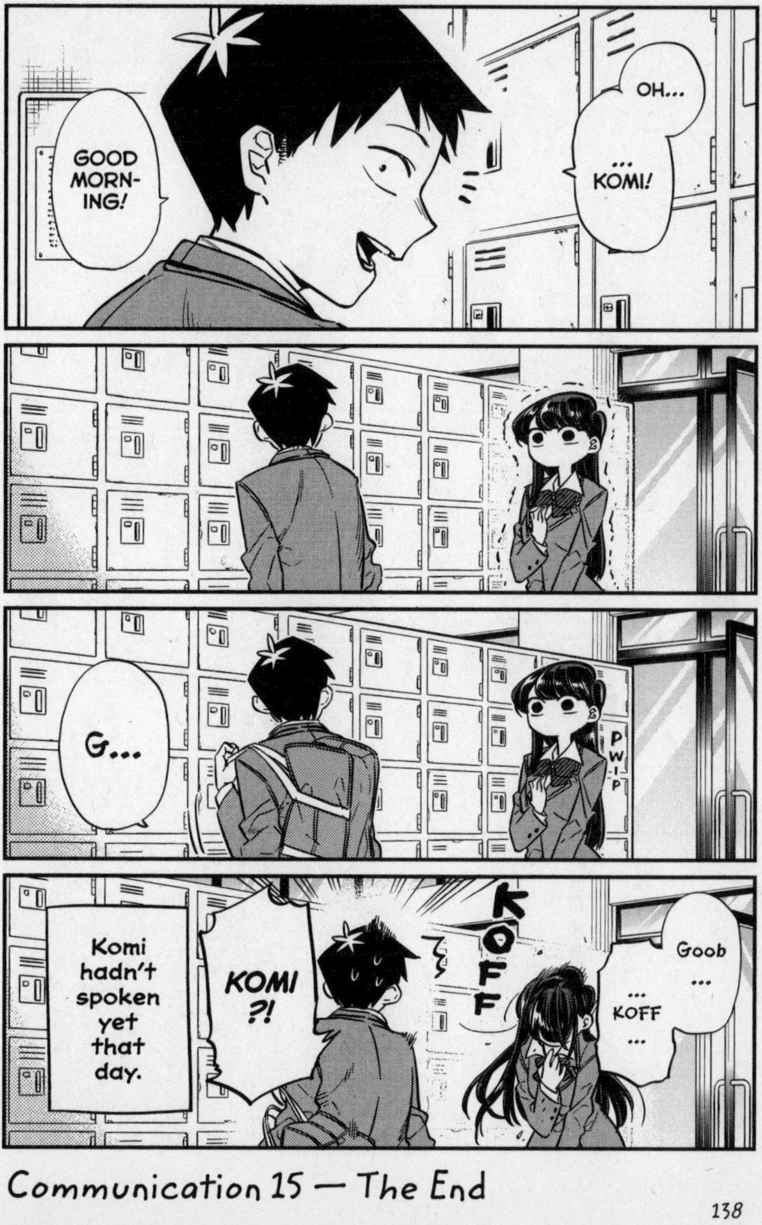
OH... ...KOMI!
GOOD MORN-ING!
G...
PWIP
Goob ... ... KOFF ...
KOFF KOFF
KOMI ?!
Komi hadn't spoken yet that day.

Communication 15 — The End

Komi Can't Communicate

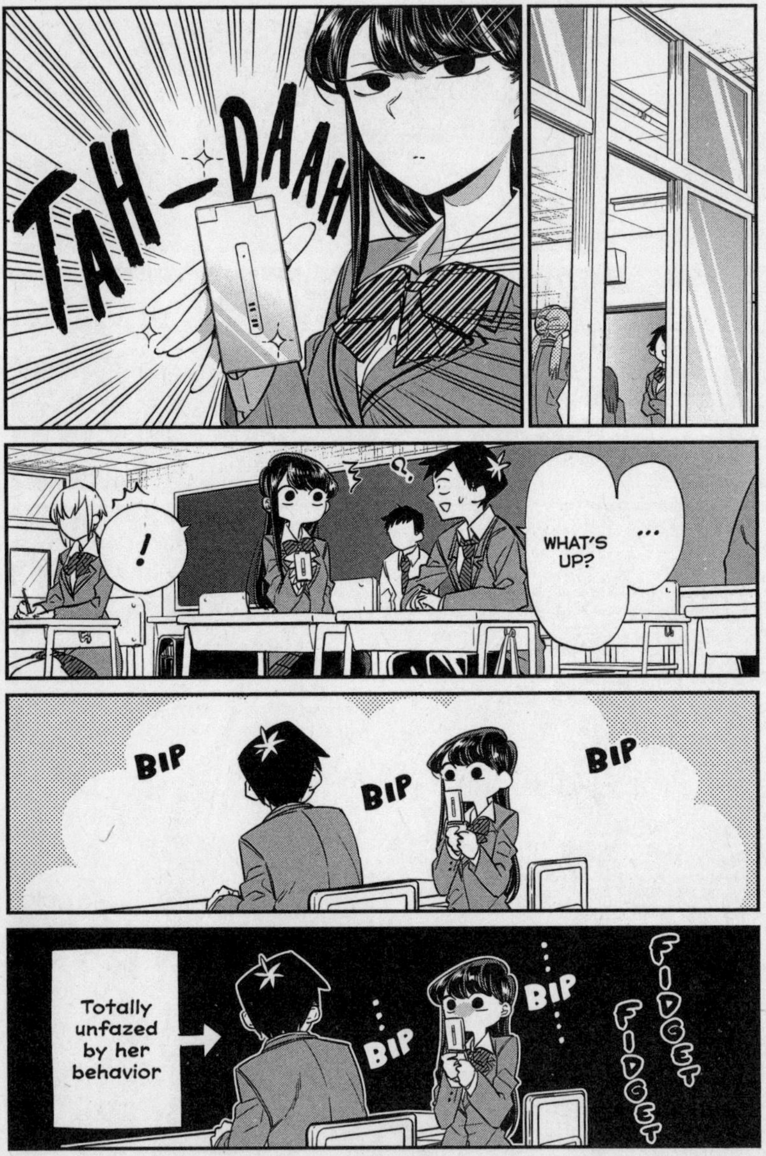
TAH-DAAH
WHAT'S UP? ...
!
BIP
BIP
BIP
FIDGET FIDGET
... BIP ...
... BIP
Totally unfazed by her behavior

Communication 16: Cell Phone

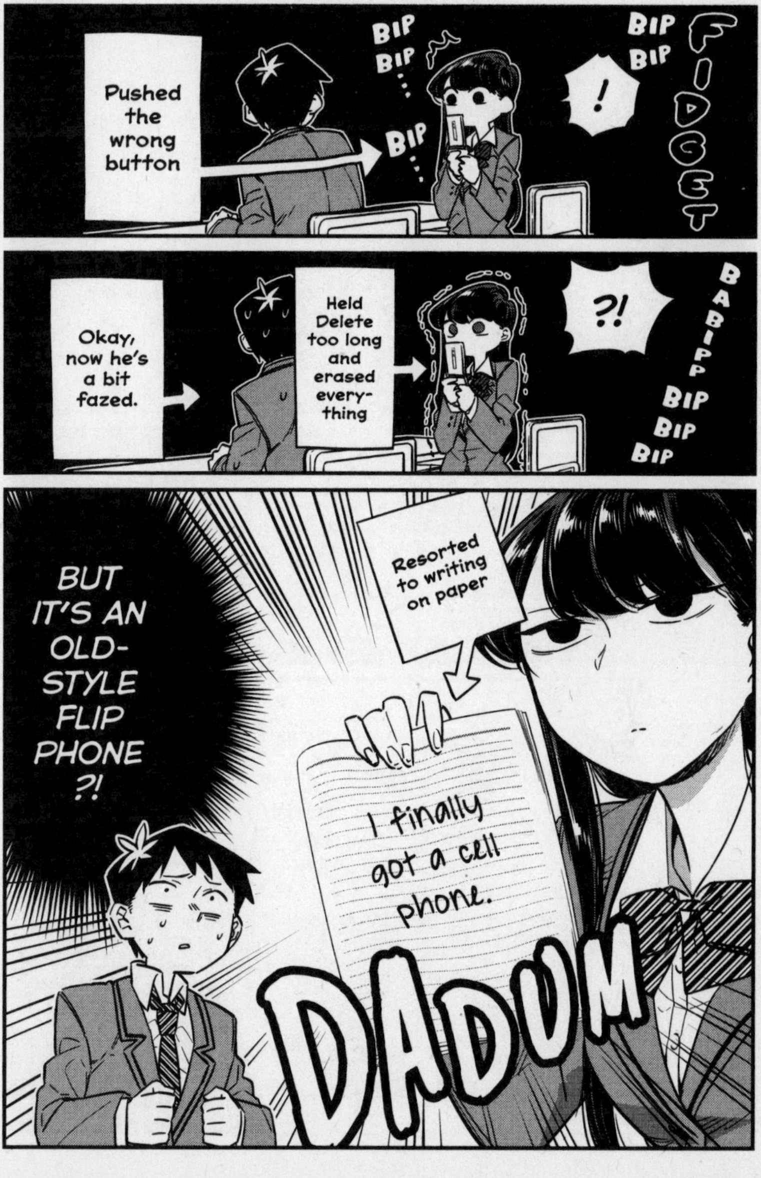
FIDGET
BIP BIP
!
BIP BIP... BIP...
Pushed the wrong button
BABIPP BIP BIP BIP
?!
Held Delete too long and erased every-thing
Okay, now he's a bit fazed.
Resorted to writing on paper
I finally got a cell phone.
BUT IT'S AN OLD-STYLE FLIP PHONE ?!
DADUM

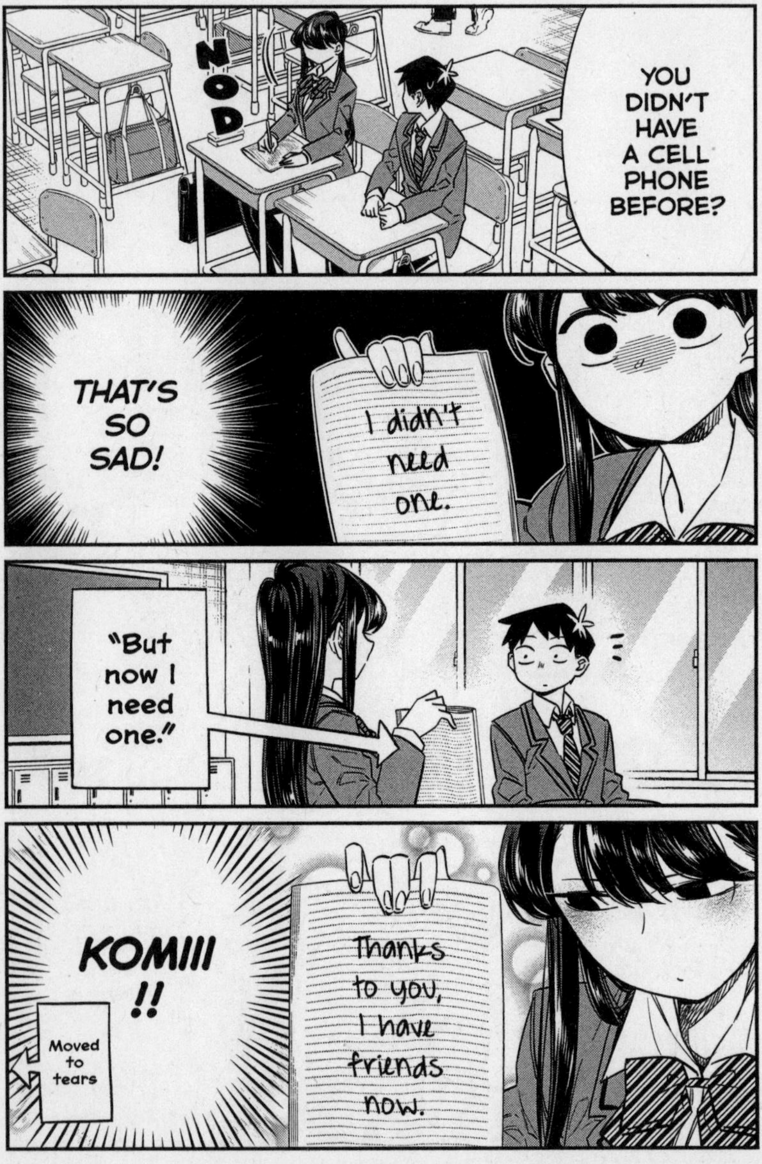
YOU DIDN'T HAVE A CELL PHONE BEFORE?
NOD
I didn't need one.
THAT'S SO SAD!
"But now I need one."
Thanks to you, I have friends now.
KOMIII !!
Moved to tears

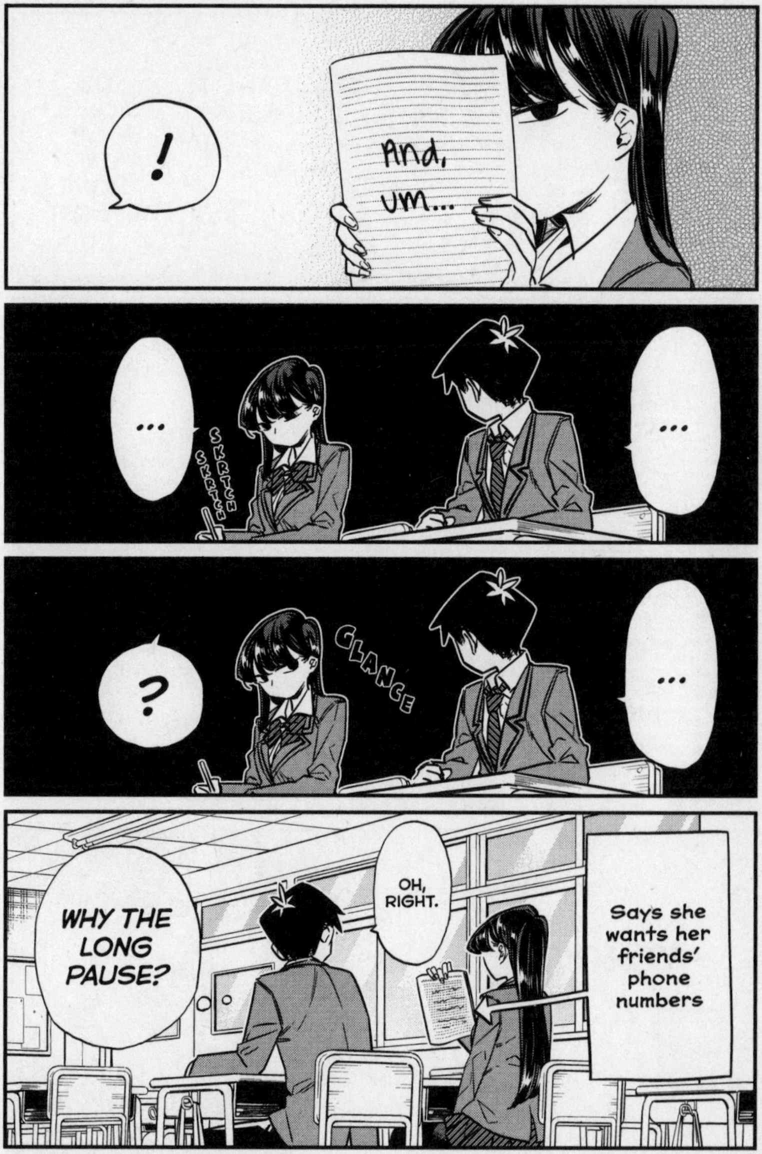
And, um...
!
...
SKRTCH SKRTCH
...
...
GLANCE
?
Says she wants her friends' phone numbers
OH, RIGHT.
WHY THE LONG PAUSE?

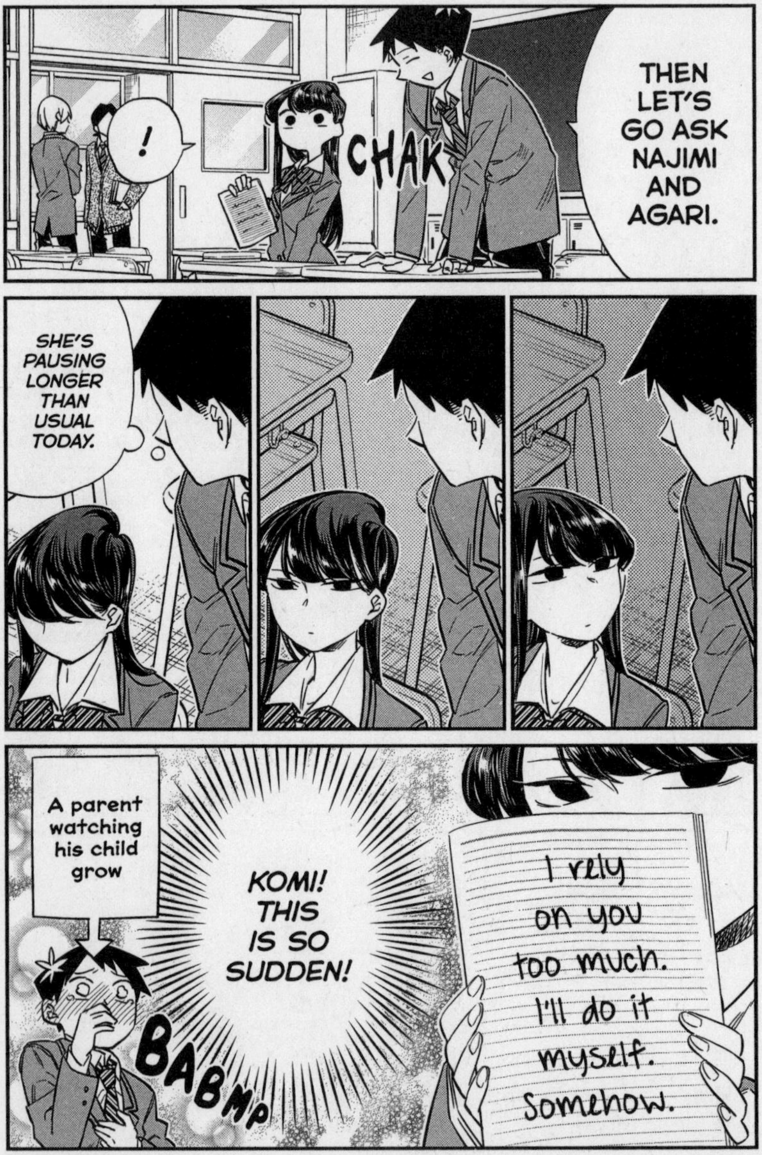
THEN LET'S GO ASK NAJIMI AND AGARI.
CHAK
!
SHE'S PAUSING LONGER THAN USUAL TODAY.
I rely on you too much. I'll do it myself. Somehow.
KOMI! THIS IS SO SUDDEN!
BABMP
A parent watching his child grow

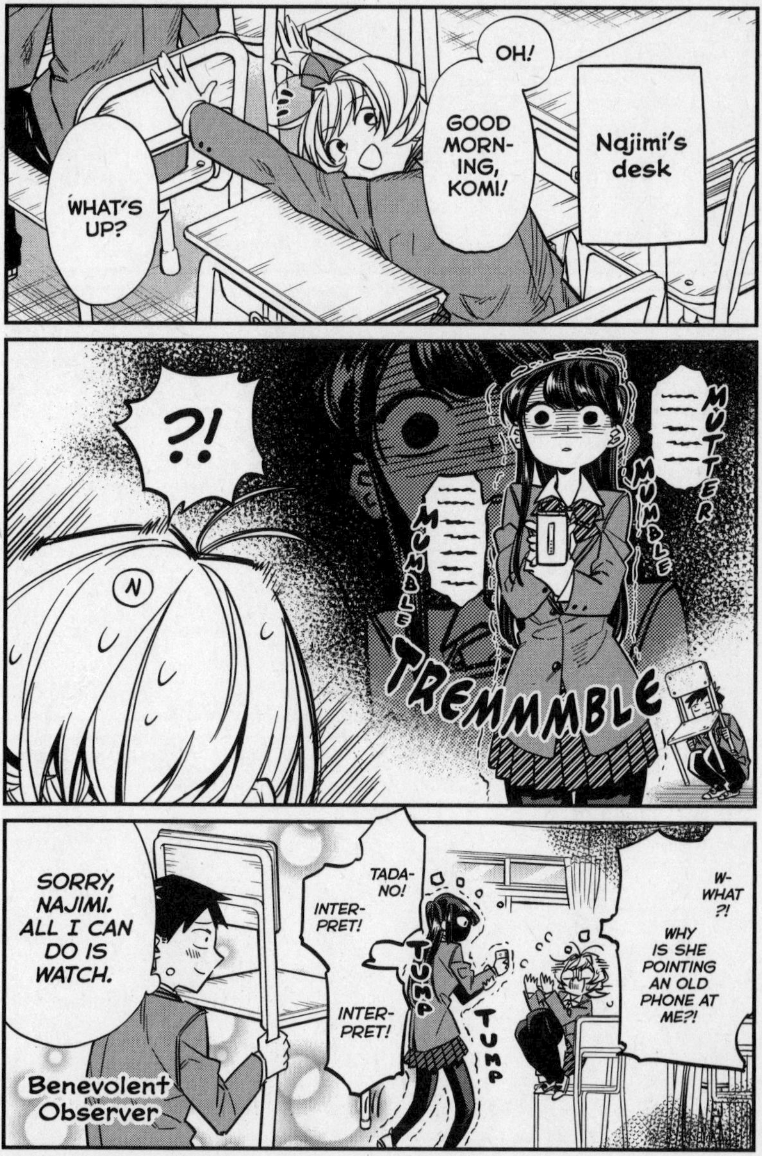
Najimi's desk
OH!
GOOD MORNING, KOMI!
WHAT'S UP?
MUTTER
MUMBLE
MUMBLE
?!
TREMMMBLE
N
W-WHAT?!
WHY IS SHE POINTING AN OLD PHONE AT ME?!
TUMP
TUMP
TADA-NO!
INTER-PRET!
INTER-PRET!
SORRY, NAJIMI. ALL I CAN DO IS WATCH.
Benevolent Observer

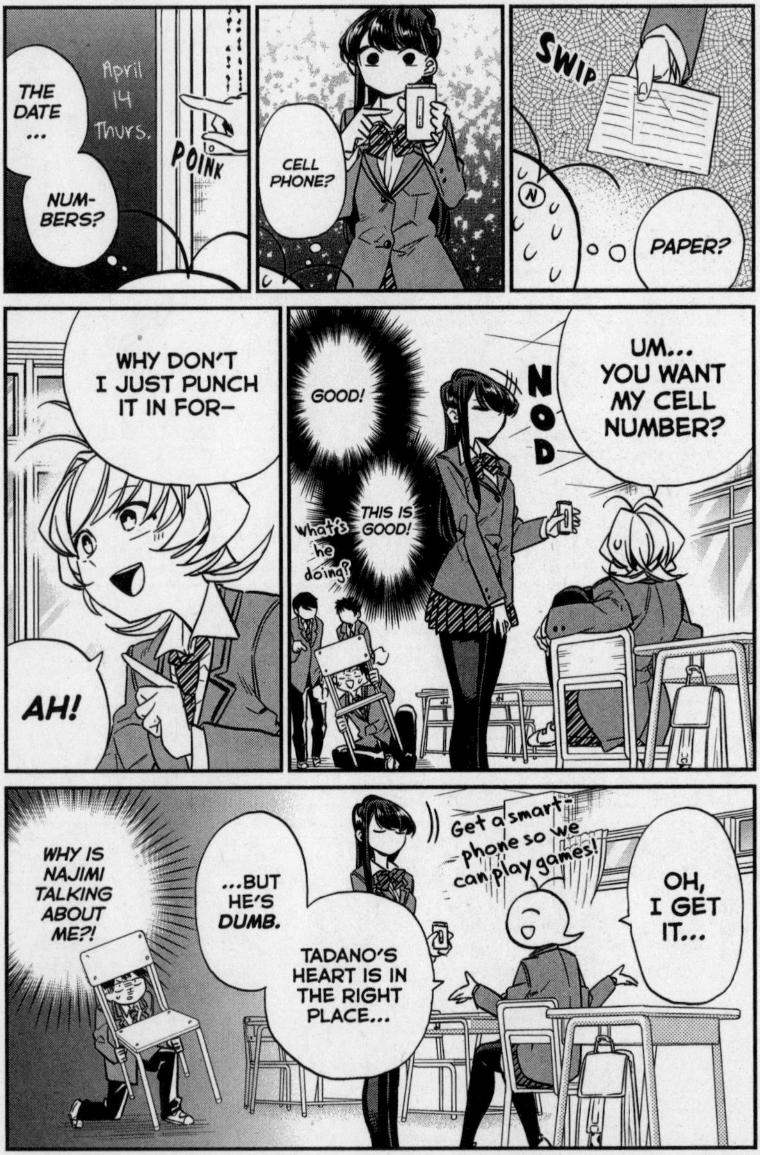
SWIP
PAPER?
CELL PHONE?
THE DATE...
April 14 Thurs.
POINK
NUM-BERS?
UM... YOU WANT MY CELL NUMBER?
NOD
GOOD!
THIS IS GOOD!
What's he doing?
WHY DON'T I JUST PUNCH IT IN FOR—
AH!
OH, I GET IT...
Get a smart-phone so we can play games!
TADANO'S HEART IS IN THE RIGHT PLACE...
...BUT HE'S DUMB.
WHY IS NAJIMI TALKING ABOUT ME?!

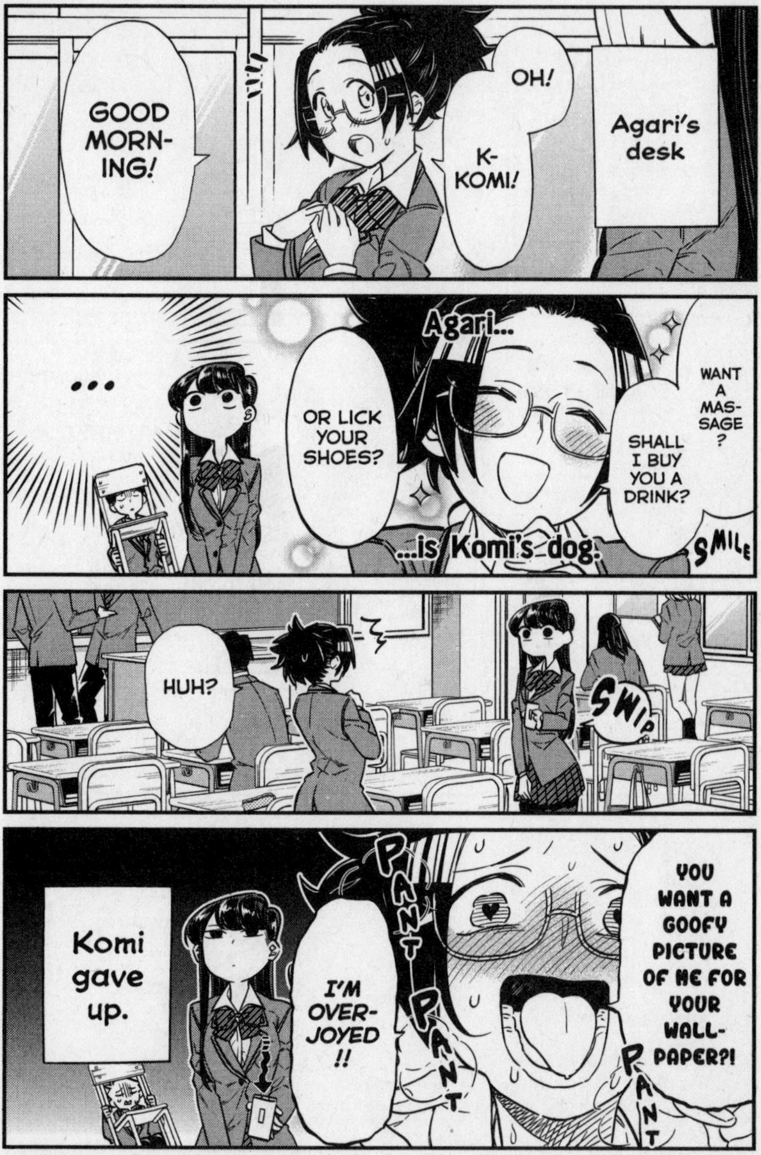
Agari's desk
OH! K-KOMI!
GOOD MORNING!
WANT A MASSAGE?
SHALL I BUY YOU A DRINK?
SMILE
Agari... ...is Komi's dog.
OR LICK YOUR SHOES?
...
SWIP
HUH?
YOU WANT A GOOFY PICTURE OF ME FOR YOUR WALLPAPER?!
PANT
PANT
PANT
PANT
I'M OVERJOYED!!
Komi gave up.

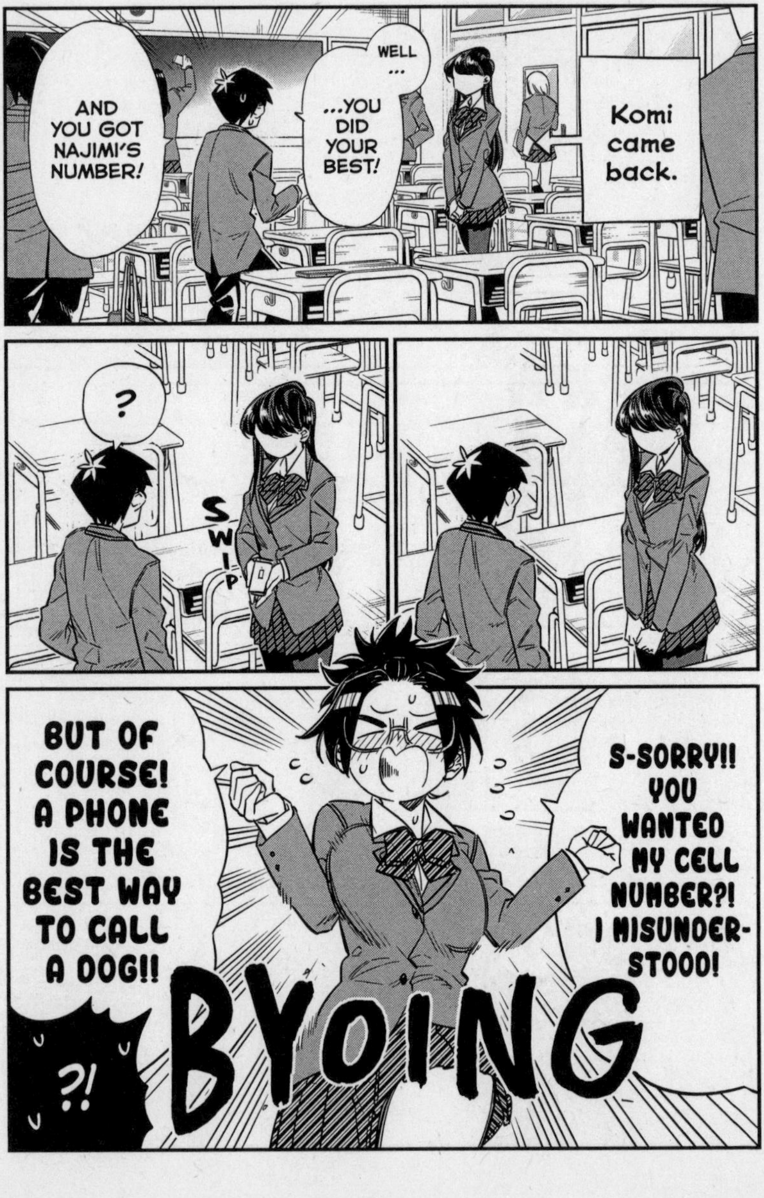
Komi came back.
WELL ... ...YOU DID YOUR BEST!
AND YOU GOT NAJIMI'S NUMBER!
?
SWIP
S-SORRY!! YOU WANTED MY CELL NUMBER?! I MISUNDER-STOOD!
BUT OF COURSE! A PHONE IS THE BEST WAY TO CALL A DOG!!
BYOING
?!

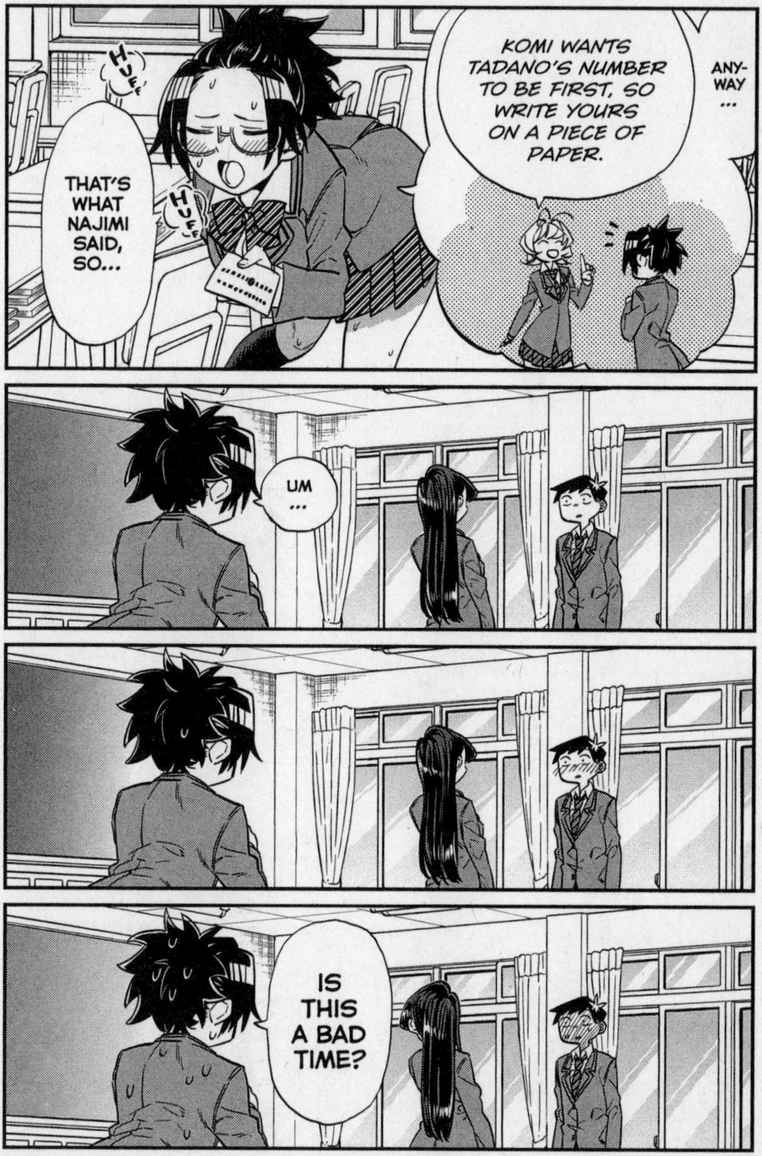

ANY-WAY...
KOMI WANTS TADANO'S NUMBER TO BE FIRST, SO WRITE YOURS ON A PIECE OF PAPER.
HUFF
HUFF
THAT'S WHAT NAJIMI SAID, SO...
UM...
IS THIS A BAD TIME?

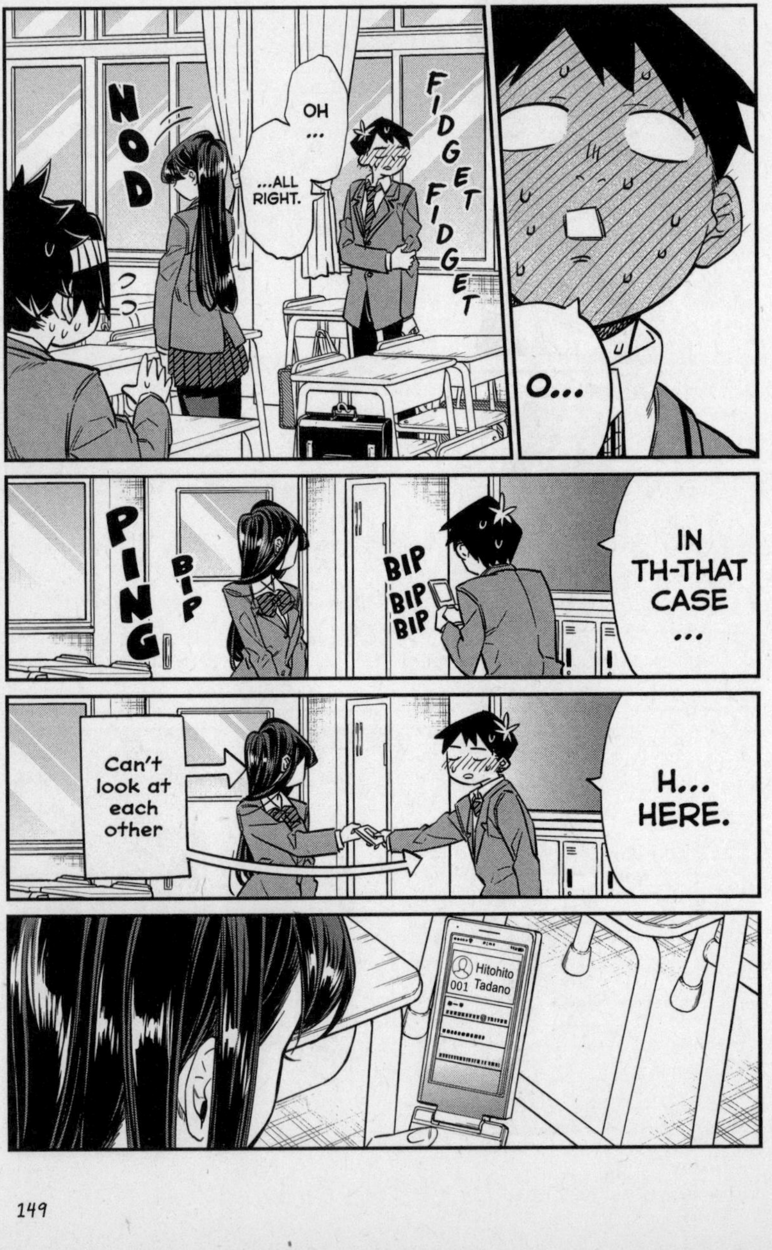
O...
FIDGET FIDGET
OH ... ...ALL RIGHT.
NOD
IN TH-THAT CASE ...
BIP BIP BIP
BIP BIP
PING
H... HERE.
Can't look at each other
Hitohito Tadano
001

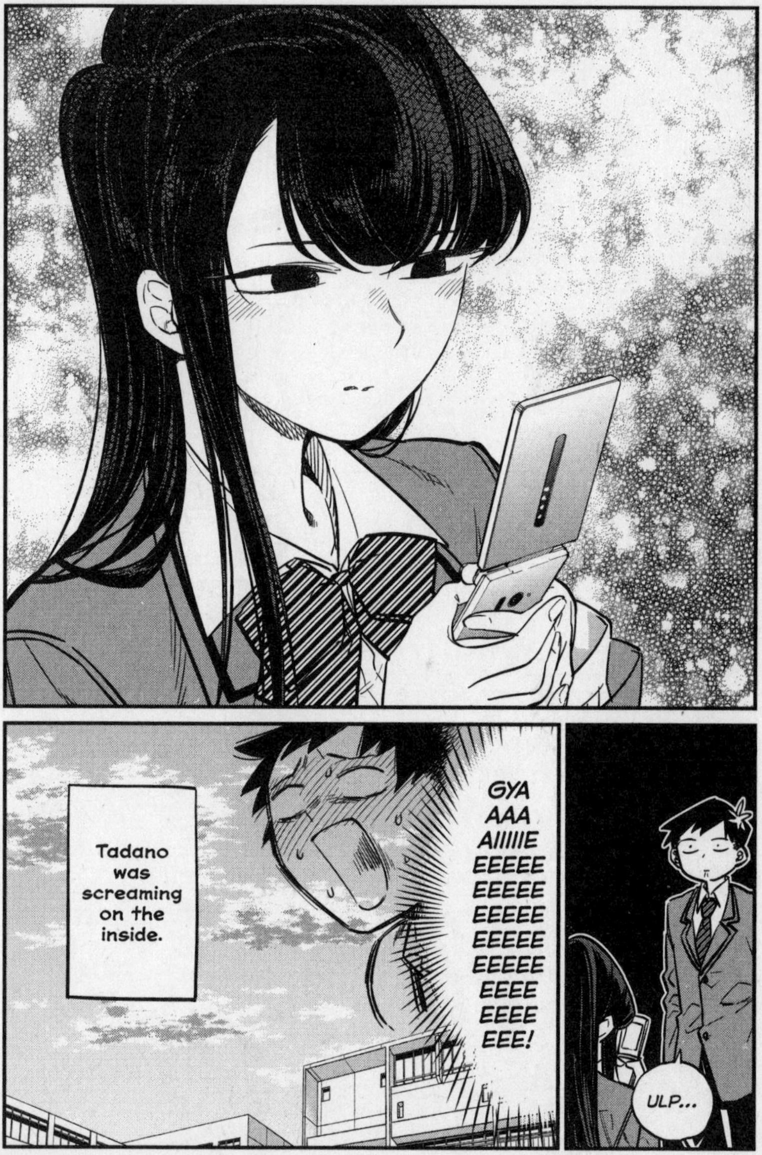
Tadano was screaming on the inside.
GYA AAA AIIIIIE EEEEE EEEEE EEEEE EEEEE EEEEE EEEE EEEE EEE!
ULP...

Communication 16 — The End

Komi Can't Communicate

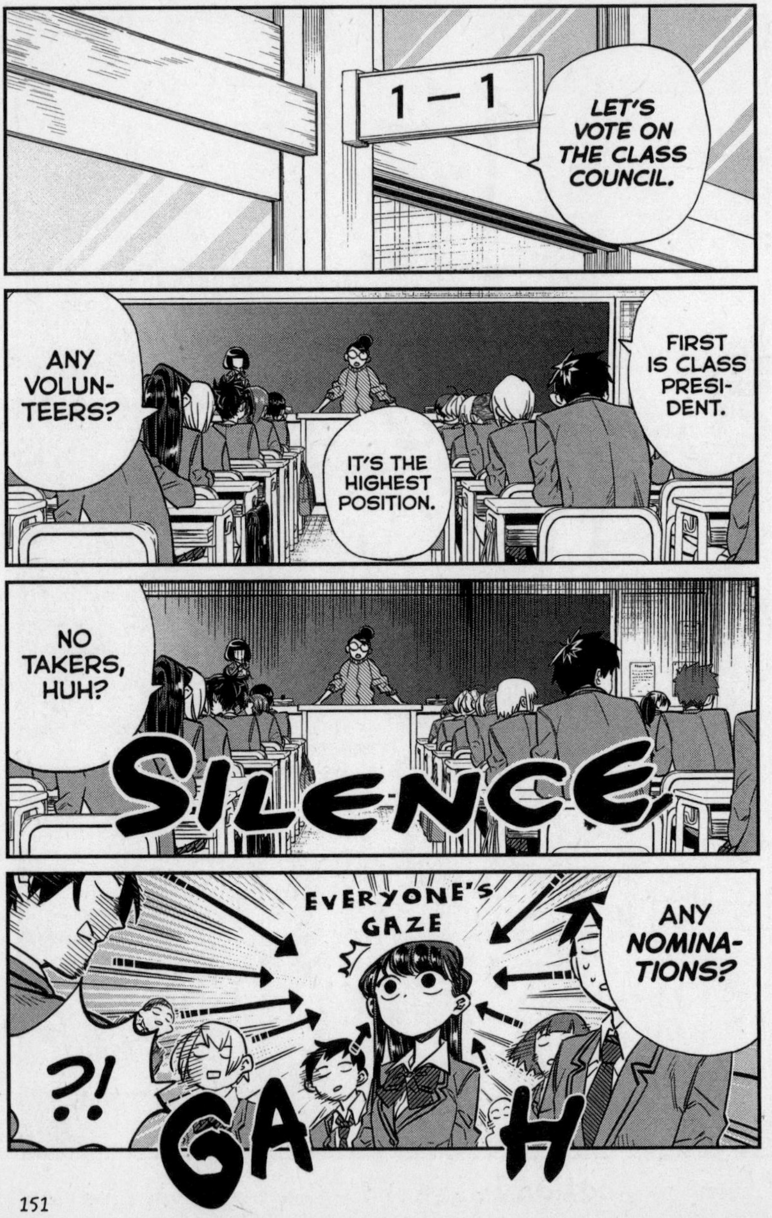
1-1
LET'S VOTE ON THE CLASS COUNCIL.
FIRST IS CLASS PRESIDENT.
IT'S THE HIGHEST POSITION.
ANY VOLUNTEERS?
NO TAKERS, HUH?
SILENCE
ANY NOMINATIONS?
EVERYONE'S GAZE
?!
GAH

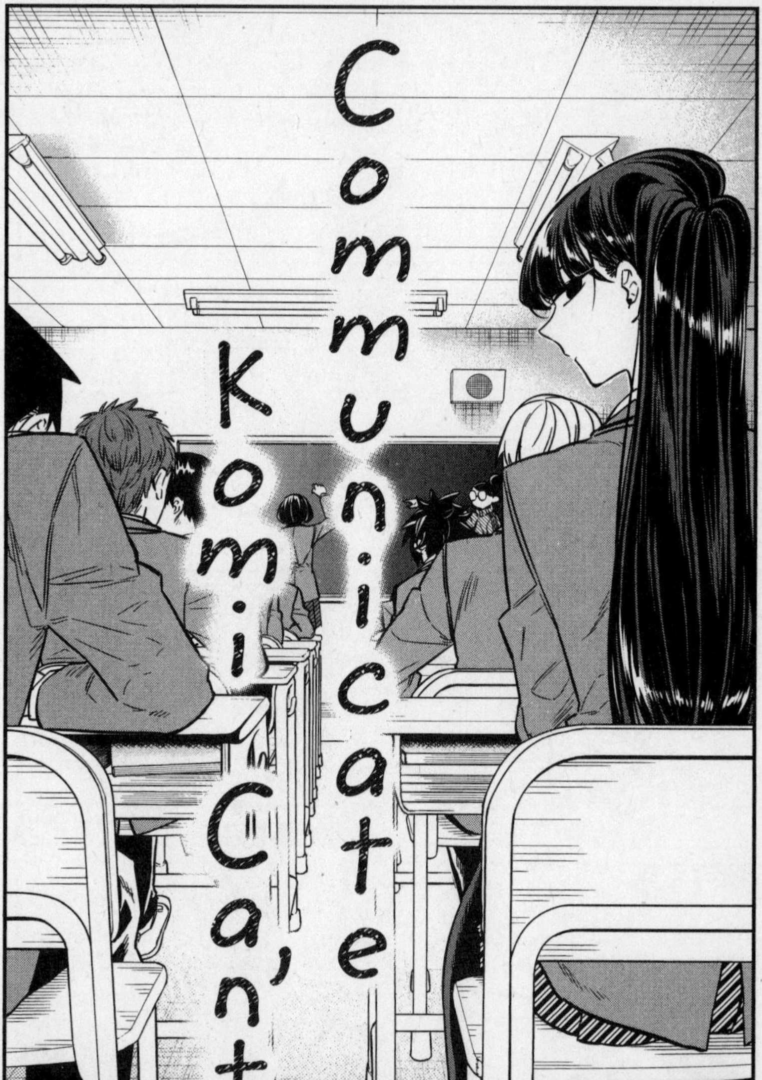
Komi Can't Communicate

Communication 17: Class Council Election

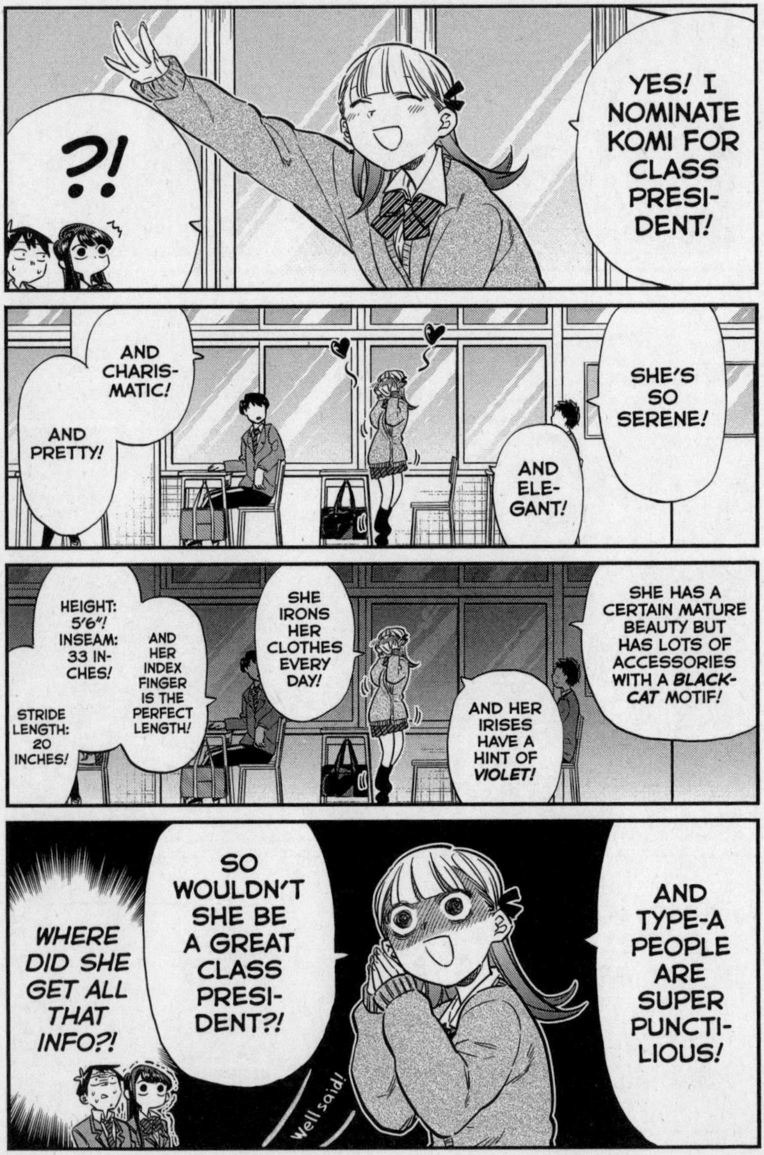
YES! I NOMINATE KOMI FOR CLASS PRESIDENT!
?!
SHE'S SO SERENE!
AND ELEGANT!
AND CHARISMATIC!
AND PRETTY!
SHE HAS A CERTAIN MATURE BEAUTY BUT HAS LOTS OF ACCESSORIES WITH A *BLACK-CAT* MOTIF!
AND HER IRISES HAVE A HINT OF *VIOLET!*
SHE IRONS HER CLOTHES EVERY DAY!
AND HER INDEX FINGER IS THE PERFECT LENGTH!
HEIGHT: 5'6"! INSEAM: 33 INCHES!
STRIDE LENGTH: 20 INCHES!
AND TYPE-A PEOPLE ARE SUPER PUNCTILIOUS!
SO WOULDN'T SHE BE A GREAT CLASS PRESIDENT?!
Well said!
WHERE DID SHE GET ALL THAT INFO?!

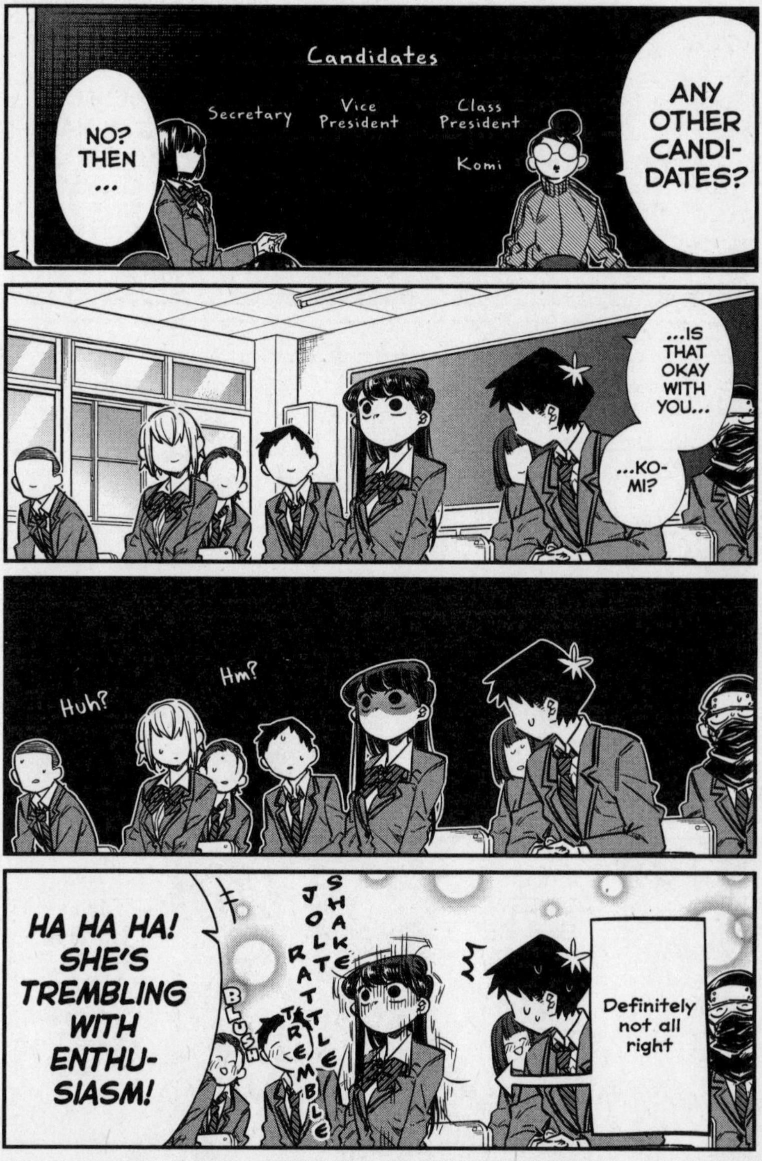
ANY OTHER CANDI-DATES?
Candidates
Class President
Komi
Vice President
Secretary
NO? THEN ...
...IS THAT OKAY WITH YOU...
...KO-MI?
Hm?
Huh?
Definitely not all right
SHAKE
JOLT
RATTLE
TREMBLE
BLUSH
HA HA HA! SHE'S TREMBLING WITH ENTHU-SIASM!

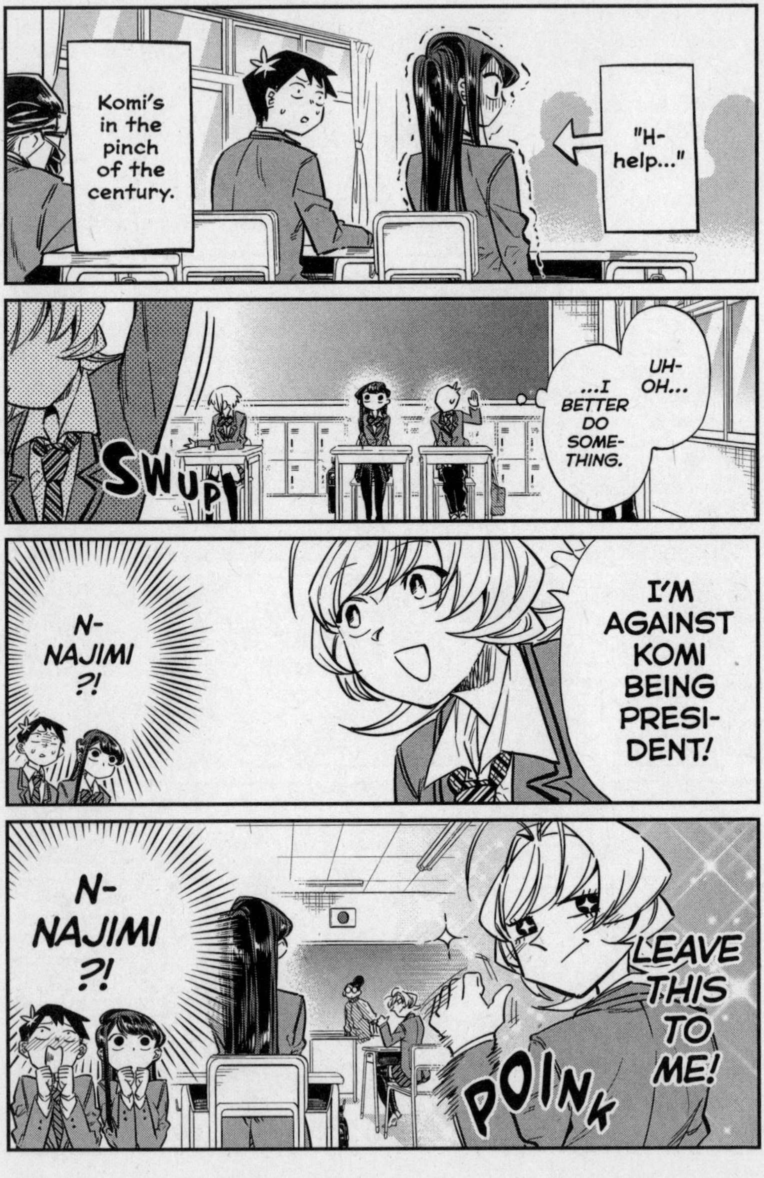
"H-help..."
Komi's in the pinch of the century.
UH-OH... ...I BETTER DO SOMETHING.
SWUP
I'M AGAINST KOMI BEING PRESIDENT!
N-NAJIMI?!
LEAVE THIS TO ME!
POINK
N-NAJIMI?!

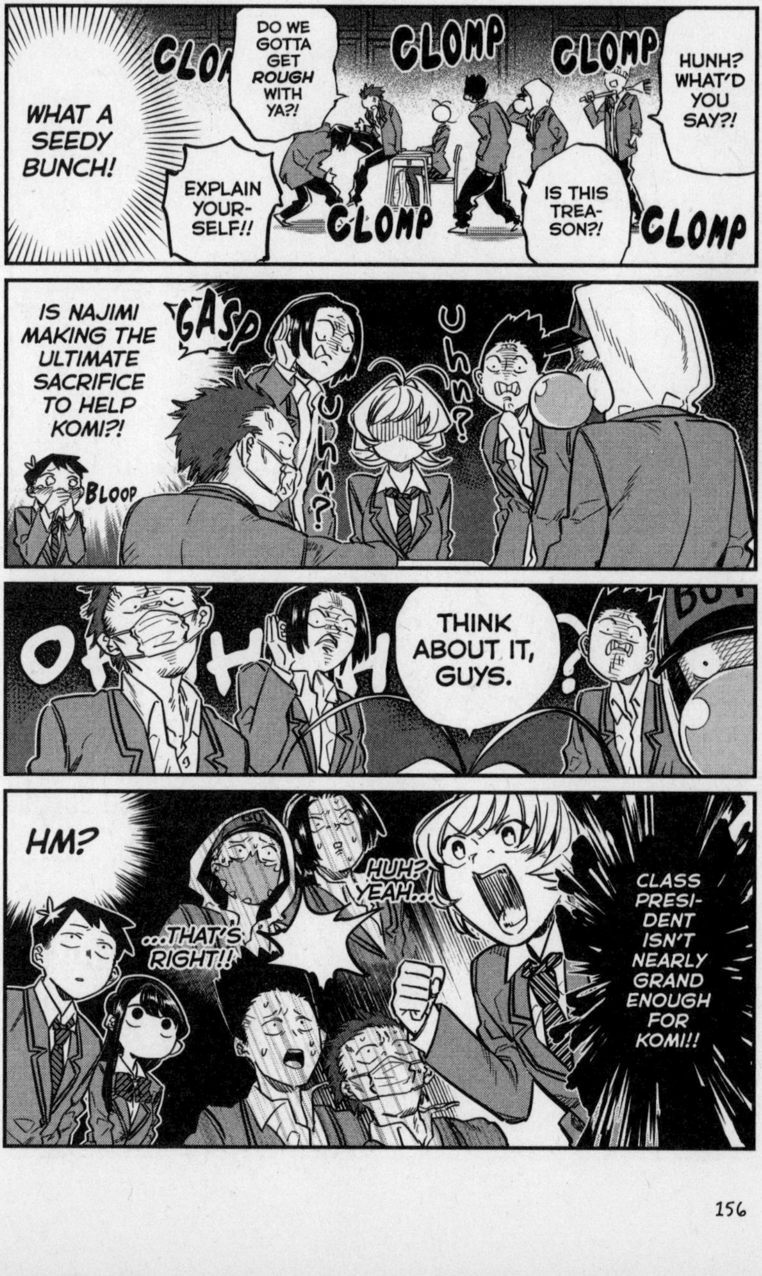
HUNH? WHAT'D YOU SAY?!
CLOMP
IS THIS TREASON?!
CLOMP
CLOMP
DO WE GOTTA GET ROUGH WITH YA?!
EXPLAIN YOURSELF!!
CLOMP
CLOM
WHAT A SEEDY BUNCH!
Uhhn?
Uhhn?
GASP
IS NAJIMI MAKING THE ULTIMATE SACRIFICE TO HELP KOMI?!
BLOOP
?
THINK ABOUT IT, GUYS.
OHH
CLASS PRESIDENT ISN'T NEARLY GRAND ENOUGH FOR KOMI!!
HUH? YEAH...!
...THAT'S RIGHT!!
HM?

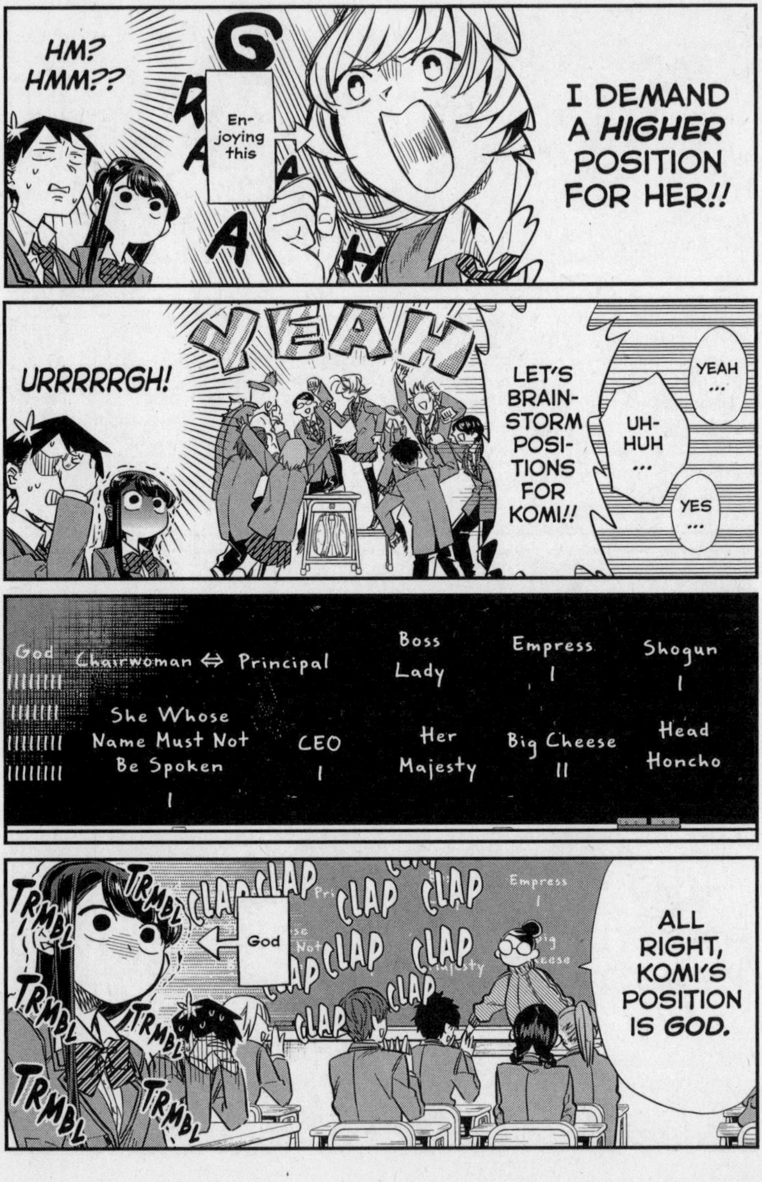
I DEMAND A HIGHER POSITION FOR HER!!
GRAAAH
En-joying this
HM? HMM??
YEAH...
UH-HUH...
YES...
LET'S BRAIN-STORM POSI-TIONS FOR KOMI!!
YEAH
URRRRRGH!
God
Chairwoman ⇔ Principal
Boss Lady
Empress
Shogun
She Whose Name Must Not Be Spoken
CEO
Her Majesty
Big Cheese
Head Honcho
ALL RIGHT, KOMI'S POSITION IS GOD.
CLAP CLAP CLAP CLAP CLAP CLAP CLAP CLAP CLAP CLAP
God
TRMBL TRMBL TRMBL TRMBL TRMBL TRMBL

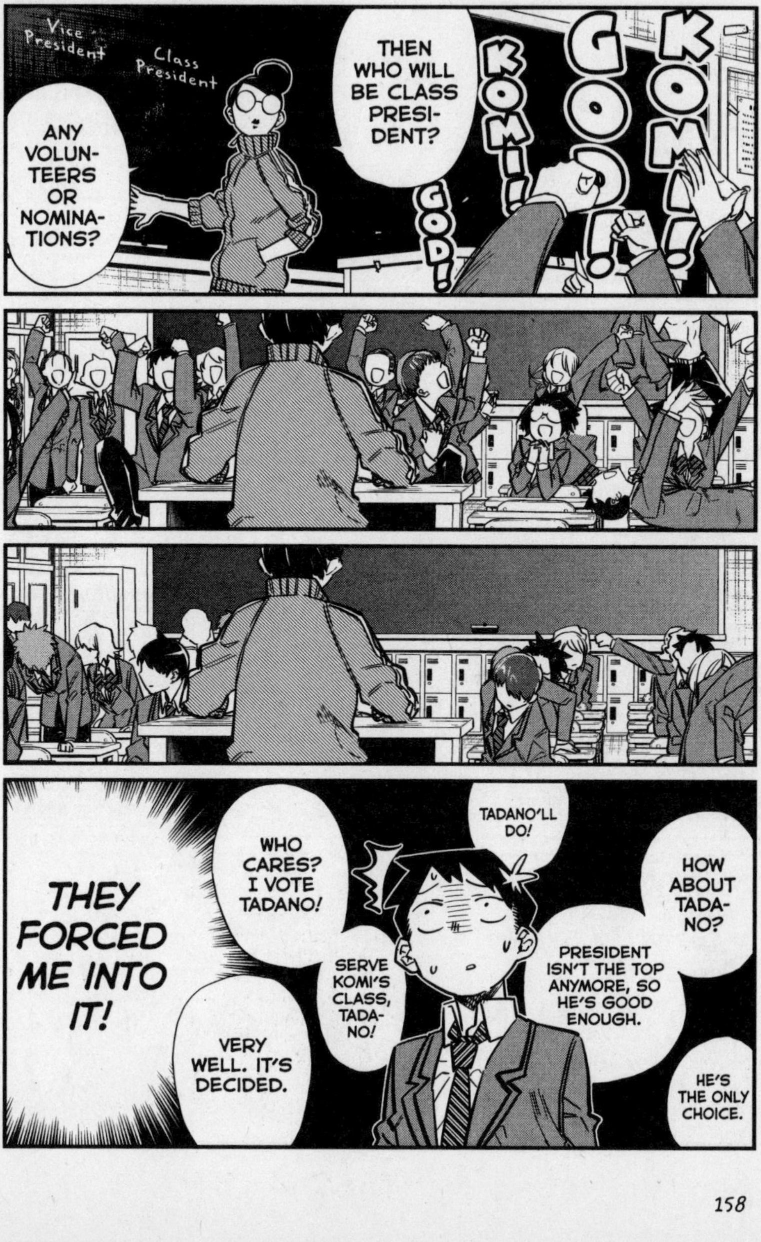
Vice President
Class President
THEN WHO WILL BE CLASS PRESIDENT?
ANY VOLUNTEERS OR NOMINATIONS?
KOMI!
GOD!
KOMI!
GOD!
TADANO'LL DO!
HOW ABOUT TADANO?
WHO CARES? I VOTE TADANO!
PRESIDENT ISN'T THE TOP ANYMORE, SO HE'S GOOD ENOUGH.
SERVE KOMI'S CLASS, TADANO!
HE'S THE ONLY CHOICE.
VERY WELL. IT'S DECIDED.
THEY FORCED ME INTO IT!

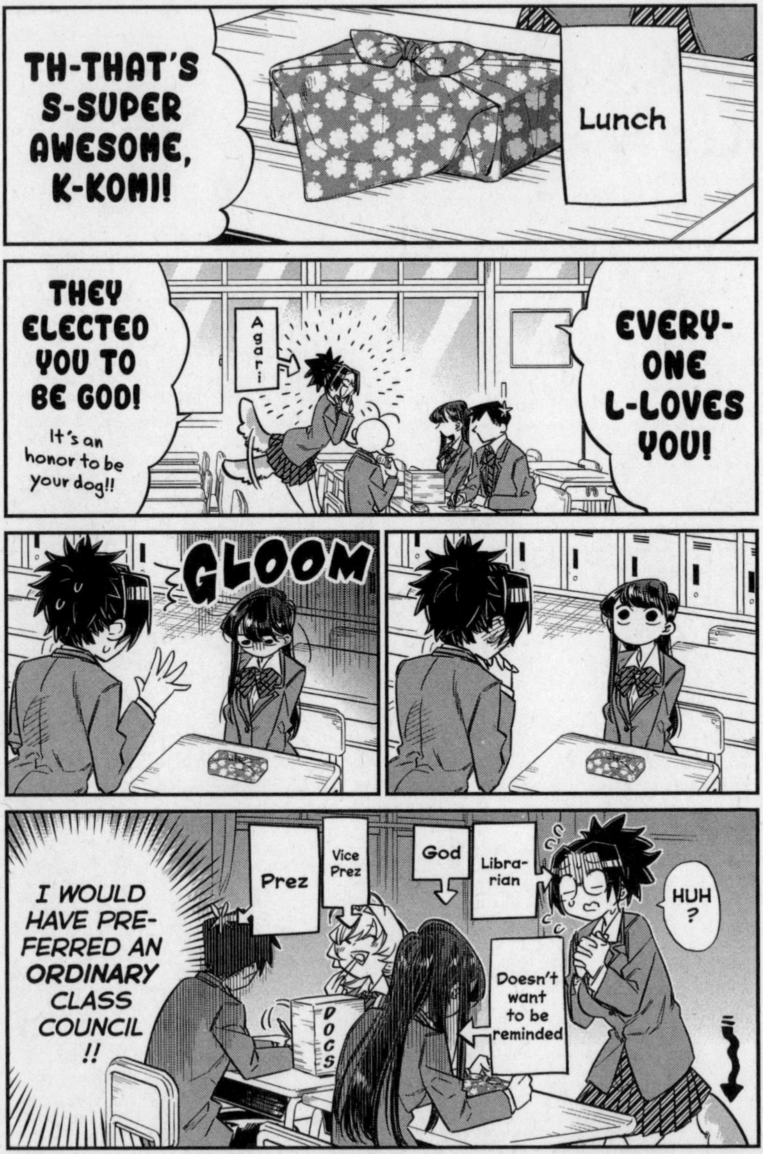
Lunch
TH-THAT'S S-SUPER AWESOME, K-KOMI!
EVERY-ONE L-LOVES YOU!
Agari
THEY ELECTED YOU TO BE GOD!
It's an honor to be your dog!!
GLOOM
HUH?
Librarian
God
Doesn't want to be reminded
Vice Prez
Prez
DOCS
I WOULD HAVE PRE-FERRED AN ORDINARY CLASS COUNCIL !!

Communication 17 — The End

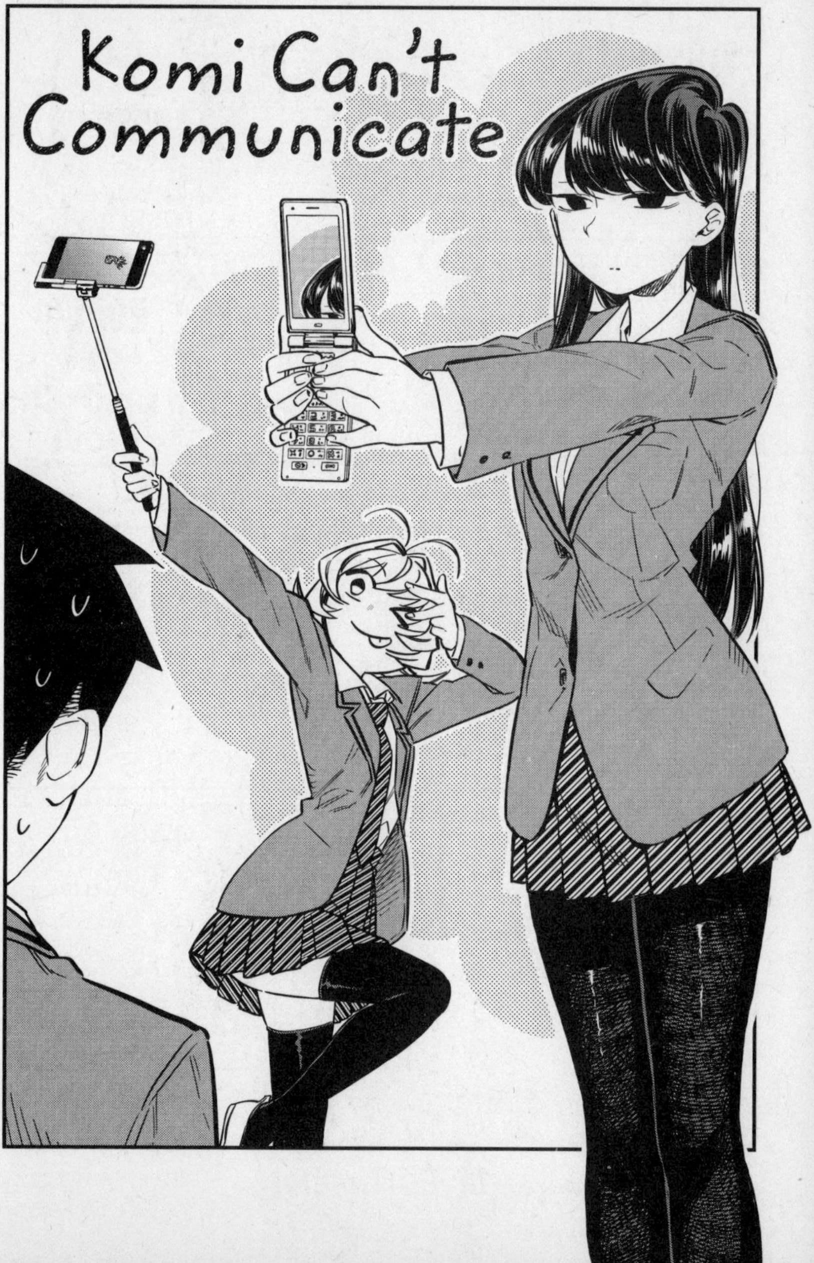
Komi Can't
Communicate

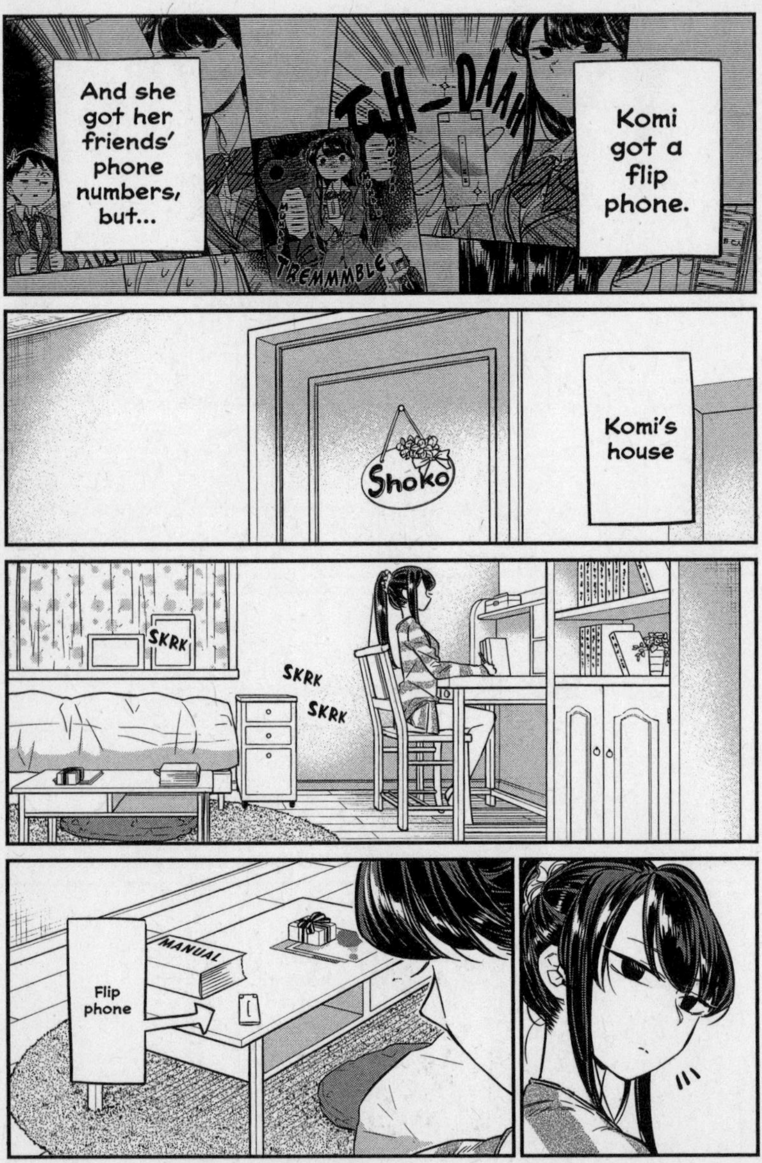
Komi got a flip phone.
TAH-DAAH
And she got her friends' phone numbers, but...
TREMMMBLE
Komi's house
Shoko
SKRK
SKRK
SKRK
MANUAL
Flip phone

Communication 18: Accidental Phone Call

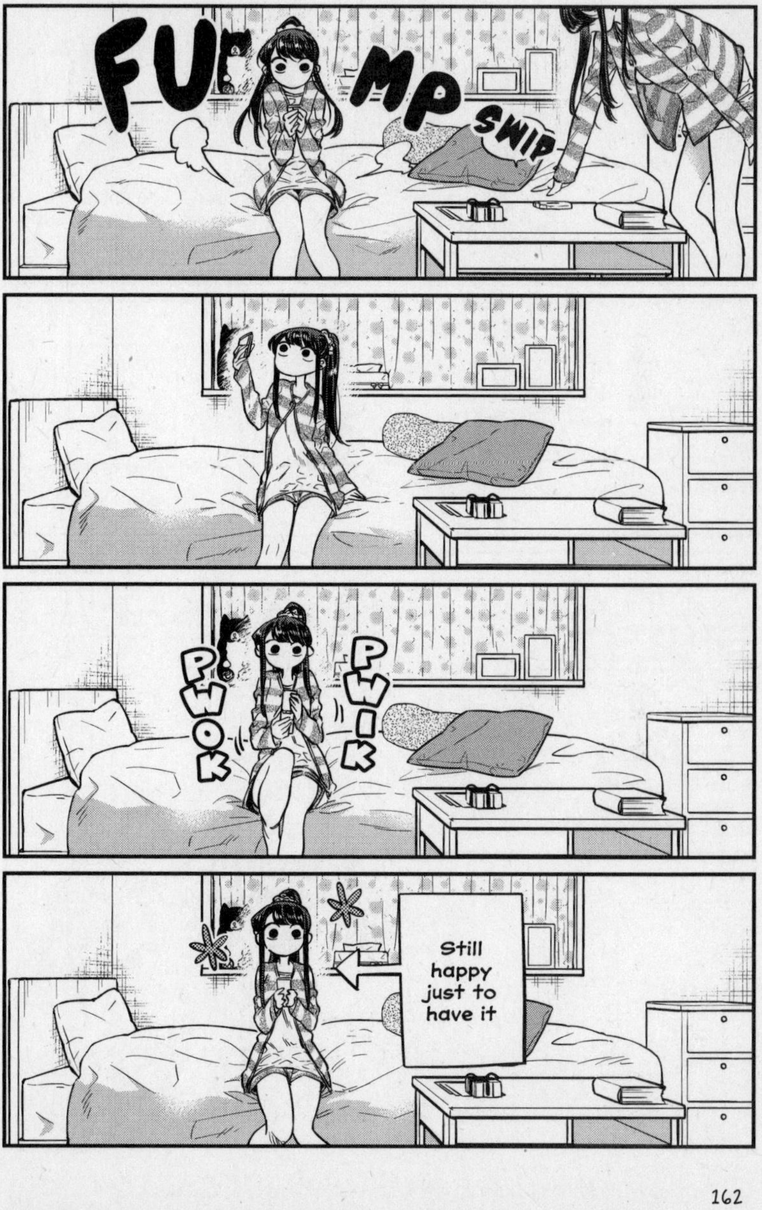
FUMP
SWIP
PWIK
PWOK
Still happy just to have it

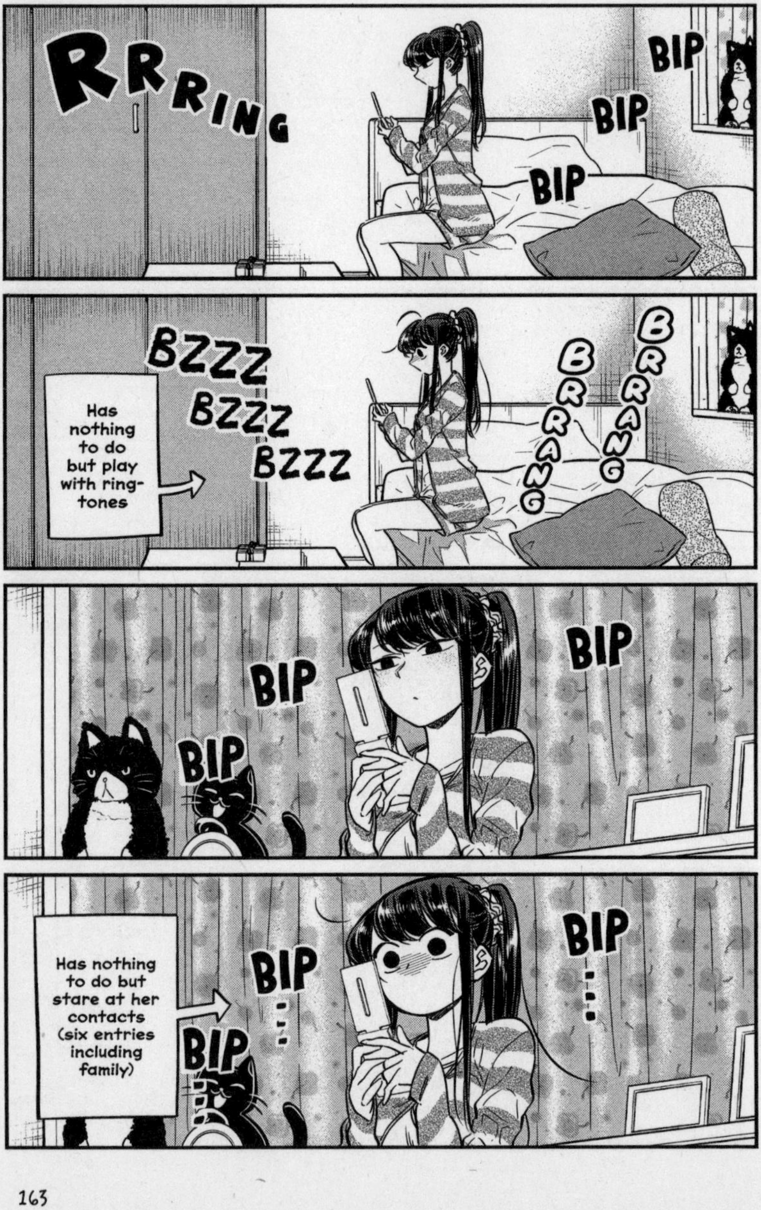
BIP
BIP
BIP
RRRING
BRRANG
BRRANG
BZZZ
BZZZ
BZZZ
Has nothing to do but play with ring-tones
BIP
BIP
BIP
BIP...
BIP...
BIP...
Has nothing to do but stare at her contacts (six entries including family)

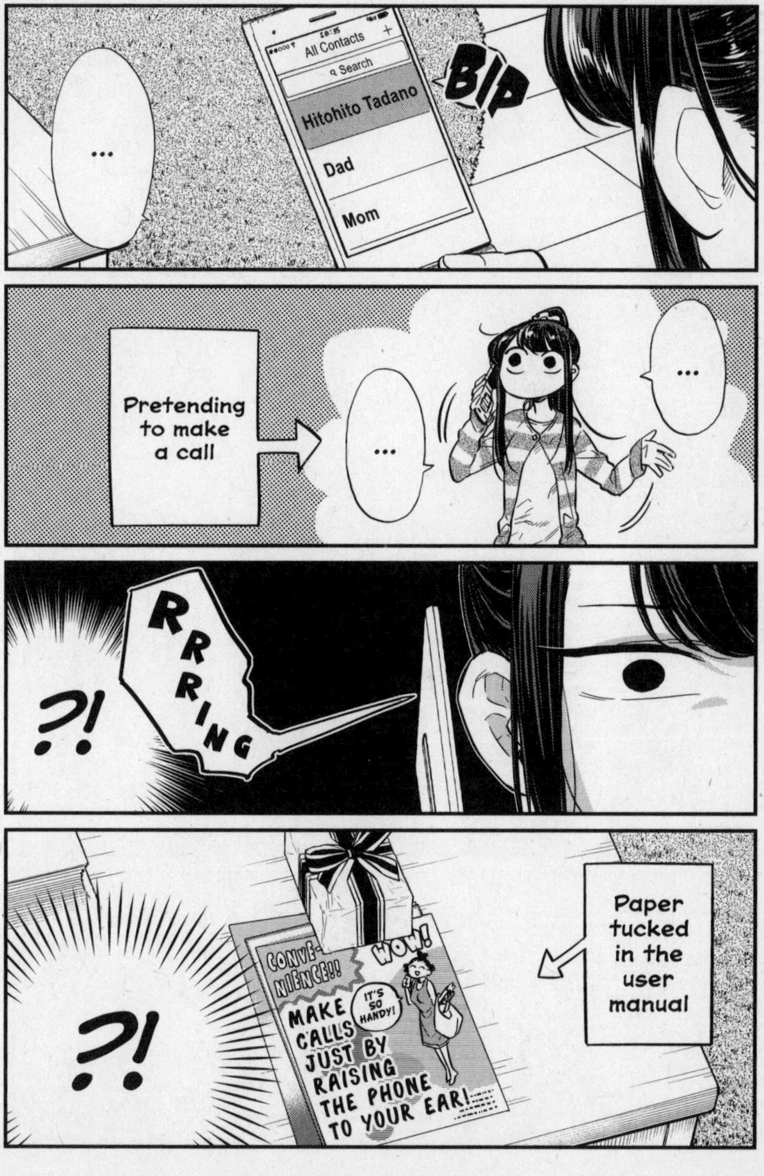
BIP
All Contacts
Search
Hitohito Tadano
Dad
Mom
...
...
...
Pretending to make a call
RRRING
?!
Paper tucked in the user manual
WOW!
CONVE-NIENCE!!
IT'S SO HANDY!
MAKE CALLS JUST BY RAISING THE PHONE TO YOUR EAR!
?!

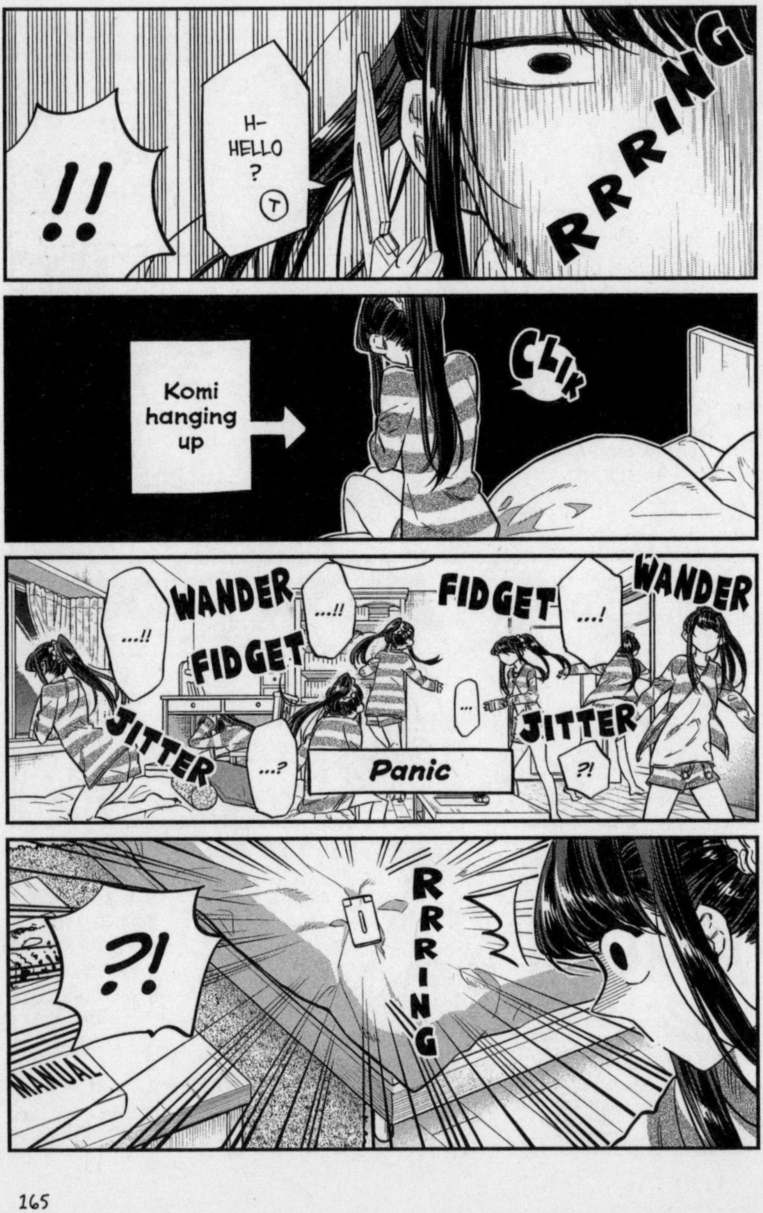
RRRING
H-HELLO?
(T)
!!
CLIK
Komi hanging up
WANDER
...!
FIDGET
JITTER
?!
...
...!!
Panic
WANDER
FIDGET
...!!
JITTER
...?
RRRING
?!
MANUAL

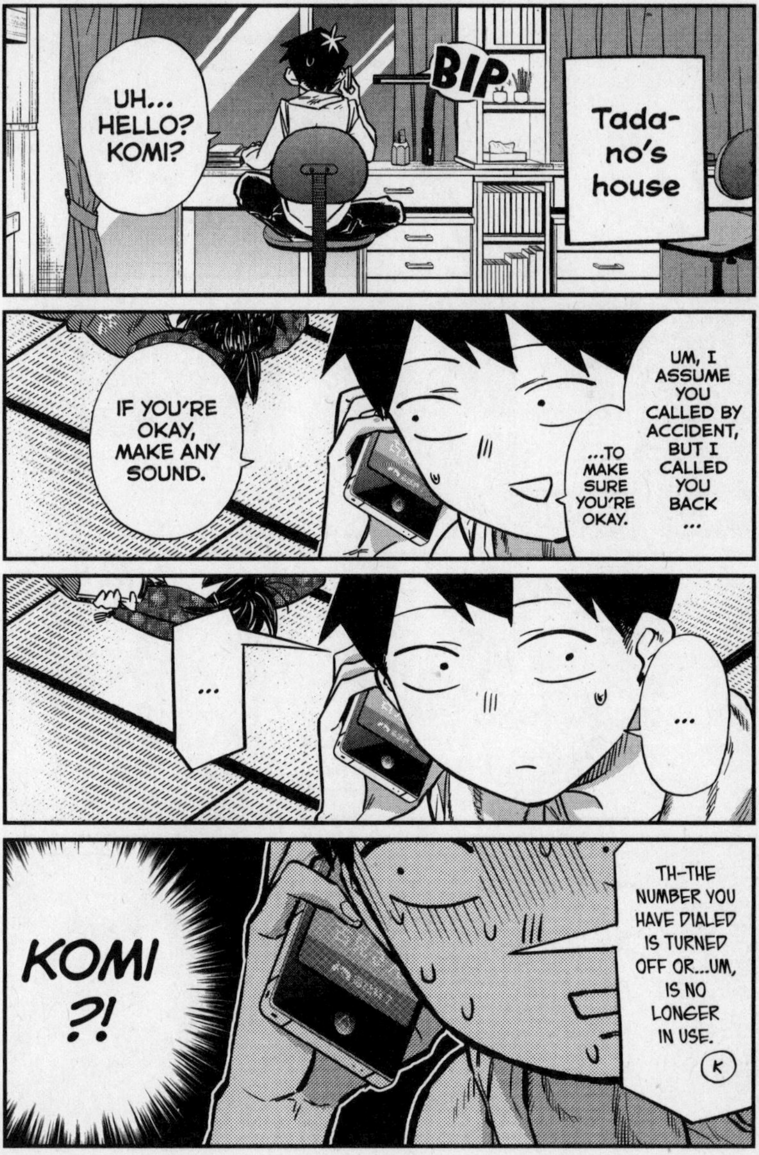
Tada-no's house
BIP
UH... HELLO? KOMI?
UM, I ASSUME YOU CALLED BY ACCIDENT, BUT I CALLED YOU BACK ...
...TO MAKE SURE YOU'RE OKAY.
IF YOU'RE OKAY, MAKE ANY SOUND.
...
...
TH-THE NUMBER YOU HAVE DIALED IS TURNED OFF OR...UM, IS NO LONGER IN USE.
KOMI ?!

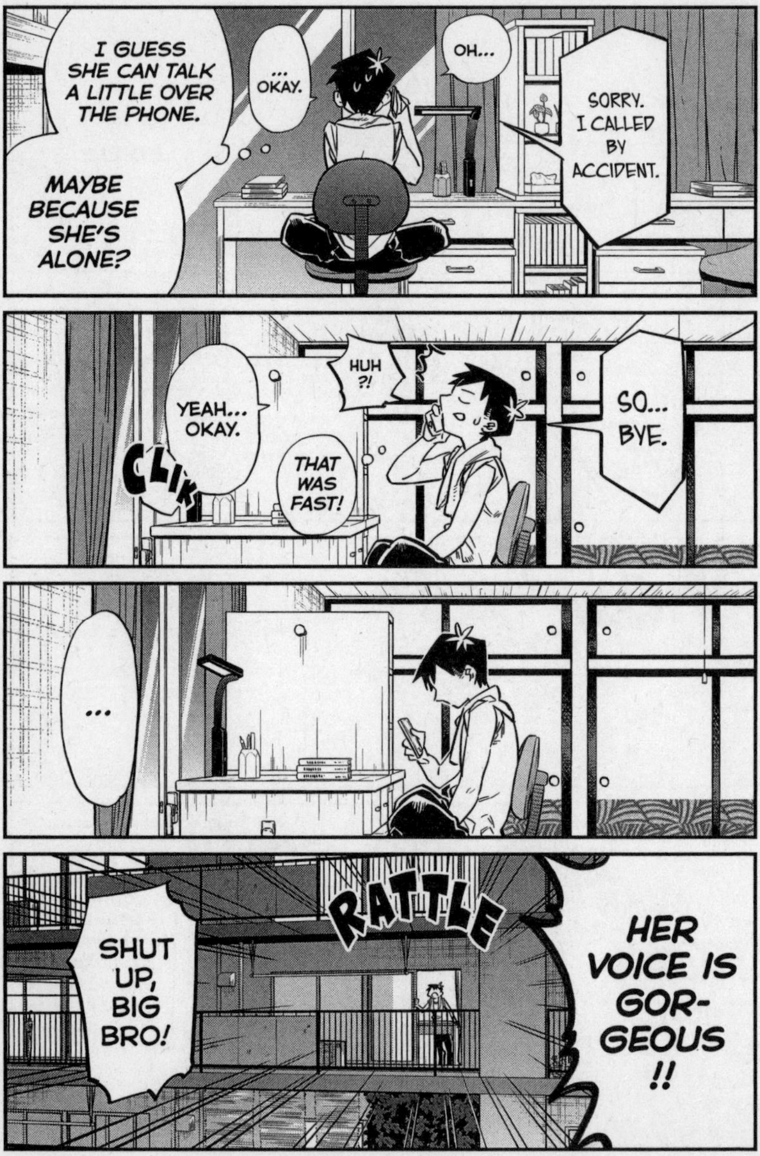
SORRY. I CALLED BY ACCIDENT.
OH...
... OKAY.
I GUESS SHE CAN TALK A LITTLE OVER THE PHONE.
MAYBE BECAUSE SHE'S ALONE?
SO... BYE.
HUH ?!
THAT WAS FAST!
YEAH... OKAY.
CLIK
...
HER VOICE IS GOR-GEOUS !!
RATTLE
SHUT UP, BIG BRO!

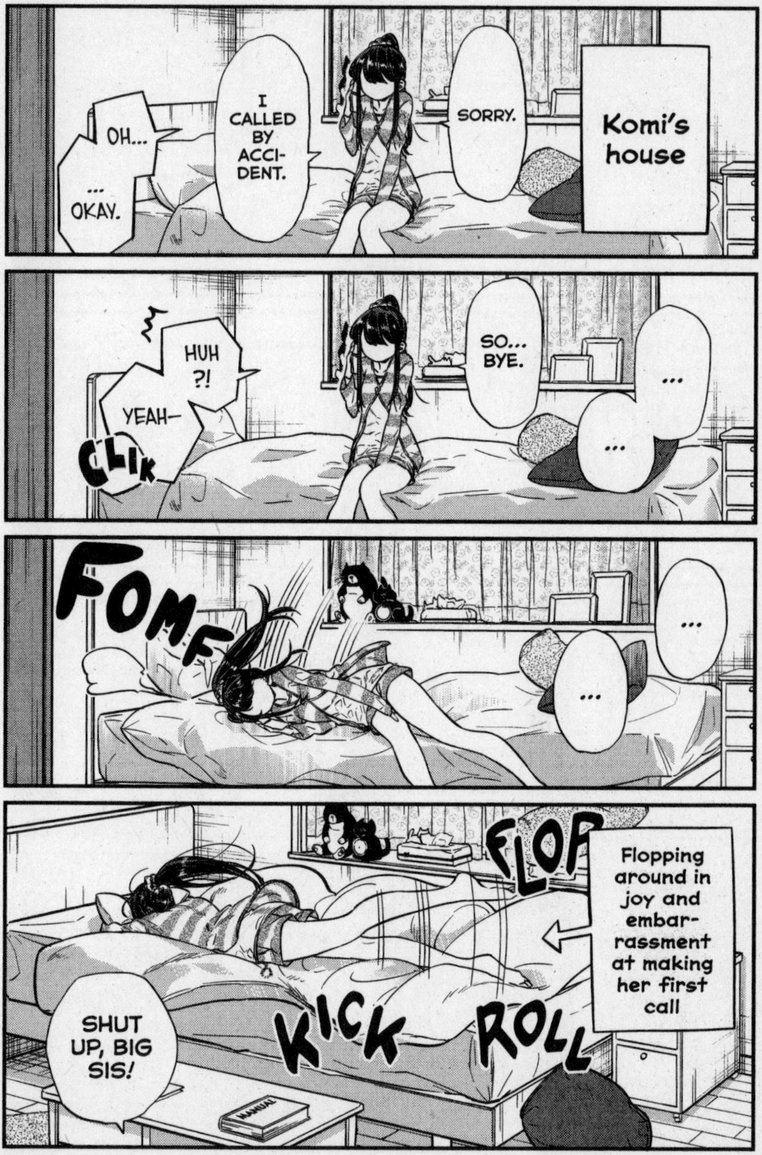
Komi's house
SORRY.
I CALLED BY ACCIDENT.
OH...
... OKAY.
...
...
SO... BYE.
HUH ?!
YEAH-
CLIK
...
...
FOMF
Flopping around in joy and embarrassment at making her first call
FLOP
ROLL
KICK
SHUT UP, BIG SIS!
MANUAL

Communication 18 — The End

Komi Can't Communicate

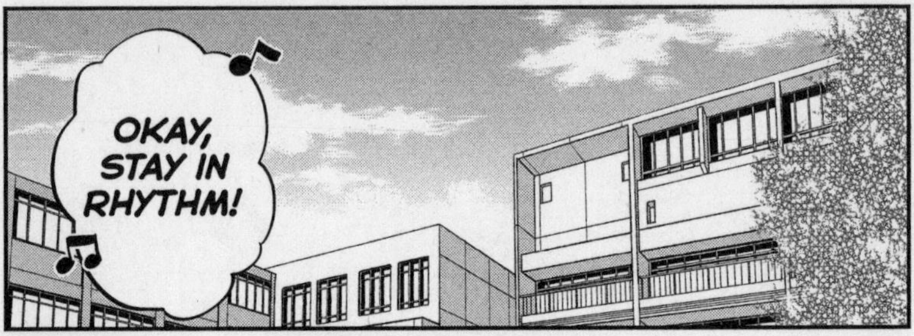
OKAY, STAY IN RHYTHM!

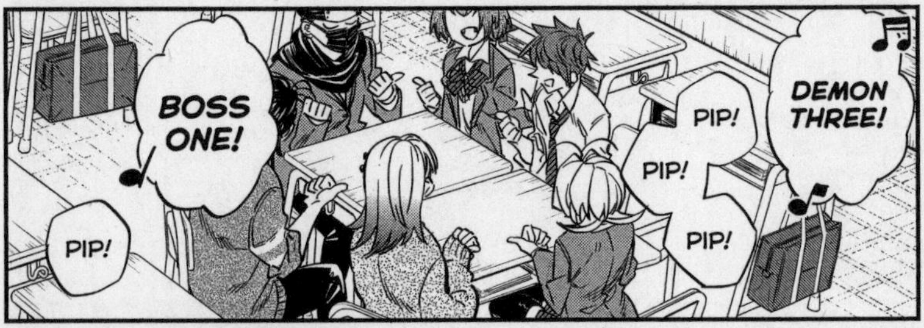
DEMON THREE!
PIP!
PIP!
PIP!
BOSS ONE!
PIP!

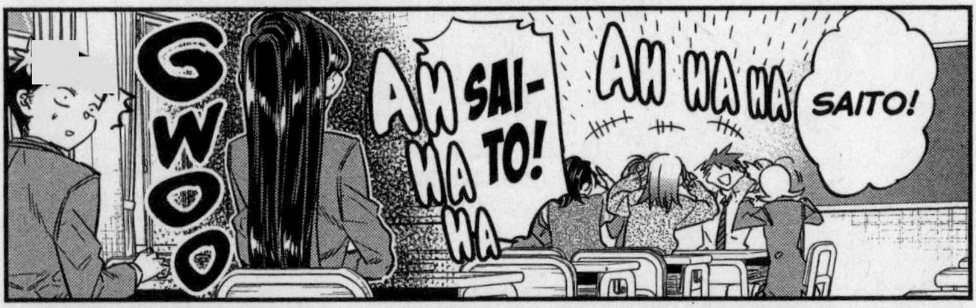
SAITO!
AH HA HA
SAI- TO!
AH HA HA HA
GWOO

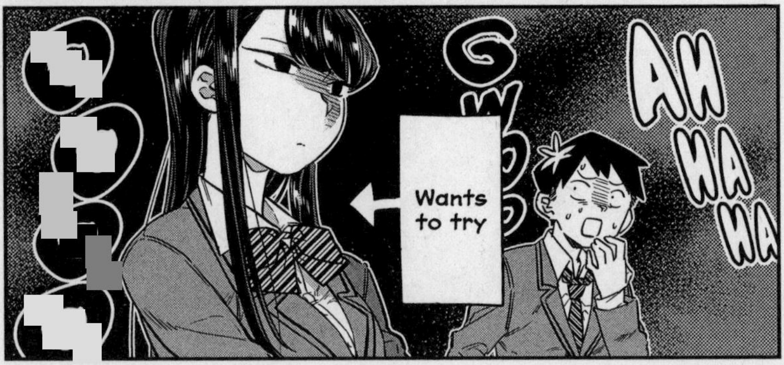
AH HA HA HA
GWOO
Wants to try

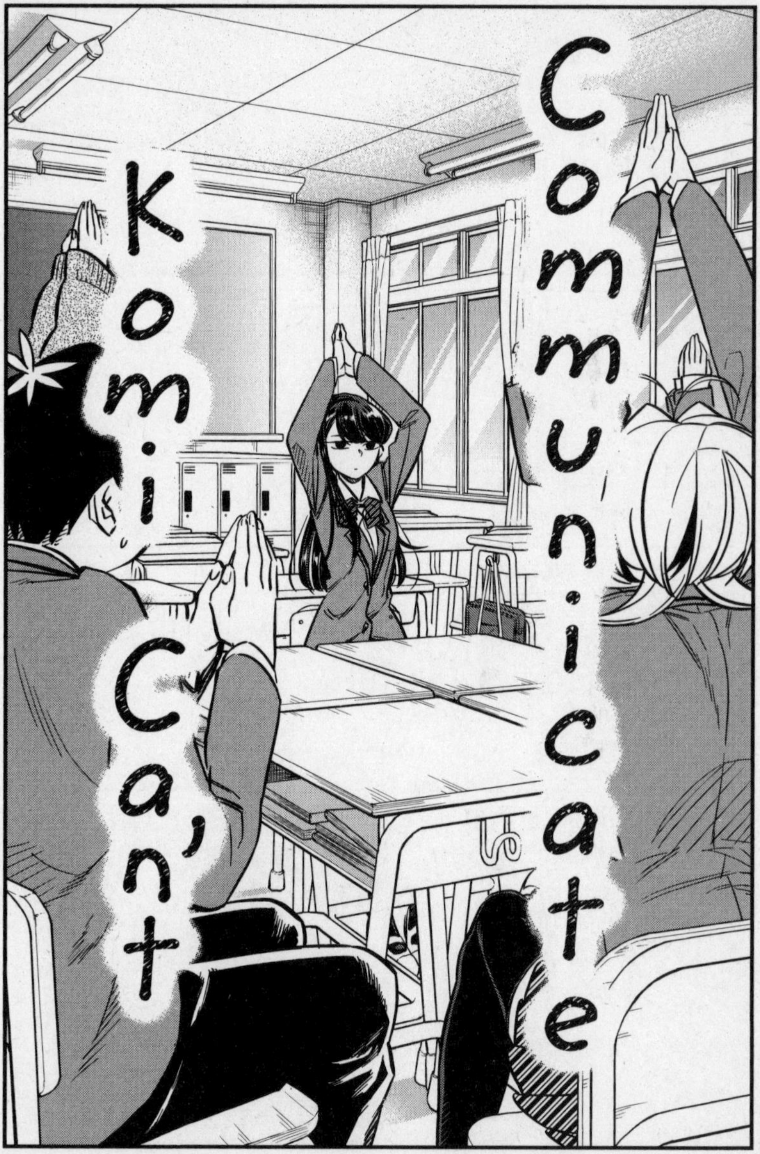
Komi Can't
Communicate

Communication 19: Saito

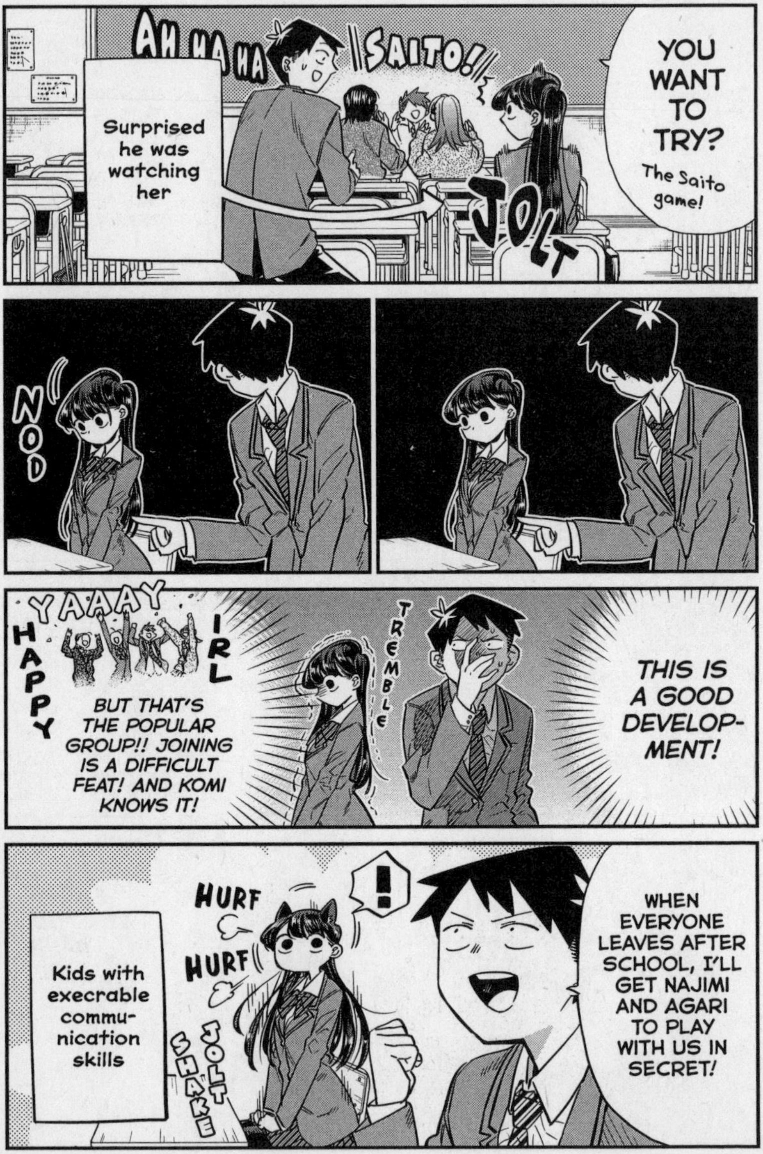
YOU WANT TO TRY?
The Saito game!
SAITO!
AH HA HA
Surprised he was watching her
JOLT
NOD
THIS IS A GOOD DEVELOP-MENT!
TREMBLE
IRL
YAAAY
HAPPY
BUT THAT'S THE POPULAR GROUP!! JOINING IS A DIFFICULT FEAT! AND KOMI KNOWS IT!
WHEN EVERYONE LEAVES AFTER SCHOOL, I'LL GET NAJIMI AND AGARI TO PLAY WITH US IN SECRET!
!
HURF
HURF
JOLT
SHAKE
Kids with execrable commu-nication skills

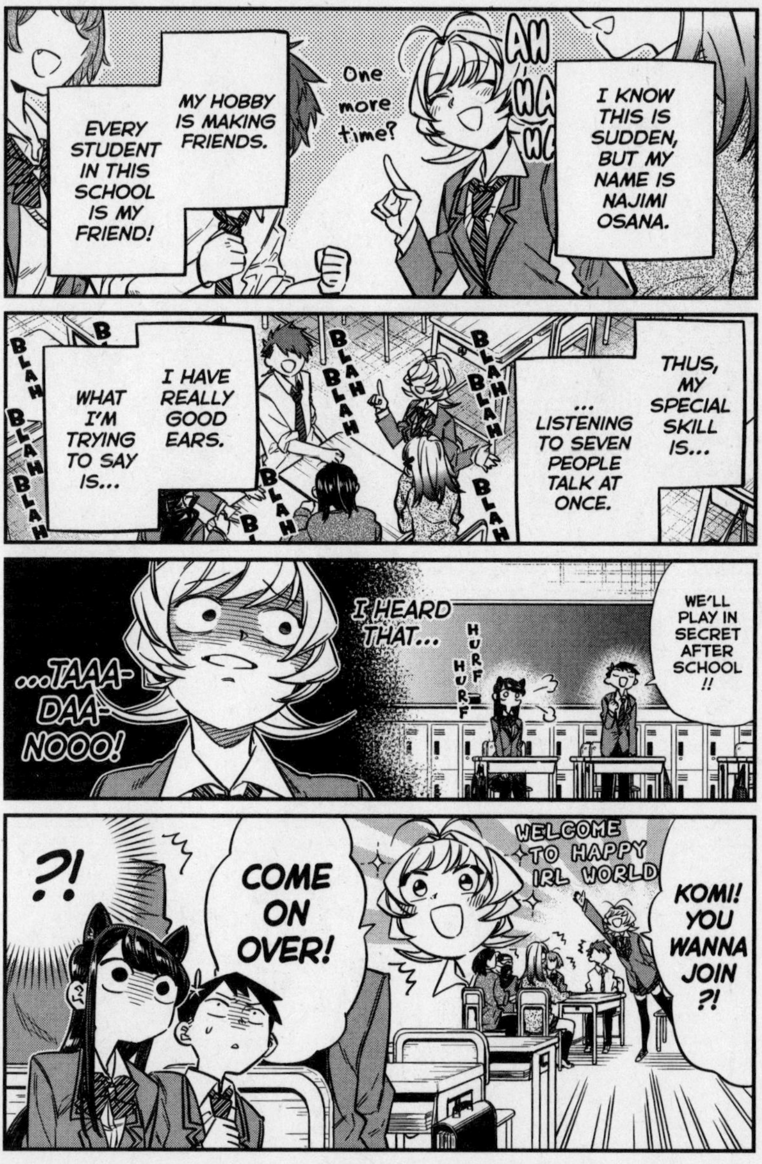
I KNOW THIS IS SUDDEN, BUT MY NAME IS NAJIMI OSANA.
AH HA HA
One more time?
MY HOBBY IS MAKING FRIENDS.
EVERY STUDENT IN THIS SCHOOL IS MY FRIEND!
THUS, MY SPECIAL SKILL IS...
... LISTENING TO SEVEN PEOPLE TALK AT ONCE.
BLAH BLAH BLAH
BLAH BLAH
BLAH BLAH
I HAVE REALLY GOOD EARS.
WHAT I'M TRYING TO SAY IS...
BLAH BLAH BLAH
WE'LL PLAY IN SECRET AFTER SCHOOL !!
HURF HURF
I HEARD THAT...
...TAAA-DAA-NOOO!
KOMI! YOU WANNA JOIN ?!
WELCOME TO HAPPY IRL WORLD
COME ON OVER!
?!

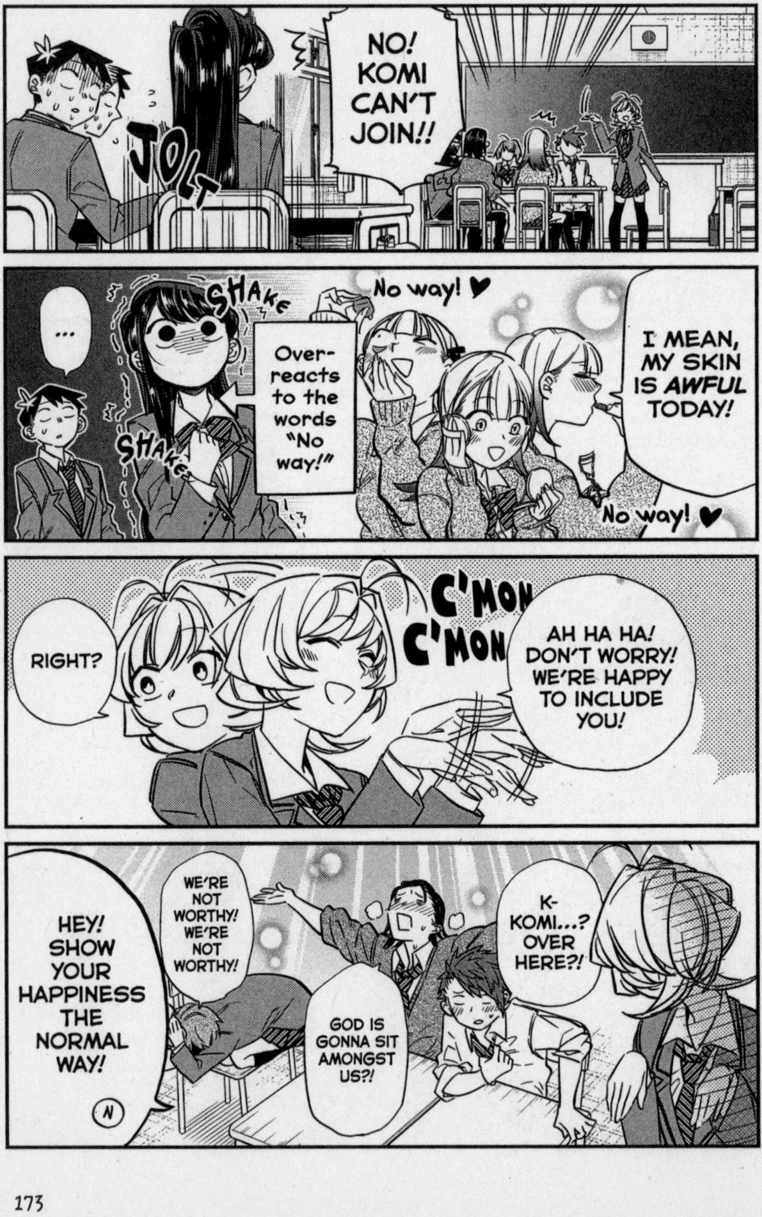
NO! KOMI CAN'T JOIN!!
JOLT
I MEAN, MY SKIN IS AWFUL TODAY!
No way! ♥
No way! ♥
Over-reacts to the words "No way!"
SHAKE
SHAKE
...
AH HA HA! DON'T WORRY! WE'RE HAPPY TO INCLUDE YOU!
C'MON C'MON
RIGHT?
K-KOMI...? OVER HERE?!
WE'RE NOT WORTHY! WE'RE NOT WORTHY!
GOD IS GONNA SIT AMONGST US?!
HEY! SHOW YOUR HAPPINESS THE NORMAL WAY!
N

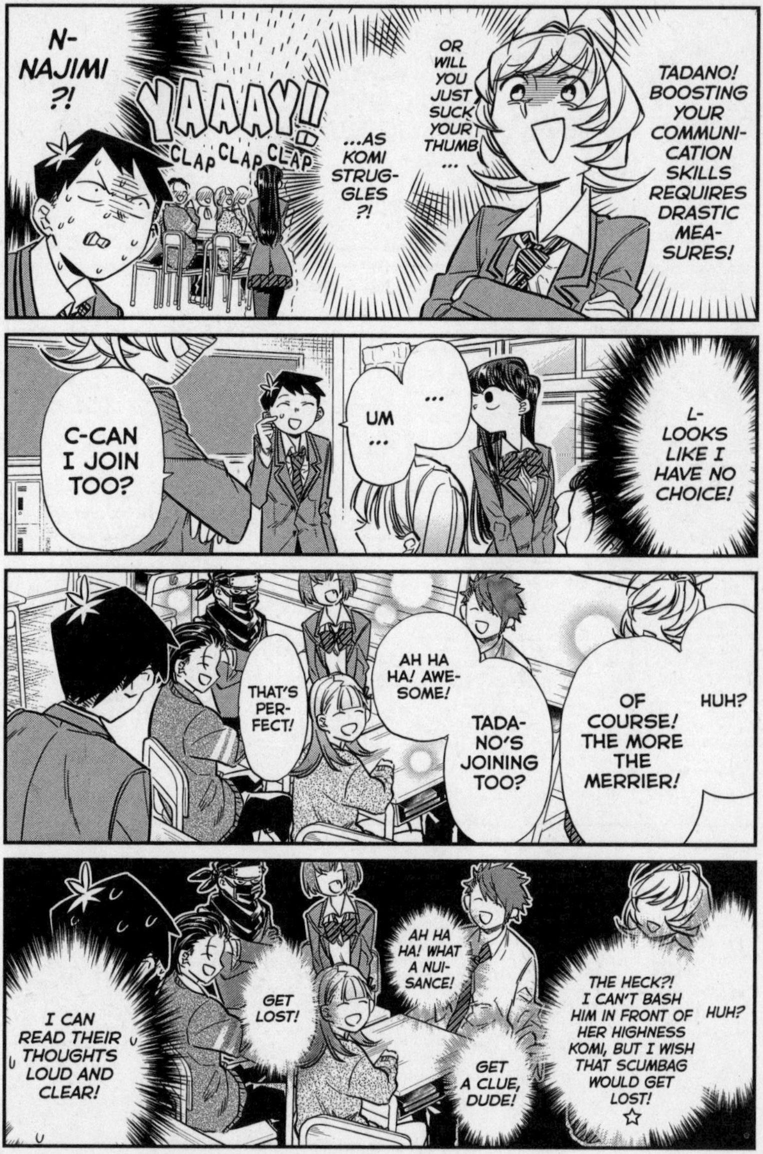
TADANO! BOOSTING YOUR COMMUNICATION SKILLS REQUIRES DRASTIC MEASURES!
OR WILL YOU JUST SUCK YOUR THUMB ...
...AS KOMI STRUGGLES?!
YAAAY!!
CLAP CLAP CLAP
N-NAJIMI?!
L-LOOKS LIKE I HAVE NO CHOICE!
...
UM ...
C-CAN I JOIN TOO?
HUH?
OF COURSE! THE MORE THE MERRIER!
TADANO'S JOINING TOO?
AH HA HA! AWESOME!
THAT'S PERFECT!
HUH?
THE HECK?! I CAN'T BASH HIM IN FRONT OF HER HIGHNESS KOMI, BUT I WISH THAT SCUMBAG WOULD GET LOST! ☆
AH HA HA! WHAT A NUISANCE!
GET A CLUE, DUDE!
GET LOST!
I CAN READ THEIR THOUGHTS LOUD AND CLEAR!

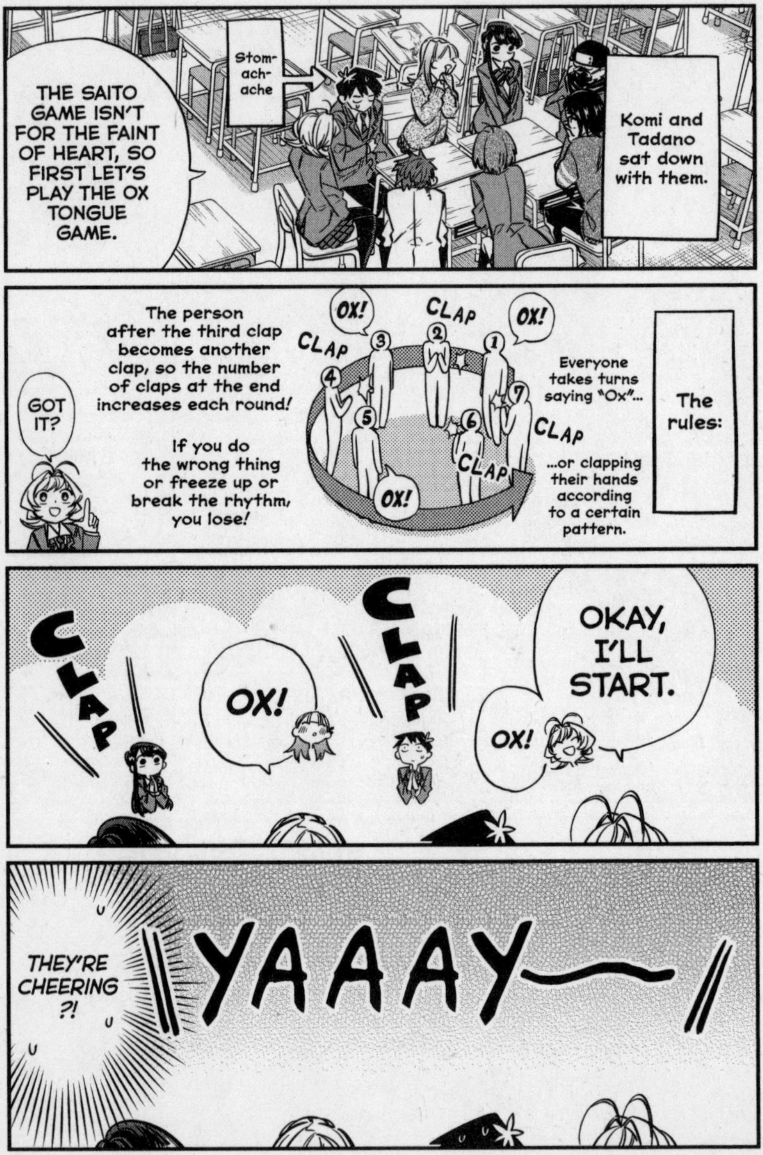
Komi and Tadano sat down with them.
Stom-ach-ache
THE SAITO GAME ISN'T FOR THE FAINT OF HEART, SO FIRST LET'S PLAY THE OX TONGUE GAME.
The rules:
Everyone takes turns saying "Ox"...
...or clapping their hands according to a certain pattern.
OX!
CLAP
OX!
CLAP
OX!
CLAP
CLAP
The person after the third clap becomes another clap, so the number of claps at the end increases each round!
If you do the wrong thing or freeze up or break the rhythm, you lose!
GOT IT?
OKAY, I'LL START.
OX!
CLAP
OX!
CLAP
YAAAY—
THEY'RE CHEERING?!

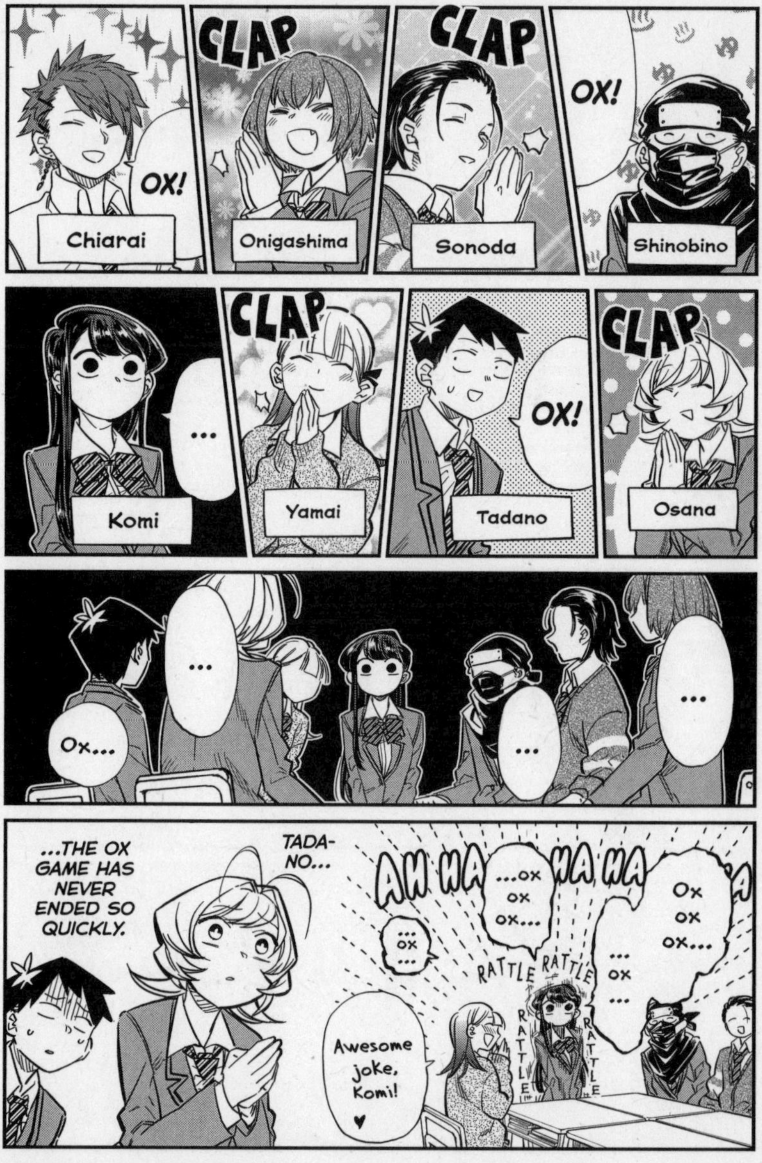
OX!
Shinobino
CLAP
Sonoda
CLAP
Onigashima
OX!
Chiarai
CLAP
Osana
OX!
Tadano
CLAP
Yamai
...
Komi
...
...
...
Ox...
AH HA HA HA
Ox ox ox...
... ox ...
...ox ox ox...
RATTLE RATTLE
RATTLE RATTLE
...ox...
Awesome joke, Komi! ♥
TADANO...
...THE OX GAME HAS NEVER ENDED SO QUICKLY.

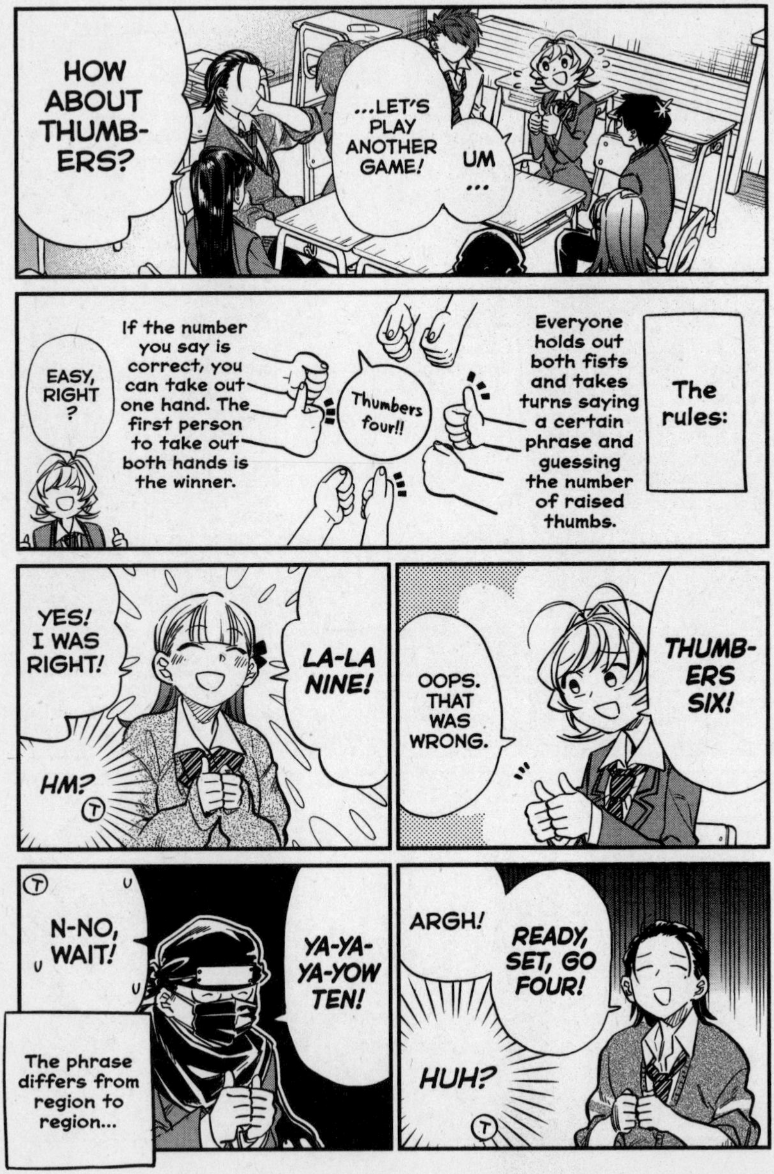
UM ...
...LET'S PLAY ANOTHER GAME!
HOW ABOUT THUMBERS?
The rules:
Everyone holds out both fists and takes turns saying a certain phrase and guessing the number of raised thumbs.
Thumbers four!!
If the number you say is correct, you can take out one hand. The first person to take out both hands is the winner.
EASY, RIGHT?
THUMBERS SIX!
OOPS. THAT WAS WRONG.
LA-LA NINE!
YES! I WAS RIGHT!
HM?
READY, SET, GO FOUR!
ARGH!
HUH?
YA-YA-YA-YOW TEN!
N-NO, WAIT!
The phrase differs from region to region...

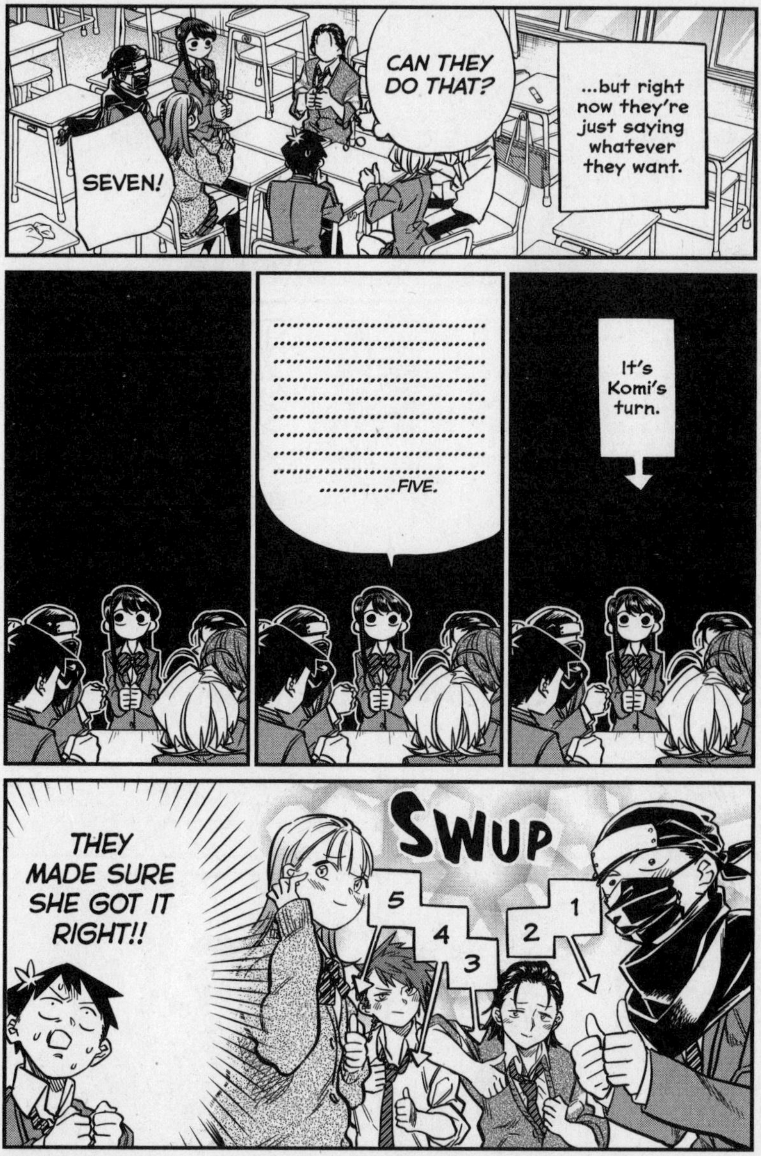
SEVEN!
CAN THEY DO THAT?
...but right now they're just saying whatever they want.
It's Komi's turn.
....
....
....
....
....
....
....
....
....
............FIVE.
SWUP
1
2
3
4
5
THEY MADE SURE SHE GOT IT RIGHT!!

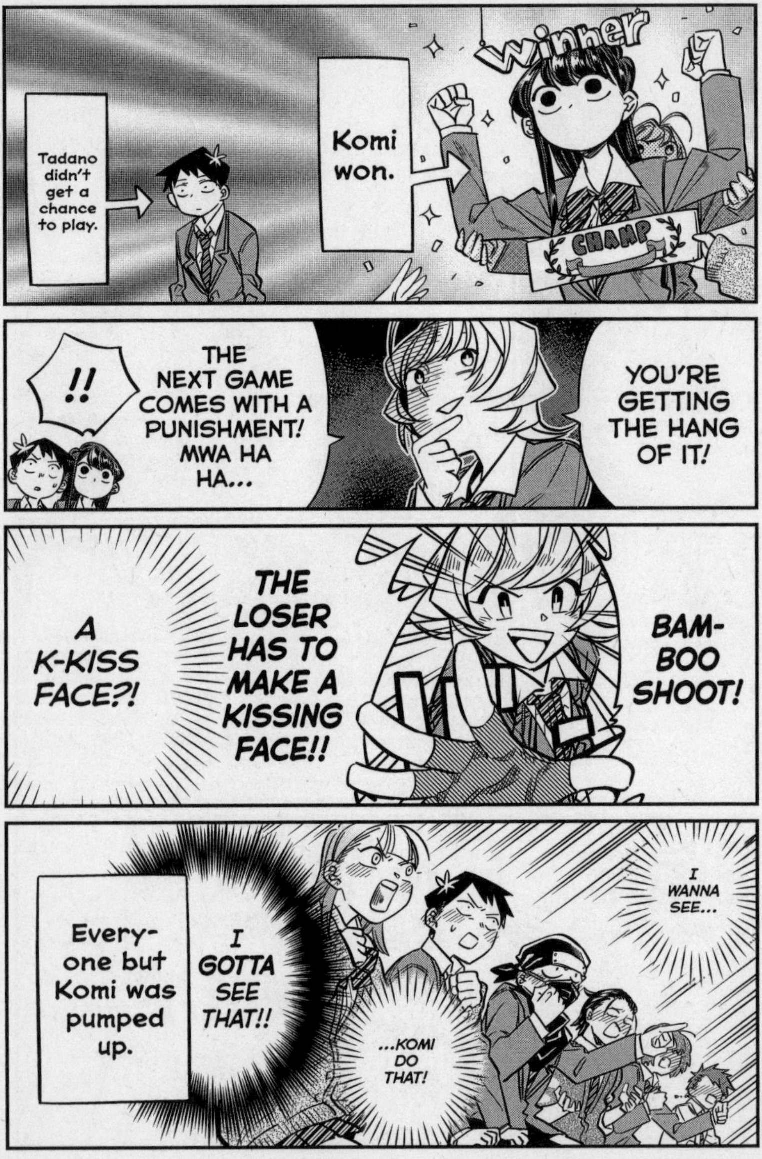
Winner
Komi won.
CHAMP
Tadano didn't get a chance to play.
YOU'RE GETTING THE HANG OF IT!
THE NEXT GAME COMES WITH A PUNISHMENT! MWA HA HA...
!!
BAMBOO SHOOT!
THE LOSER HAS TO MAKE A KISSING FACE!!
A K-KISS FACE?!
I WANNA SEE...
...KOMI DO THAT!
I GOTTA SEE THAT!!
Everyone but Komi was pumped up.

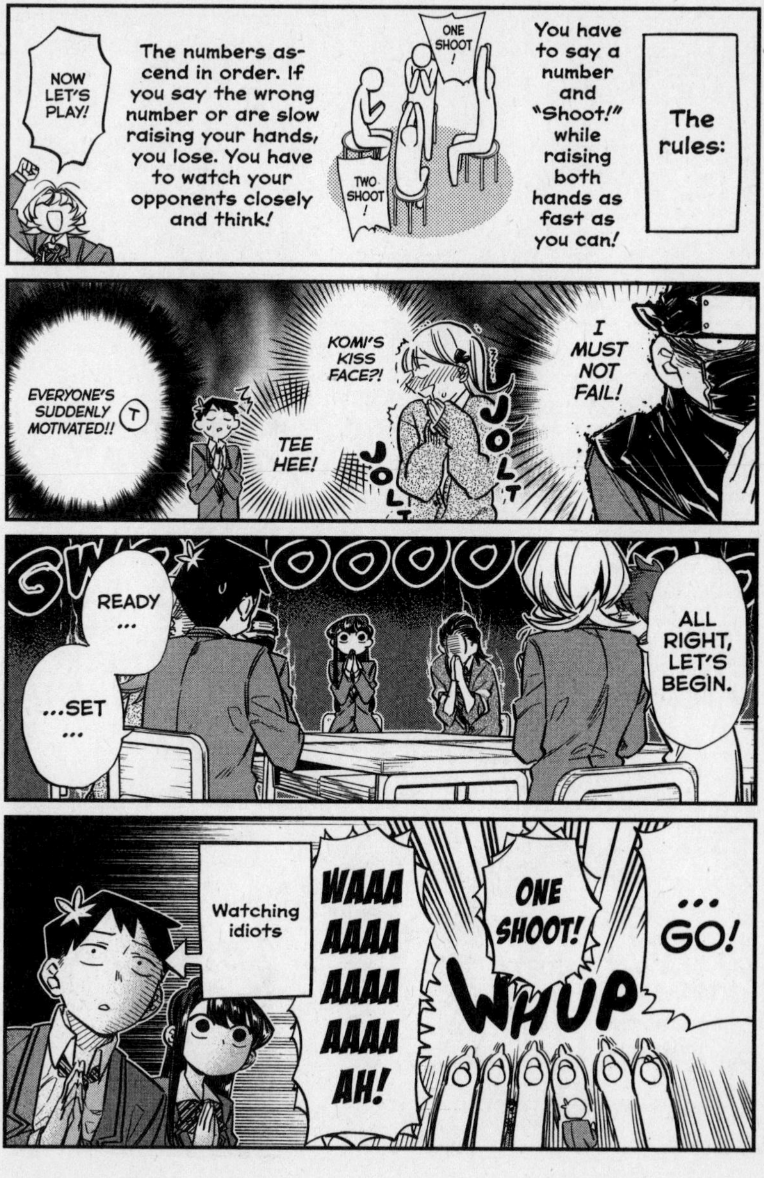
The rules:
You have to say a number and "Shoot!" while raising both hands as fast as you can!
ONE SHOOT!
TWO SHOOT!
The numbers ascend in order. If you say the wrong number or are slow raising your hands, you lose. You have to watch your opponents closely and think!
NOW LET'S PLAY!
I MUST NOT FAIL!
JOLT
JOLT
KOMI'S KISS FACE?!
TEE HEE!
EVERYONE'S SUDDENLY MOTIVATED!! T
ALL RIGHT, LET'S BEGIN.
READY ...
...SET ...
... GO!
ONE SHOOT!
WHUP
WAAAAAAAAAAAAAAAAAAH!
Watching idiots

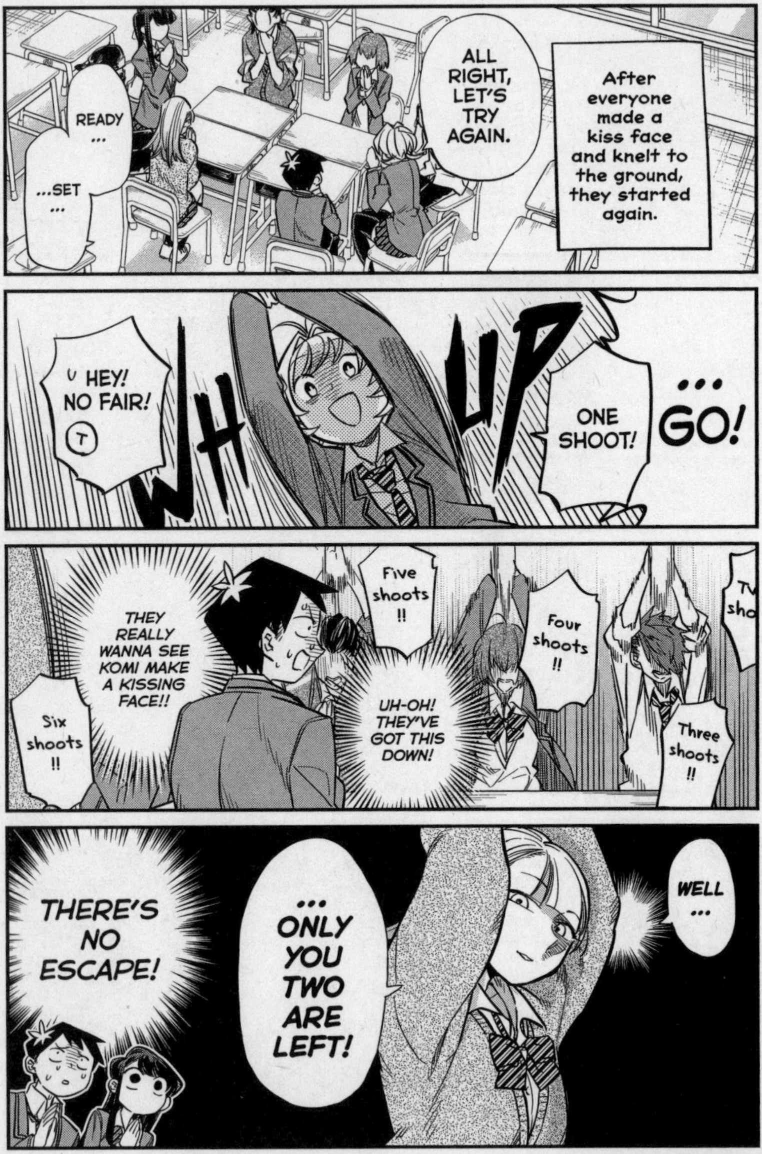
After everyone made a kiss face and knelt to the ground, they started again.
ALL RIGHT, LET'S TRY AGAIN.
READY ...
...SET ...
... GO!
ONE SHOOT!
WHUP
HEY! NO FAIR!
Three shoots !!
Four shoots !!
Five shoots !!
UH-OH! THEY'VE GOT THIS DOWN!
THEY REALLY WANNA SEE KOMI MAKE A KISSING FACE!!
Six shoots !!
WELL ...
... ONLY YOU TWO ARE LEFT!
THERE'S NO ESCAPE!

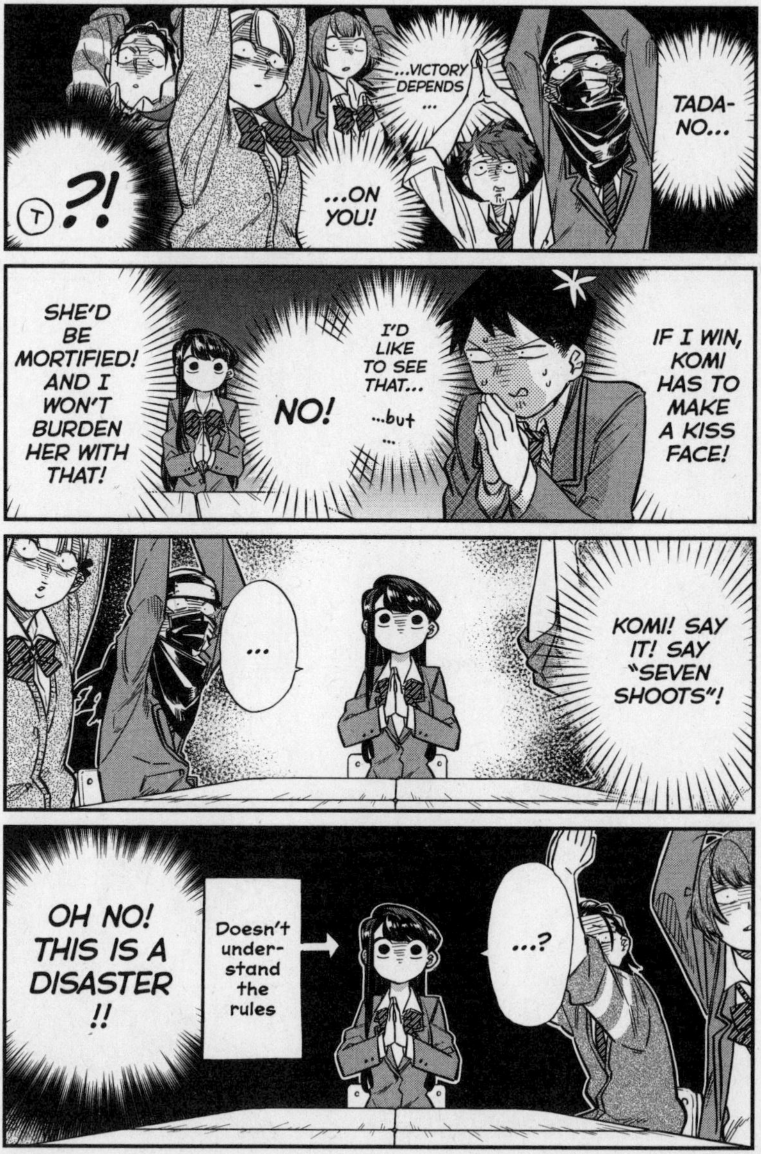
TADA-NO...
...VICTORY DEPENDS ...
...ON YOU!
?!
IF I WIN, KOMI HAS TO MAKE A KISS FACE!
I'D LIKE TO SEE THAT...
...but ...
NO!
SHE'D BE MORTIFIED! AND I WON'T BURDEN HER WITH THAT!
KOMI! SAY IT! SAY "SEVEN SHOOTS"!
...
...?
Doesn't under-stand the rules
OH NO! THIS IS A DISASTER !!

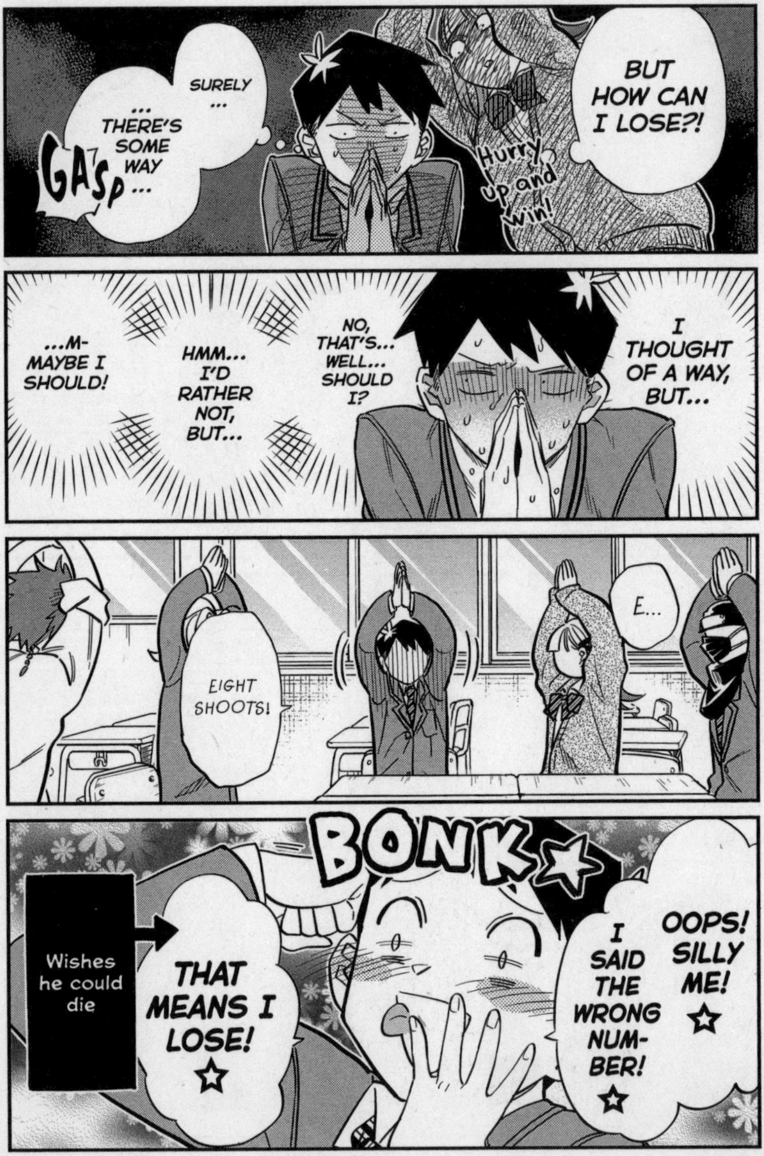
BUT HOW CAN I LOSE?!
Hurry up and win!
SURELY ... ... THERE'S SOME WAY ...
GASP
I THOUGHT OF A WAY, BUT...
NO, THAT'S... WELL... SHOULD I?
HMM... I'D RATHER NOT, BUT...
...M-MAYBE I SHOULD!
E...
EIGHT SHOOTS!
BONK☆
OOPS! SILLY ME! ☆
I SAID THE WRONG NUMBER! ☆
THAT MEANS I LOSE! ☆
Wishes he could die

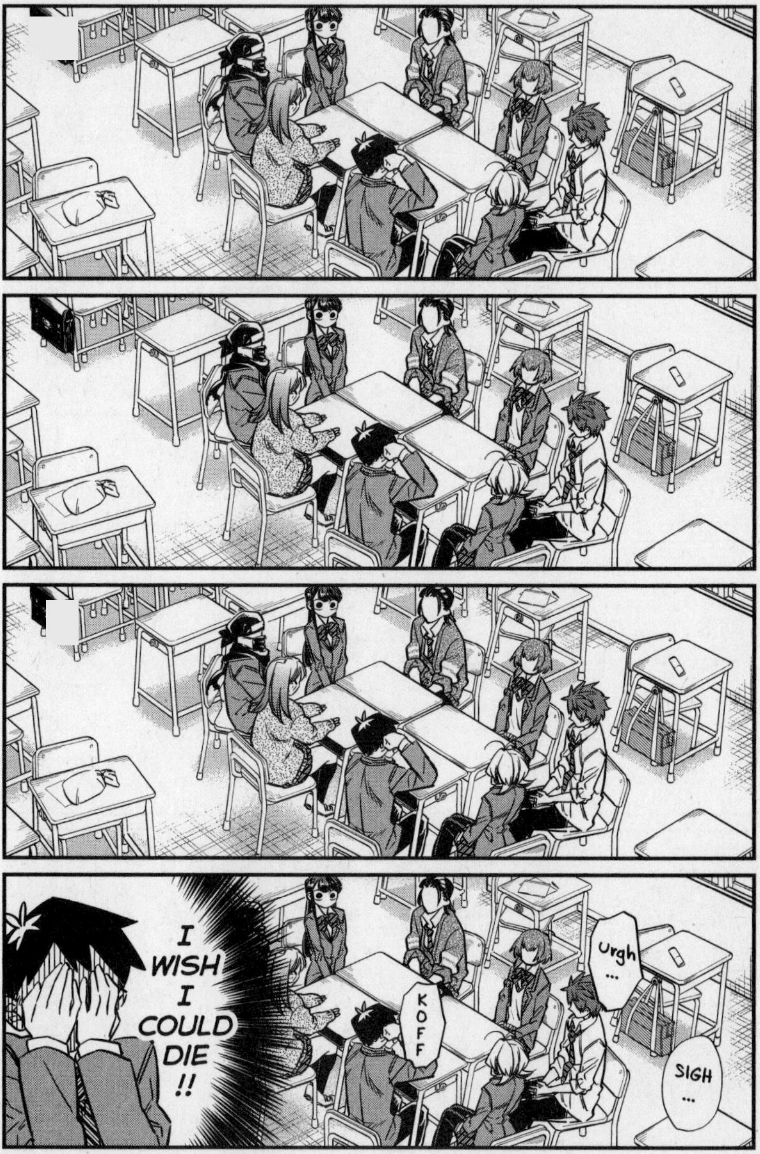
Urgh ...
SIGH ...
KOFF
I WISH I COULD DIE !!

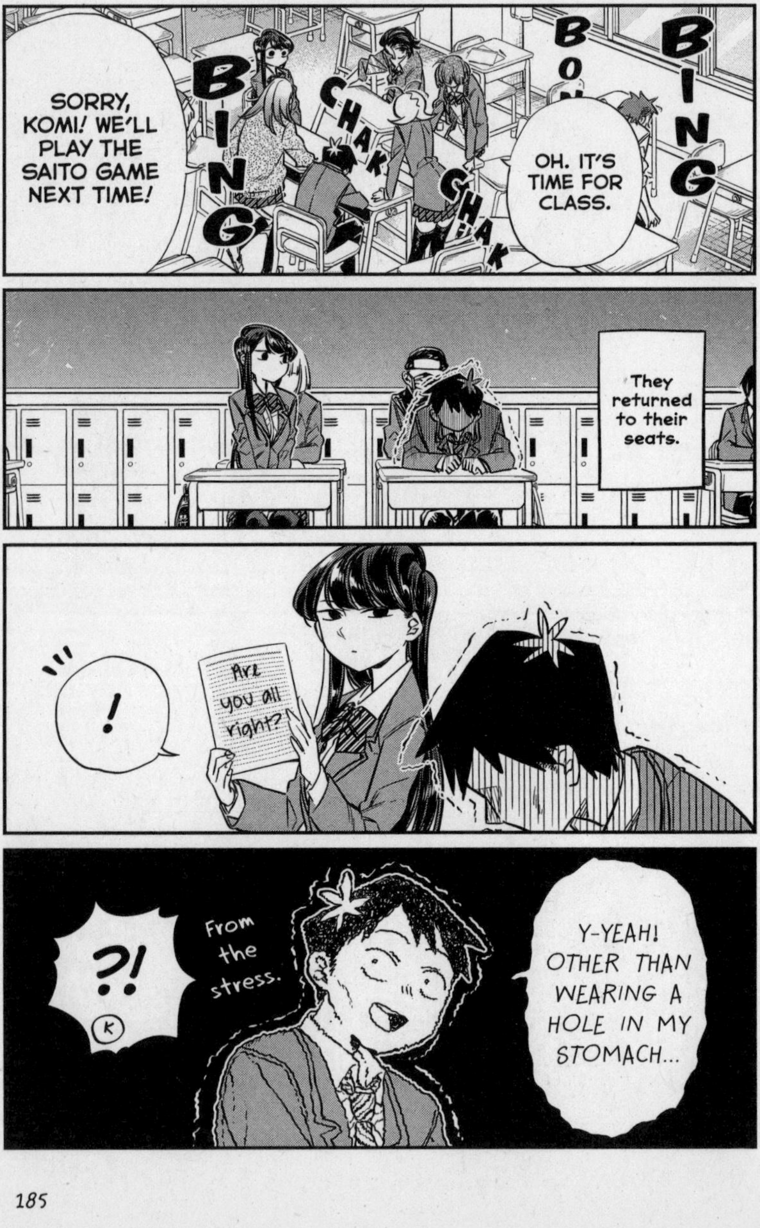
BING
BONG
OH. IT'S TIME FOR CLASS.
CHAK
CHAK
BING
SORRY, KOMI! WE'LL PLAY THE SAITO GAME NEXT TIME!
They returned to their seats.
Are you all right?
!
Y-YEAH! OTHER THAN WEARING A HOLE IN MY STOMACH...
From the stress.
?!
K

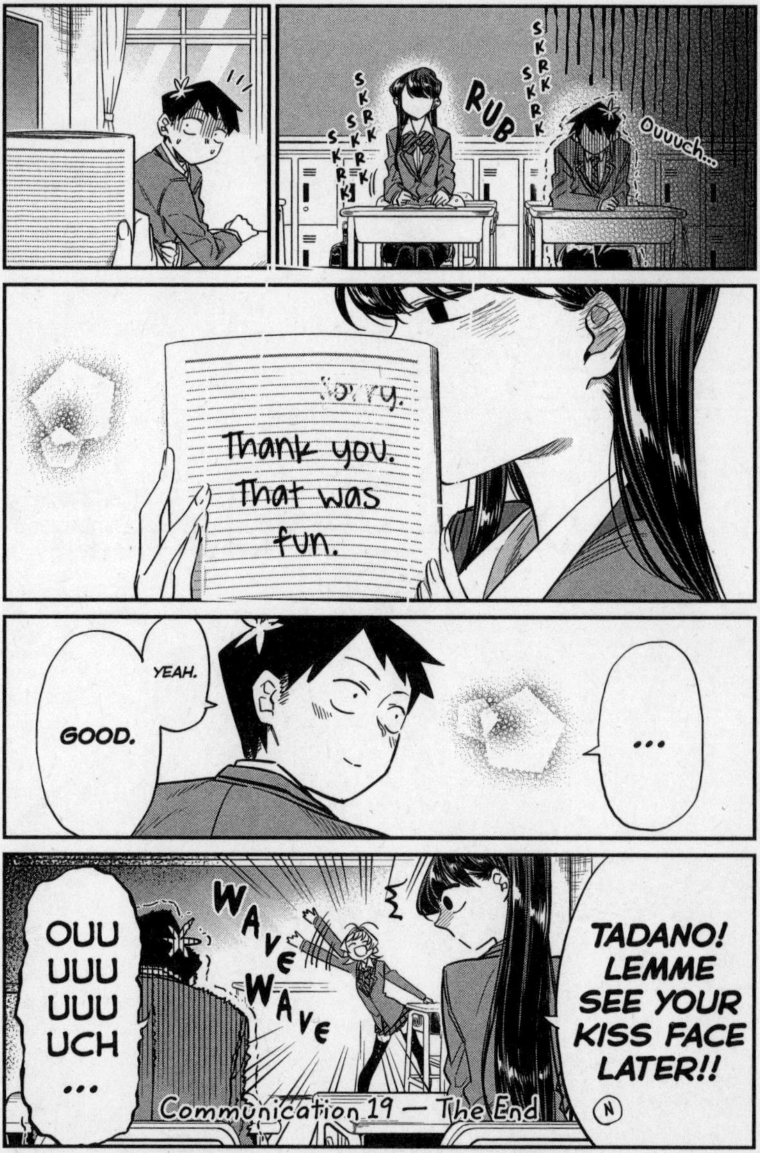
SKRK SKRK
RUB
SKRK SKRK
Ouuuch...
Sorry.
Thank you. That was fun.
...
YEAH. GOOD.
TADANO! LEMME SEE YOUR KISS FACE LATER!!
WAVE WAVE
OUUUUUUUUUUCH...
Communication 19 — The End

Komi Can't Communicate vol. 1 — The End

Komi Can't Communicate

Komi Can't Communicate

Can She Make a Hundred Friends?

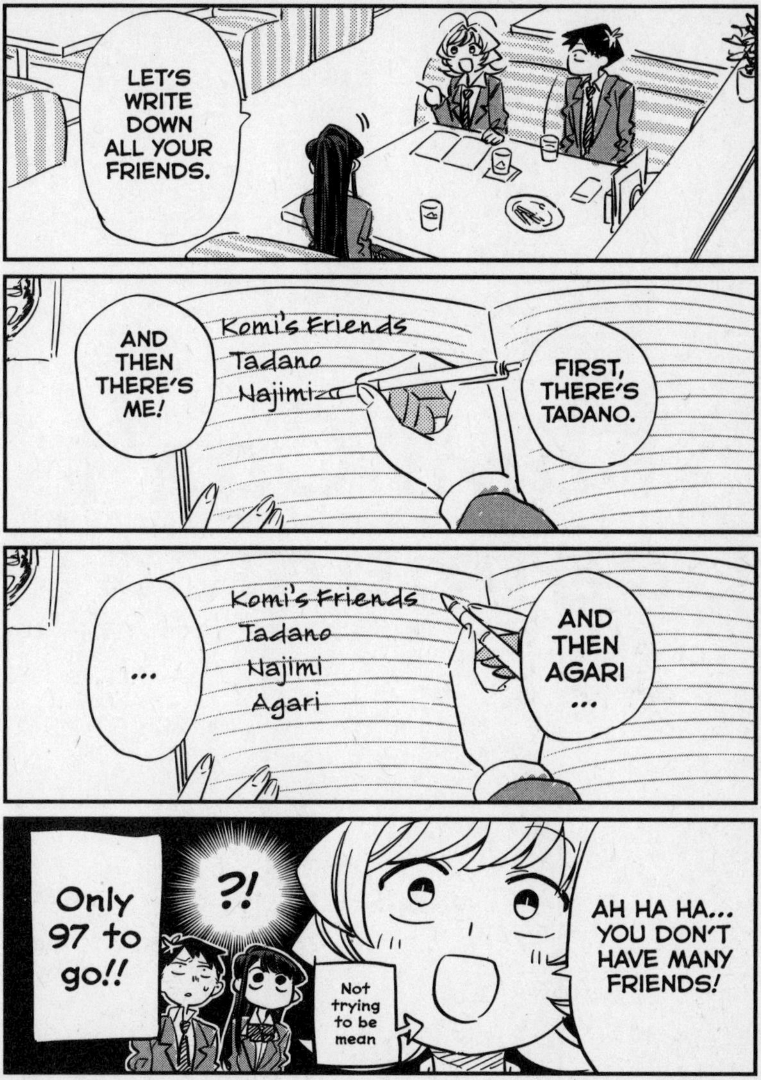
LET'S WRITE DOWN ALL YOUR FRIENDS.
FIRST, THERE'S TADANO.
Komi's Friends
Tadano
Najimi
AND THEN THERE'S ME!
AND THEN AGARI ...
Komi's Friends
Tadano
Najimi
Agari
...
AH HA HA... YOU DON'T HAVE MANY FRIENDS!
Not trying to be mean
?!
Only 97 to go!!

Komi Can't Communicate

A Distant Gaze

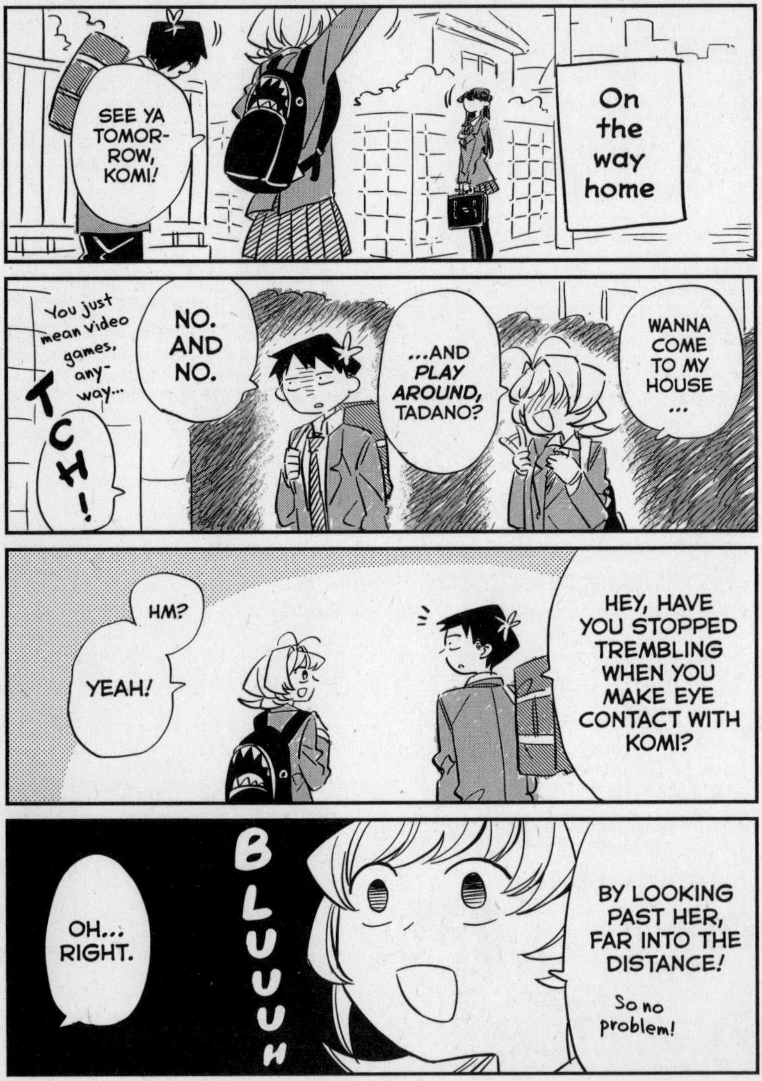
On the way home
SEE YA TOMORROW, KOMI!
WANNA COME TO MY HOUSE ...
...AND *PLAY AROUND,* TADANO?
NO. AND NO.
You just mean video games, anyway...
TCH!
HEY, HAVE YOU STOPPED TREMBLING WHEN YOU MAKE EYE CONTACT WITH KOMI?
HM?
YEAH!
BY LOOKING PAST HER, FAR INTO THE DISTANCE!
So no problem!
BLUUUH
OH... RIGHT.

Komi Can't Communicate

VOL. 1
Shonen Sunday Edition

Story and Art by Tomohito Oda

English Translation & Adaptation/John Werry
Touch-Up Art & Lettering/Eve Grandt
Design/Julian [JR] Robinson
Editor/Pancha Diaz

COMI-SAN WA, COMYUSHO DESU. Vol.1
by Tomohito ODA
© 2016 Tomohito ODA
All rights reserved.
Original Japanese edition published by SHOGAKUKAN.
English translation rights in the United States of America, Canada, the United
Kingdom, Ireland, Australia and New Zealand arranged with SHOGAKUKAN.

Original Cover Design/Masato ISHIZAWA + Bay Bridge Studio

Printed in the U.S.A.

Published by VIZ Media, LLC
P.O. Box 77010
San Francisco, CA 94107

10 9 8 7 6 5 4
First printing, June 2019
Fourth printing, March 2020

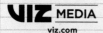

viz.com

shonensunday.com

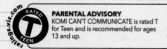

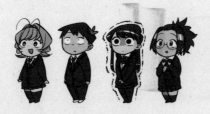

Tomohito Oda won the grand prize for *World Worst One* in the 70th Shogakukan New Comic Artist Awards in 2012. Oda's series *Digicon*, about a tough high school girl who finds herself in control of an alien with plans for world domination, ran from 2014 to 2015. In 2015, *Komi Can't Communicate* debuted as a one-shot in *Weekly Shonen Sunday* and was picked up as a full series by the same magazine in 2016.

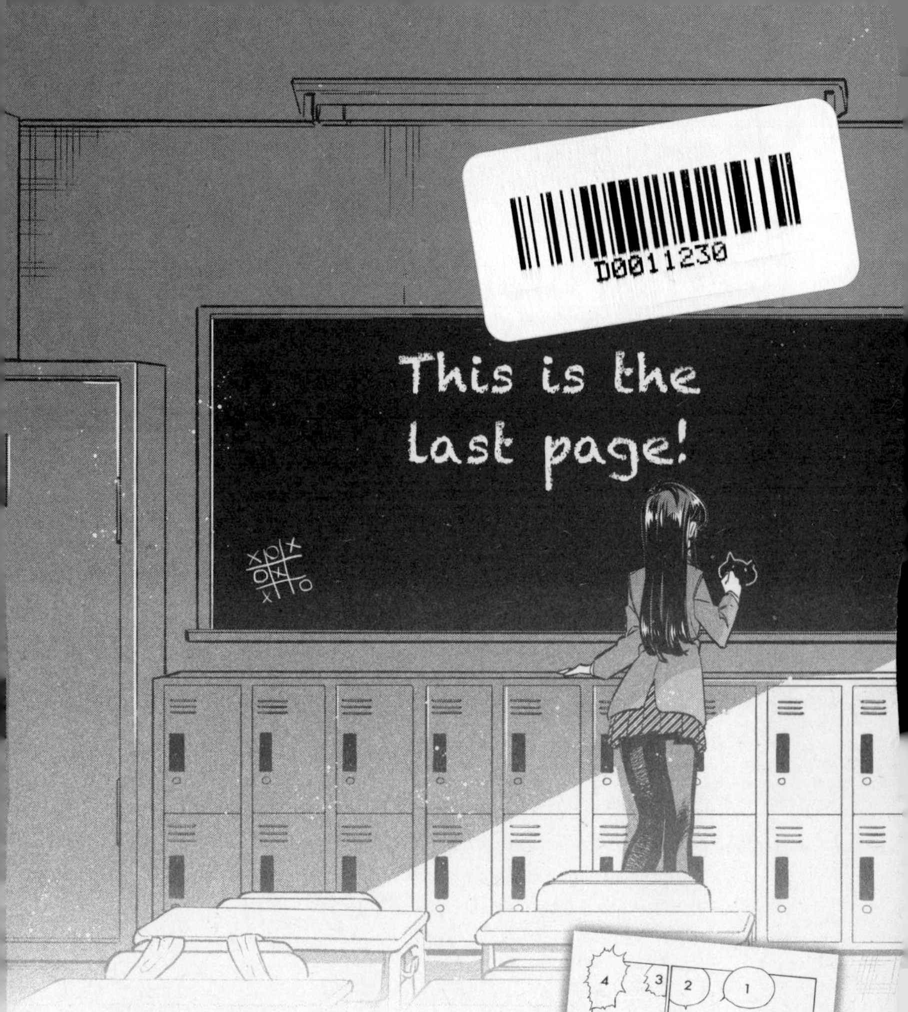
This is the last page!

Komi Can't Communicate has been printed in the original Japanese format to preserve the orientation of the artwork.

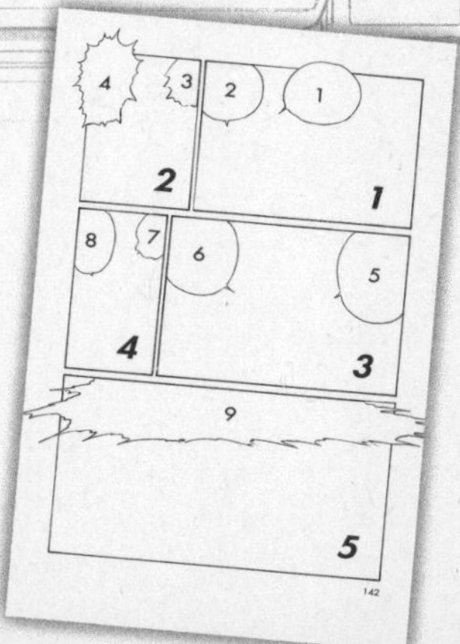

Follow the action this way.